Guided Reading
and Study Workbook
(Level B)

Prentice Hall
Earth
Science

Boston, Massachusetts • Glenview, Illinois • Parsippany, New Jersey • Shoreview, Minnesota • Upper Saddle River, New Jersey

13-digit ISBN 978-0-13-362756-5
10-digit ISBN 0-13-362756-X

1 2 3 4 5 6 7 8 9 10   11 10 09 08 07

How to use the *Guided Reading and Study Workbook, Level B*

Did you know that learning to study more effectively can make a real difference in students' performance at school? Students who master study skills are more confident and have more fun learning. This book, the *Guided Reading and Study Workbook, Level B* for Prentice Hall *Earth Science*, is designed to help your students acquire the skills that will allow them to study Earth science more effectively.

The *Guided Reading and Study Workbook, Level B* can be used to

- preview a chapter,
- learn key vocabulary terms,
- master difficult concepts, and
- review for chapter and unit tests.

The *Guided Reading and Study Workbook, Level B* concentrates on the Key Concepts presented in each chapter of the textbook. Each chapter in the *Guided Reading and Study Workbook, Level B* begins with a chapter summary. This review material stresses the Key Concepts and facts you should focus on in that particular chapter.

An alternate way of using the chapter summary is to assign students to read it before you cover the chapter in the textbook. In that way, students will be alerted to the important facts contained in the chapter. Used in this manner, the summary can be a prereading guide to the chapter material.

Following the chapter summary, you will find specific workbook activities designed to help students read and understand the textbook. Completing these worksheets will help students master the Key Concepts in each section.

The final part of many chapters consists of a WordWise vocabulary review. The vocabulary reviews take a variety of formats including crossword puzzles, multiple-choice questions, and matching exercises.

Contents

Chapter 1 Introduction to Earth Science

Summary

1.1 What Is Earth Science?

◕ **Earth science is the name for the group of sciences that deals with Earth and its neighbors in space.**

- **Geology** means "study of Earth." Geology is divided into physical geology and historical geology.
- **Oceanography** is the study of the Earth's oceans, as well as coastal processes, seafloor topography, and marine life.
- **Meteorology** is the study of atmosphere and the processes that produce weather and climate.
- **Astronomy** is the study of the universe.

◕ **The nebular hypothesis suggests that the bodies of our solar system evolved from an enormous rotating cloud called the solar nebula. It was made up mostly of hydrogen and helium, with a small percentage of heavier elements.**

- Shortly after the Earth formed, melting occurred in the Earth's interior. Gravity caused denser elements to sink to Earth's center. Less dense elements floated toward the surface. As a result, Earth is made up of layers of materials that have different properties.

1.2 A View of Earth

◕ **Earth can be thought of as consisting of four major spheres: the hydrosphere, atmosphere, geosphere, and biosphere.**

- The **hydrosphere** is the water portion of Earth.
- The **atmosphere** is an envelope of gases that surrounds Earth.
- The **geosphere** is the layer of Earth under both the atmosphere and the oceans. It includes the core, the mantle, and the crust.
- The **biosphere** is made up of all life on Earth.

◕ **Because the geosphere is not uniform, it is divided into three main parts based on differences in composition—the core, the mantle, and the crust.**

- The **core**, Earth's innermost layer, is located just below the mantle.
- The **mantle** is 2890 kilometers thick. It is located below the Earth's crust and above the Earth's core.
- The **crust** is the thin, rocky, outer layer of Earth.

◕ **The theory of plate tectonics provided geologists with a model to explain how earthquakes and volcanic eruptions occur and how continents move.**

- Destructive forces wear away Earth's surface.
- Constructive forces build up the Earth's surface.
- Tectonic plates move constantly over the Earth's mantle.

Chapter 1   Introduction to Earth Science

1.3 Representing Earth's Surface

☛ **Latitude is the distance north or south of the equator, measured in degrees. Longitude is the distance east or west of the prime meridian, measured in degrees.**

- The equator divides Earth into two hemispheres—the northern and the southern.
- The prime meridian and the 180° meridian divide Earth into eastern and western hemispheres.

☛ **No matter what kind of map is made, some portion of the surface will always look either too small, too big, or out of place. Mapmakers have, however, found ways to limit the distortion of shape, size, distance, and direction.**

☛ **Topographic maps show elevation using contour lines.**

- A **topographic map** represents Earth's three-dimensional surface in two dimensions.
- A **contour line** indicates the elevation of the land.
- A **contour interval** tells the difference in elevation between adjacent contour lines.
- A scale helps to determine distances on a map.

☛ **A geologic map shows the type and age of exposed rocks.**

☛ **Today's technology provides us with the ability to more precisely analyze Earth's physical properties.**

- Satellites and computers provide more accurate maps.

1.4 Earth System Science

☛ **Earth system science aims to understand Earth as a system made up of interacting parts, or subsystems.**

☛ **A system can be any size group of interacting parts that form a complex whole.**

- In a closed system, matter does not enter or leave the system.
- In an open system, energy and matter flow into and out of the system.
- Most natural systems are open systems.
- The Earth system is powered by energy from two sources.

☛ **One source of energy for Earth systems is the sun, which drives external processes that occur in the atmosphere, hydrosphere, and at Earth's surface.**

- The sun's energy drives weather, climate, ocean circulation, and erosion.

Chapter 1   Introduction to Earth Science

👆 **Earth's interior is the second source of energy for Earth systems.**

- Heat powers the internal processes that cause volcanoes, earthquakes, and mountains.
- The Earth system's processes are interlinked. A change in one part of the system can affect the whole system.

👆 **Our actions produce changes in all of the other parts of the Earth system.**

- Environment refers to things that surround and influence an organism.
- Environmental science focuses on the relationships between people and Earth.
- Resources include water, soil, metallic and nonmetallic minerals, and energy.

👆 **Renewable resources can be replenished over relatively short time spans.**

- Plants, animals, and energy such as water, wind, and the sun are some examples of renewable resources.

👆 **Although these and other resources continue to form, the processes that create them are so slow that it takes millions of years for significant deposits to accumulate.**

- Iron, aluminum, copper, oil, natural gas, and coal are examples of nonrenewable resources.
- Population growth equals an increase in demand for resources.

👆 **Significant threats to the environment include air pollution, acid rain, ozone depletion, and global warming.**

- Understanding Earth's environment and the impact of humans on limited resources is necessary for the survival and well-being of the planet.

1.5 What Is Scientific Inquiry?

👆 **Once data have been gathered, scientists try to explain how or why things happen in the manner observed. Scientists do this by stating a possible explanation called a scientific hypothesis.**

- A hypothesis becomes a scientific theory if it survives tests and analyses.

👆 **A scientific theory is well tested and widely accepted by the scientific community and best explains certain observable facts.**

- Scientific investigations often have four steps—collecting facts; developing a hypothesis; observing and experimenting; and accepting, modifying, or rejecting the hypothesis.

Chapter 1   Introduction to Earth Science

Section 1.1 What Is Earth Science?
(pages 2–5)

This section explains what Earth science is and what Earth scientists study.

Reading Strategy (page 2)

Categorizing As you read about the different branches of Earth science, list some of the things that are studied in each branch. For more information on this Reading Strategy, see the **Reading and Study Skills** in the **Skills and Reference Handbook** at the end of your textbook.

geology	a.
oceanography	b.
meteorology	c.
astronomy	d.

Overview of Earth Science (pages 2–3)

1. ◓ Circle the letters of the topics studied in Earth science.

    a. Earth's atmosphere

    b. Earth's surface

    c. Earth's neighbors in space

2. What does the word *geology* mean? _____

    _____

3. Is the following sentence true or false? Geology is divided into two broad

    areas—physical geology and historical geology. _____

4. What do physical geologists study? _____

    _____

    _____

5. Rocks and minerals form in response to Earth's internal and

    _____ processes.

Chapter 1   Introduction to Earth Science

6. Historical geologists try to establish a timeline of the vast number of

   _____ and biological changes that have occurred in the past.

7. What do oceanographers study? _____

   _____

8. The study of the atmosphere and the processes that produce

   weather and climate is _____. Circle the correct answer.

   astronomy   meteorology   physics

Formation of Earth (pages 3–5)

9. ☞ The _____ hypothesis suggests that the bodies
   of our solar system evolved from an enormous rotating cloud
   called the solar nebula. Choose the correct answer.

nebular   solar   cloud

Look at the diagram. It shows the first two stages of the formation of the
solar system according to the nebular hypothesis. Complete the sentences
below about these stages using the terms in the box.

cloud   heat   helium   sun

10. Our solar system began as an enormous _____ of dust and

    gases made up mostly of hydrogen and _____ .

11. Then the cloud started to rotate and collapse toward the center of the

    cloud. _____ was generated at the center, which enventually

    formed the _____ .

Chapter 1   Introduction to Earth Science

Section 1.2 A View of Earth
(pages 7–10)

This section explains the physical structure of Earth.

Reading Strategy (page 7)

Predicting Before you read, predict the meaning of the vocabulary terms. After you read, revise your definition if your prediction was incorrect. For more information on this Reading Strategy, see the **Reading and Study Skills** in the **Skills and Reference Handbook** at the end of your textbook.

Vocabulary Term	Before You Read	After You Read
hydrosphere	a.	b.
atmosphere	c.	d.
geosphere	e.	f.
biosphere	g.	h.
core	i.	j.
mantle	k.	l.
crust	m.	n.

Earth's Major Spheres (pages 7–9)

1. Earth can be thought of as consisting of four major spheres: the

    hydrosphere, atmosphere, geosphere, and _____.

Match each term to its description.

Term	Description
_____ **2.** hydrosphere	a. all life-forms on Earth
_____ **3.** atmosphere	b. composed of the core, mantle, and crust
_____ **4.** geosphere	c. the water portion of Earth
_____ **5.** biosphere	d. the gaseous envelope around Earth

Chapter 1   Introduction to Earth Science

6. What does each letter in the diagram below represent? Use these
vocabulary words.

crust
inner core
lower mantle
outer core
upper mantle

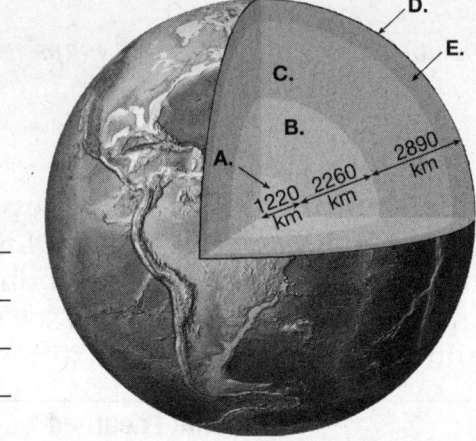

A. _____

B. _____

C. _____

D. _____

E. _____

Plate Tectonics (pages 9–10)

7. Is the following sentence true or false? Forces such as weathering and
erosion that work to wear away high points and flatten out Earth's

surface are called constructive forces. _____

8. Circle the letter of each type of constructive force.

a. gravity   b. mountain building   c. volcanism

9. Is the following sentence true or false? Constructive forces depend on

Earth's internal heat for their source of energy. _____

10. ● Circle the letter of the theory that provided geologists with a model
to explain how earthquakes and volcanic eruptions occur and how
continents move.

a. continental drift   b. evolution   c. plate tectonics

11. Use one of these terms to fill in the blank.

heat	rock	water

Plates move slowly and continuously due to the unequal

distribution of _____ within Earth.

Chapter 1   Introduction to Earth Science

Section 1.3 Representing Earth's Surface
(pages 11–17)

This section explains various types of globes and maps used to represent Earth's surface.

Reading Strategy (page 11)

Monitoring Your Understanding Preview the Key Concepts, topic headings, vocabulary, and figures in this section. List two things you expect to learn. After reading, state what you learned about each item you listed. For more information on this Reading Strategy, see the **Reading and Study Skills** in the **Skills and Reference Handbook** at the end of your textbook.

What I Expect to Learn	What I Learned
a.	b.
c.	d.

Determining Location (pages 11–12)

Match each description to its term.

Description

_____ 1. the distance north or south of the equator

_____ 2. the distance east or west of the prime meridian

_____ 3. the line of latitude around the middle of the globe at 0 degrees

_____ 4. the line of longitude at 0 degrees

_____ 5. the two hemispheres formed by the prime meridian and the 180° meridian

Term

a. longitude

b. eastern, western

c. prime meridian

d. latitude

e. equator

Chapter 1   Introduction to Earth Science

Maps and Mapping (pages 12–13)

6. Match the name of the map type with the correct example below.

Robinson Projection   Mercator Projection
Gnomonic Projection   Conic Projection

A. _____   B. _____

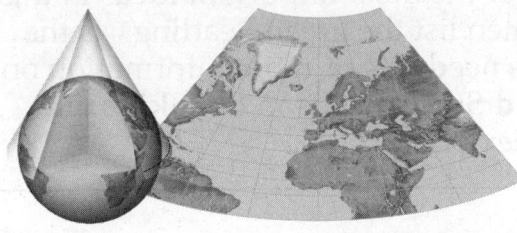
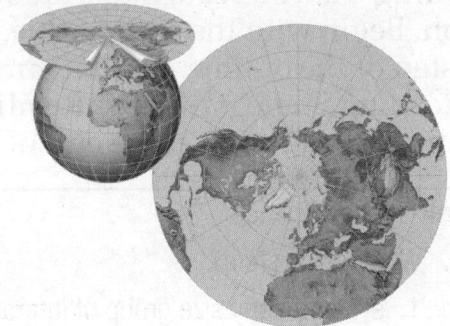

C. _____   D. _____

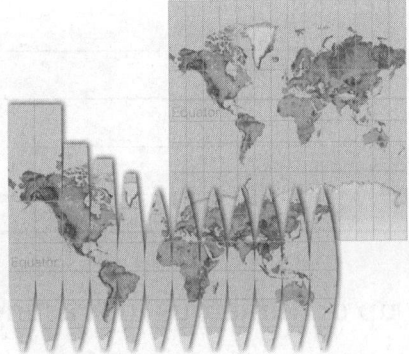
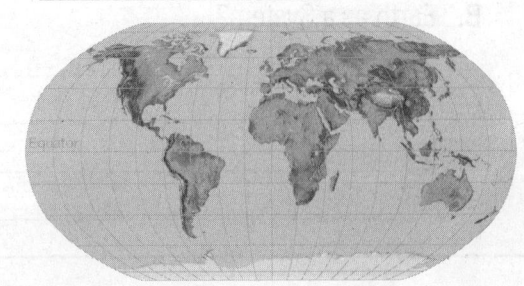

Topographic Maps (pages 14–15)

7. 👆 Is the following sentence true or false? Topographical maps show the

elevation of Earth's surface. _____

Advanced Technology (pages 16–17)

8. Circle the things scientists can study using satellite remote sensing.

a. rivers and oceans   b. fires   c. pollution

Chapter 1   Introduction to Earth Science

Section 1.4 Earth System Science
(pages 18–22)

This section describes Earth as a system of interacting parts.

Reading Strategy (page 18)

Outlining As you read, make an outline of the most important ideas in this section. Begin with the section title, and then list the green headings as the next step of the outline. Outline further as needed. For more information on this Reading Strategy, see the **Reading and Study Skills** in the **Skills and Reference Handbook** at the end of your textbook.

I. Earth System Science

    A. What Is a System?

        1. system—any size group of interacting parts forming a whole

        2. types of systems—closed and open

    B. Earth as a System?

        1. _____

           _____

        2. _____

           _____

---

1. Earth is a(n) _____ made up of numerous interacting parts, or subsystems.

What Is a System? (pages 18–19)

2. A system can be any size group of interacting parts that form a complex _____.

3. What is a closed system? _____

_____

_____

4. In an open system, both energy and _____ flow into and out of the system.

Earth as a System (pages 19–20)

5. Is the following sentence true or false? The Earth system is powered by energy from the sun and Earth's exterior. _____

Chapter 1   Introduction to Earth Science

6. ☞ Is the following sentence true or false? The sun drives external processes that occur in the atmosphere, hydrosphere, and at Earth's surface. _____

7. Use the phrases in the box to complete the concept map below

> habitats eliminated
> lower temperatures
> rivers and streams rerouted

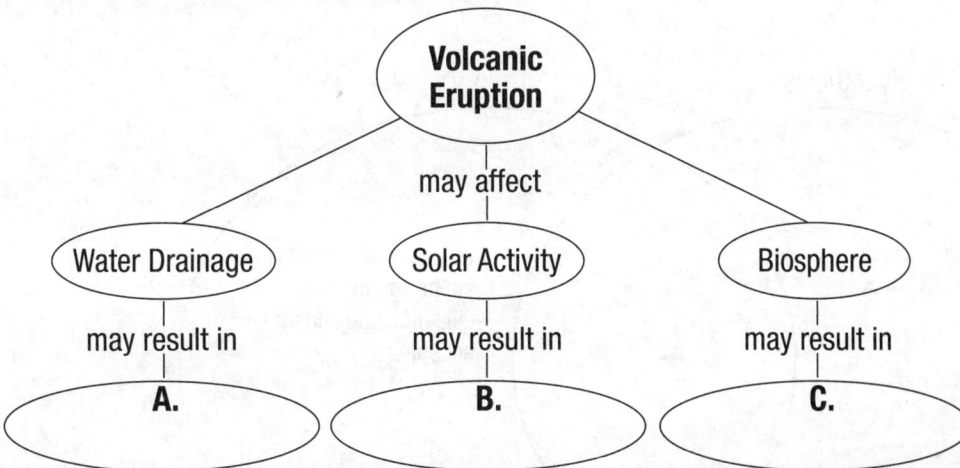

People and the Environment (pages 20–21)

8. Circle the letter of each statement that is true about nonliving things that make up the environment.

   a. Water and air are nonliving things that make up the environment.

   b. Plants, animals, and microscopic organisms are nonliving things that make up the environment.

   c. Temperature, humidity, and sunlight are conditions that make up the environment.

9. ☞ What are renewable resources? _____

   _____

   _____

10. ☞ Circle the letter of each item that is a nonrenewable resource.

    a. iron   b. petroleum   c. natural fibers

Environmental Problems (pages 21–22)

11. ☞ Significant threats to the environment include air pollution, acid rain,

    ozone depletion, and _____ .

Chapter 1   Introduction to Earth Science

Section 1.5 What Is Scientific Inquiry?
(pages 23–24)

This section describes methods used for scientific inquiry.

Reading Strategy (page 23)

Comparing and Contrasting As you read, complete the Venn diagram by listing the ways that a hypothesis and a theory are alike and how they differ. For more information on this Reading Strategy, see the **Reading and Study Skills** in the **Skills and Reference Handbook** at the end of your textbook.

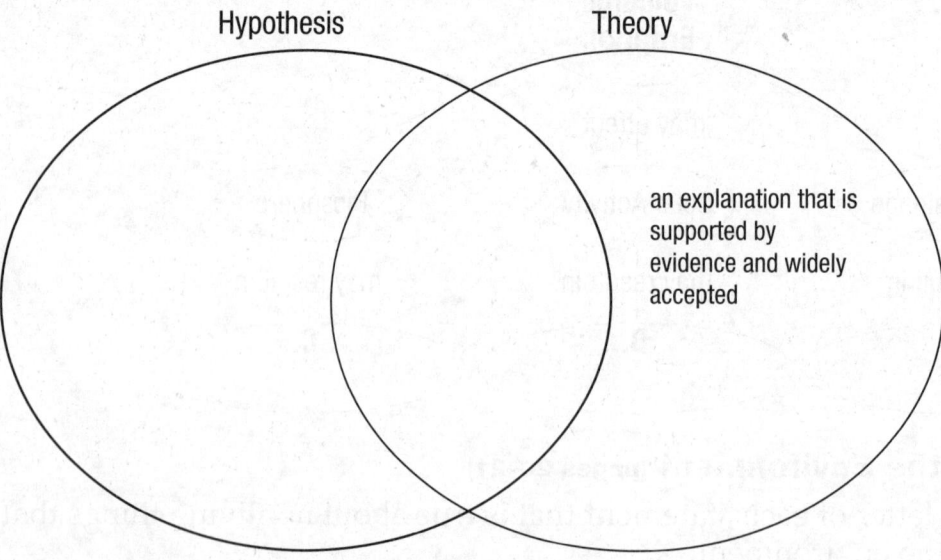

Hypothesis   Theory

an explanation that is supported by evidence and widely accepted

Hypothesis (pages 23–24)

1. What is a hypothesis? _____

    _____

2. Is the following sentence true or false? Before a hypothesis can become an accepted part of scientific knowledge, it must be tested and analyzed.

    _____

3. Circle the letter of each sentence that is true about hypotheses.

    a. If a hypothesis can't be tested, it is not scientifically useful.

    b. Hypotheses that fail rigorous testing are discarded.

    c. A hypothesis is a well-tested and widely accepted principle.

4. Is the following sentence true or false? Sometimes more than one hypothesis is developed to explain the same set of observations.

    _____

Chapter 1   Introduction to Earth Science

Theory (page 24)

5. ◕ A scientific _____ is well tested and widely accepted by the scientific community and best explains certain observable facts.

6. Describe a scientific theory that is currently accepted as true. _____

_____

_____

_____

Scientific Methods (page 24)

7. Circle the letter that best answers the question. What is the process of gathering facts through observations and formulating scientific hypotheses and theories called?

   a. scientific hypothesis   b. scientific theory   c. scientific method

8. Using numbers 1–4, put the following basic steps of the scientific method in the correct order.

   _____ Test hypotheses using observations and/or experiments.

   _____ Collect scientific facts through observation and measurement.

   _____ After extensive testing, accept, modify, or reject the remaining hypothesis.

   _____ Develop one or more working hypothesis or models to explain observed facts or measurements.

9. Is the following sentence true or false? All scientists always follow the same steps outlined above when doing scientific research.

   _____

Chapter 1   Introduction to Earth Science

WordWise

Complete the sentences by using the vocabulary terms below.

astronomy	Earth science	hypothesis
atmosphere	geology	latitude
biosphere	geosphere	longitude
contour lines	hydrosphere	meteorology

The name of the group of sciences that deal with Earth and its neighbors in

space is called _____.

All the water on Earth makes up the _____.

A word that means "study of Earth" is _____.

A distance measured in degrees north or south of the equator is called

_____.

A distance measured in degrees east or west of the prime meridian is called

_____.

Lying beneath both the atmosphere and the ocean is the _____.

An untested scientific explanation is called a _____.

The gaseous envelope surrounding Earth is called the _____.

The elevation on a topographic map is shown using _____.

The _____ includes all life on Earth.

The study of the atmosphere and the processes that produce weather and

climate is _____.

The study of the universe is _____.

Chapter 2 Minerals

Summary

2.1 Matter

☞ **An element is a substance that cannot be broken down into simpler substances by chemical or physical means.**

☞ **An atom is the smallest particle of matter that contains the characteristics of an element.**

- The central region of an atom is called the nucleus. The nucleus contains protons and neutrons.
- The number of protons in the nucleus of an atom is called the **atomic number**.
- Electrons are located in regions called **energy levels**.

☞ **Atoms with the same number of protons but different numbers of neutrons are isotopes of an element.**

- The **mass number** of an atom is the total mass of the atom expressed in atomic mass units.
- Many elements have atoms whose nuclei are unstable. These atoms disintegrate by radioactive decay.

☞ **A compound is a substance that consists of two or more elements that are chemically combined in specific proportions.**

☞ **When an atom's outermost energy level does not contain the maximum number of electrons, the atom is likely to form a chemical bond with one or more other atoms.**

- Chemical combinations of the atoms of elements are called **compounds**.
- **Chemical bonds** are the forces that hold atoms together in a compound. There are three principal types of chemical bonds: ionic, covalent, and metallic.
- An atom can gain or lose one or more electrons. The atom then has an electrical charge and is called an **ion**.

☞ **Ionic bonds form between positive and negative ions.**

☞ **Covalent bonds form when atoms share electrons.**

☞ **Metallic bonds form when electrons are shared by metal ions.**

Chapter 2   Minerals

2.2 Minerals

👁 **A mineral is a naturally occurring, inorganic solid with an orderly crystalline structure and a definite chemical composition.**

- Minerals form by natural processes.
- Minerals are solids in normal temperature ranges on Earth.
- Minerals are crystalline. Their atoms or ions are arranged in an orderly and repetitive way.
- Minerals have definite chemical composition. They usually are compounds formed of two or more elements.
- Most minerals are inorganic chemical compounds.

👁 **There are four major processes by which minerals form: crystallization from magma, precipitation, changes in pressure and temperature, and formation from hydrothermal solutions.**

- Magma is molten rock from deep in the Earth. As it cools, it forms minerals.
- Substances dissolved in water may react to form minerals.
- Changes in temperature and pressure can make new minerals form.
- When hot solutions touch exisiting minerals, chemical reactions take place and form new minerals.

👁 **Common minerals, together with the thousands of others that form on Earth, can be classified into groups based on their composition.**

👁 **Silicon and oxygen combine to form a structure called the silicon-oxygen tetrahedron.**

- **Silicates** are made of silicon and oxygen. They are the most common group of minerals on Earth.
- Most silicate minerals crystallize from cooling magma.

👁 **Carbonates are minerals that contain the elements carbon, oxygen, and one or more other metallic elements.**

👁 **Oxides are minerals that contain oxygen and one or more other elements, which are usually metals.**

👁 **Sulfates and sulfides are minerals that contain the element sulfur.**

👁 **Halides are minerals that contain a halogen ion plus one or more other elements.**

👁 **Native elements are minerals that only contain one element or type of atom.**

Chapter 2   Minerals

2.3 Properties of Minerals

Small amounts of different elements can give the same mineral different colors.

Streak is the color of a mineral in its powdered form.

Luster is used to describe how light is reflected from the surface of a mineral.

Crystal form is the visible expression of a mineral's internal arrangement of atoms.

The Mohs scale consists of 10 minerals arranged from 10 (hardest) to 1 (softest).

- **Hardness** is a measure of the resistance of a mineral to being scratched.
- You can test hardness by rubbing a mineral against another mineral of known hardness. One will scratch the other, unless they have the same hardness.

Cleavage is the tendency of a mineral to cleave, or break, along flat, even surfaces.

- Minerals may have cleavage in one or more directions.

Minerals that do not show cleavage when broken are said to fracture.

- **Fracture** is the uneven breakage of a mineral.

Density is a property of all matter that is the ratio of an object's mass to its volume.

Some minerals can be recognized by other distinctive properties.

Chapter 2   Minerals

Section 2.1 Matter
(pages 34–43)

This section discusses the relationship between minerals and elements. It explains the parts of an atom and defines ions, isotopes, compounds, and chemical bonds.

Reading Strategy (page 34)

Comparing and Contrasting As you read, complete the organizer to compare and contrast protons, neutrons, and electrons. For more information on this Reading Strategy, see the **Reading and Study Skills** in the **Skills and Reference Handbook** at the end of your textbook.

Protons	Electrons	Neutrons
	Differences	
		Neutron is not charged.

Similarities

Elements and the Periodic Table (pages 34–37)

1. ⬤ A substance that cannot be broken down into simpler

   substances is called a(n) _____. Circle the correct answer.

   substance   compound   element

2. The document in which elements are organized by their properties is

   known as the _____. Circle the correct answer.

   periodic table   common elements   Earth materials

Atoms (pages 35, 38)

3. ⬤ What is an atom? _____

   _____

4. The atomic number of boron is 5. What does this tell you about an atom of boron?

   _____

   _____

Chapter 2   Minerals

5. Name the three main types of particles in an atom.

_____

_____

Isotopes (pages 38–39)

6. ◉ Is the following sentence true or false? Isotopes of carbon have the same number of neutrons and different numbers of protons.

_____

7. Is the following sentence true or false? The total mass of an atom

of nitrogen is known as the atom's mass number. _____

Why Atoms Bond (pages 39–40)

8. ◉ What does a compound consist of? _____

_____

9. ◉ An atom of oxygen does not contain the maximum number of electrons in its outermost energy level. What is likely to happen to that atom?

_____

_____

Types of Chemical Bonds (pages 40–43)

Match each description with its type of chemical bond.

Description	Chemical Bond
_____ 10. ◉ when one metal ion shares electrons with another metal ion	a. covalent
_____ 11. ◉ when a positive ion is attracted to a negative ion	b. ionic
_____ 12. ◉ when one atom shares electrons with another atom	c. metallic

Chapter 2   Minerals

Section 2.2 Minerals
(pages 44–49)

This section explains what minerals are and how they are formed, classified, and grouped.

Reading Strategy (page 44)

Previewing Skim the material on mineral groups. Place each group name into one of the ovals in the organizer. As you read this section, complete the organizer with characteristics and examples of each major mineral group. For more information on this Reading Strategy, see the **Reading and Study Skills** in the **Skills and Reference Handbook** at the end of your textbook.

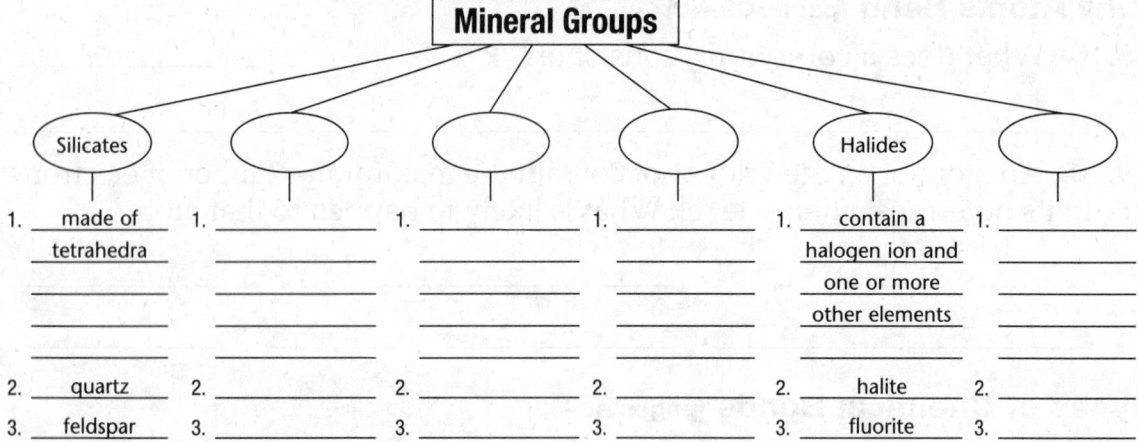

Minerals (page 45)

1. ☞ Circle the five characteristics that every mineral has.

solid	definite chemical composition
liquid	single-element composition
synthetic	crystalline structure
naturally occuring	irregular structure
regular cleavage	inorganic substance
smooth fracture	organic substance
glassy fracture	

Name _____ Class _____ Date _____

Chapter 2   Minerals

How Minerals Form (pages 45–46)

Match each description with its process of mineral formation.

Description	Process of Mineral Formation
_____ **2.** 👉 As molten rock cools, elements combine to form minerals.	a. hydrothermal solution
_____ **3.** 👉 Existing minerals recrystallize while still solid under pressure or form new minerals when temperature changes.	b. pressure and temperature changes
_____ **4.** 👉 Hot mixtures of water and dissolved substances react with existing minerals to form new minerals.	c. precipitation d. crystallization from magma
_____ **5.** 👉 Substances dissolved in water react to form new minerals when the water evaporates.	

Mineral Groups (pages 47–49)

6. 👉 What property is used to classify minerals into groups such as silicates? Circle the correct answer.

    structure   composition   density

7. 👉 What is the structure shown in the diagram?

    _____

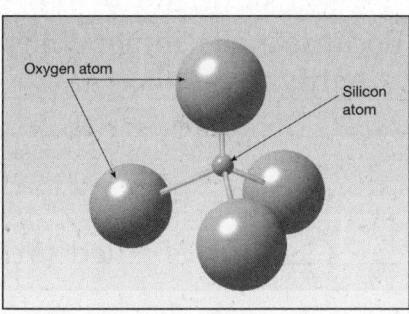

8. 👉 Circle the letter of something common to all halides.

    a. an oxygen ion

    b. a metallic element

    c. a halogen ion

9. 👉 Is the following sentence true or false? Both carbonates and oxides

    are minerals that contain the element oxygen. _____

Chapter 2   Minerals

Section 2.3 Properties of Minerals
(pages 50–55)

This section discusses the properties used to identify minerals, including color, luster, crystal form, streak, hardness, density, and some distinctive properties.

Reading Strategy (page 50)

Outlining As you read, fill in the outline. Use the headings as the main topics and add supporting details. For more information on this Reading Strategy, see the **Reading and Study Skills** in the **Skills and Reference Handbook** at the end of your textbook.

I. Properties of Minerals

    A. Color

        1. often not used to identify minerals _____

        2. _____

        _____

    B. Luster

        1. _____

        _____

        2. _____

        _____

Color (page 50)

1. Is the following sentence true or false? Because every mineral has just one color, you can always use color to identify minerals.

_____

Streak (page 51)

2. The color of a mineral in its _____ form is called *streak*. Circle the correct answer.

solid   powdered   liquid

Luster (page 51)

3. What is a mineral's luster? _____

_____

Crystal Form (page 51)

4. Is the following sentence true or false? The crystal form of a mineral

tells how its atoms are arranged. _____

Chapter 2   Minerals

Hardness (page 52)

5. 👁 Circle the letter of the hardest mineral shown on the graph.

    a. talc

    b. diamond

    c. topaz

    d. quartz

6. 👁 Circle the letter of the
    hardness number of corundum
    on the Mohs scale shown on
    the graph.

    a. 7

    b. 9

    c. 20

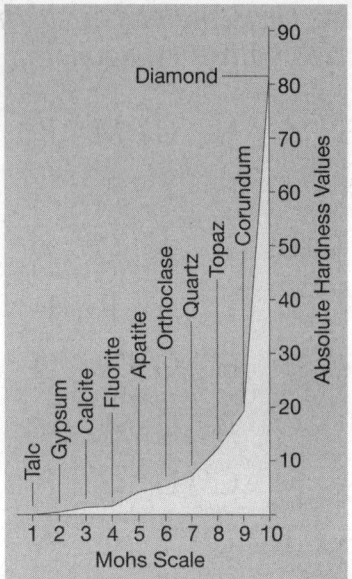

Cleavage (pages 52–53)

7. 👁 What is a mineral's cleavage?

    _____

    _____

Fracture (page 53)

8. 👁 Minerals are said to _____ if they do not show cleavage
    when broken.

Density (page 53)

9. 👁 Circle the letter of the equation that expresses the density of a
    mineral sample.

    a. density = volume/mass

    b. density = volume x mass

    c. density = mass/volume

Distinctive Properties of Minerals (pages 54–55)

10. 👁 Circle the letter of the distinctive property you could use to
    distinguish graphite from talc.

    a. color

    b. feel

    c. smell

Chapter 2   Minerals

WordWise

Use the clues and the words below to help you write the vocabulary terms from the chapter in the blanks. Then find and circle the terms in the puzzle. The terms may occur vertically, horizontally, or diagonally.

```
V E M A S S N U M B E R U N
C D Y S X T H E I M G N G I
W M E J H S P A Q X Z I O S
M I N E R A L S R E U Y J O
S C E H V T H Q N D A E I T
A X R Y P O B D T C N S L O
L I G R A M C U G P L E S P
B A Y C S I L I C A T E S E
T K L F U C L E A V A G E S
M I E G X N T E K P H T E P
A D V U L U S T E R Z P J B
C H E L E M E N T D S S T X
E X L M N B A U S S V H A L
Z P S B C E W R T N O H I A
R G C D Q R J H S M F L K P
```

atomic number
cleavage
element
energy levels
hardness
isotopes
luster
mass number
minerals
silicates

Clues   **Hidden Words**

How light is reflected from the surface of a mineral   _____

Number of protons in an atom of an element   _____

Atoms of the same element having different numbers   _____
of neutrons

Measure of how a mineral resists scratching   _____

Substance that cannot be broken down into simpler   _____
substances

Examples include quartz, copper, fluorite, and talc   _____

Regions where electrons are located   _____

Most common group of minerals on Earth   _____

Tendency of a mineral to break along flat, even surfaces   _____

Sum of protons and neutrons in the nucleus of an atom   _____

Chapter 3 Rocks

Summary

3.1 The Rock Cycle

◉ A rock is any solid mass of mineral or mineral-like matter that occurs naturally as part of our planet.

◉ The three major types of rocks are igneous rocks, sedimentary rocks, and metamorphic rocks.

◉ Interactions among Earth's water, air, and land can cause rocks to change from one type to another. The continuous processes that cause rocks to change make up the rock cycle.

◉ When magma cools and hardens beneath the surface or as the result of a volcanic eruption, igneous rock forms.
- **Magma** is molten material that forms deep beneath Earth's surface.
- **Lava** is magma that reaches the surface.
- **Weathering** is a process in which rocks are physically and chemically broken down by water, air, and living things.
- **Sediment** is made up of weathered pieces of earth materials.

◉ Eventually, sediment is compacted and cemented to form sedimentary rock.
- Sedimentary rocks buried deep within Earth's surface are subjected to great pressure and high temperatures.

◉ Under extreme pressure and temperature conditions, sedimentary rock will change in metamorphic rock.

◉ Processes driven by heat from Earth's interior are responsible for forming both igneous and metamorphic rocks. Weathering and the movement of weathered materials are external processes powered by energy from the sun and by gravity. Processes on and near Earth's surface produce sedimentary rocks.

3.2 Igneous Rocks

◉ Rocks that form when magma hardens beneath Earth's surface are called intrusive igneous rocks.
- The root word of *igneous* means "fire."

◉ When lava hardens, the rocks that form are called extrusive igneous rocks.

◉ Texture and composition are two characteristics used to classify igneous rocks.

- Texture is determined by the size, shape, and the arrangement of crystals.
- Composition is determined by the proportions of light and dark minerals.

◉ **Slow cooling results in the formation of large crystals.**

◉ **Rapid cooling of magma or lava results in rocks with small, interconnected mineral grains.**

- **Porphyritic texture** occurs in rocks with different-size minerals that cool at different rates.
- **Granitic composition** occurs when igneous rocks contain mostly quartz and feldspar.
- **Basaltic composition** occurs when rocks contain many dark silicate materials.
- **Andesitic composition** occurs in rocks with a combination of granitic and basaltic rocks.
- **Ultramafic** rocks are composed almost entirely of dark silicate minerals.

3.3 Sedimentary Rocks

◉ **Erosion involves weathering and the removal of rock. When an agent of erosion—water, wind, ice, or gravity—loses energy, it drops the sediments. This process is called deposition.**

- Sediments form when solids settle out of a fluid, such as water or air.
- **Compaction** and **cementation** change sediments into sedimentary rock.

◉ **Compaction is a process that squeezes, or compacts, sediments.**

◉ **Cementation takes place when dissolved minerals are deposited in the tiny spaces among the sediments.**

◉ **Just like igneous rocks, sedimentary rocks can be classified into two main groups according to the way they form.**

- **Clastic sedimentary rocks** are made of weathered bits of rocks and minerals.
- The size of the sediments in clastic sedimentary rocks determines their grouping.
- **Chemical sedimentary rocks** form when dissolved minerals separate from water solutions.

◉ **The many unique features of sedimentary rocks are clues to how, when, and where the rocks formed.**

- The oldest layers in sedimentary rock formations are at the bottom.
- Fossils are found in sedimentary rocks and can provide much information about the rocks that contain them.

Name _____ Class _____ Date _____

Chapter 3   Rocks

3.4 Metamorphic Rocks

👄 **Most metamorphic changes occur at elevated temperatures and pressures. These conditions are found a few kilometers below Earth's surface and extend into the upper mantle.**

- **Metamorphism** refers to the changes in mineral composition and texture of a rock subjected to high temperature and pressure within Earth.

👄 **During contact metamorphism, hot magma moves into rock.**

- This usually results in minor changes in rocks.

👄 **Regional metamorphism results in large-scale deformation and high-grade metamorphism.**

- This usually results in intense changes such as mountain building.

👄 **The agents of metamorphism are heat, pressure, and hydrothermal solutions.**

- **Hydrothermal solutions** occur when hot, water-based solutions escape from a mass of magma.

👄 **The texture of metamorphic rocks can be foliated or nonfoliated.**

- **Foliated metamorphic rocks** have a layered or banded appearance.
- **Nonfoliated metamorphic rocks** do not have a banded texture and usually contain only one mineral.

Earth Science Guided Reading and Study Workbook ▪ **27**

Chapter 3   Rocks

Section 3.1 The Rock Cycle
(pages 66–69)

This section explains the different types of rocks found on Earth and in the rock cycle.

Reading Strategy (page 66)

Building Vocabulary As you read, write down the definition for each term. For more information on this Reading Strategy, see the **Reading and Study Skills** in the **Skills and Reference Handbook** at the end of your textbook.

Term	Definition
rock	a.
igneous rock	b.
sedimentary rock	c. rock that forms when sediments become compacted and cemented
metamorphic rock	d.
rock cycle	e.
magma	f. molten material that forms deep beneath Earth's surface
lava	g.
weathering	h.
sediment	i.

Rocks (page 66)

1. 🔹 A(n) _____ is any solid mass of mineral or mineral-like matter that occurs naturally as part of Earth.

2. Most rocks occur as a solid mixture of _____. Circle the correct answer.

    minerals   pumice   lava

3. Is the following sentence true or false? A characteristic of rock is that each of the component minerals retains its properties in the mixture.

_____

4. 👁 Circle the letters that identify a type of rock.

   a. igneous   b. sedimentary   c. crystalline

The Rock Cycle (pages 67–68)

5. Use the terms in the box to fill in the blanks below in the illustration of the rock cycle.

metamorphic	sedimentary	sediment	igneous

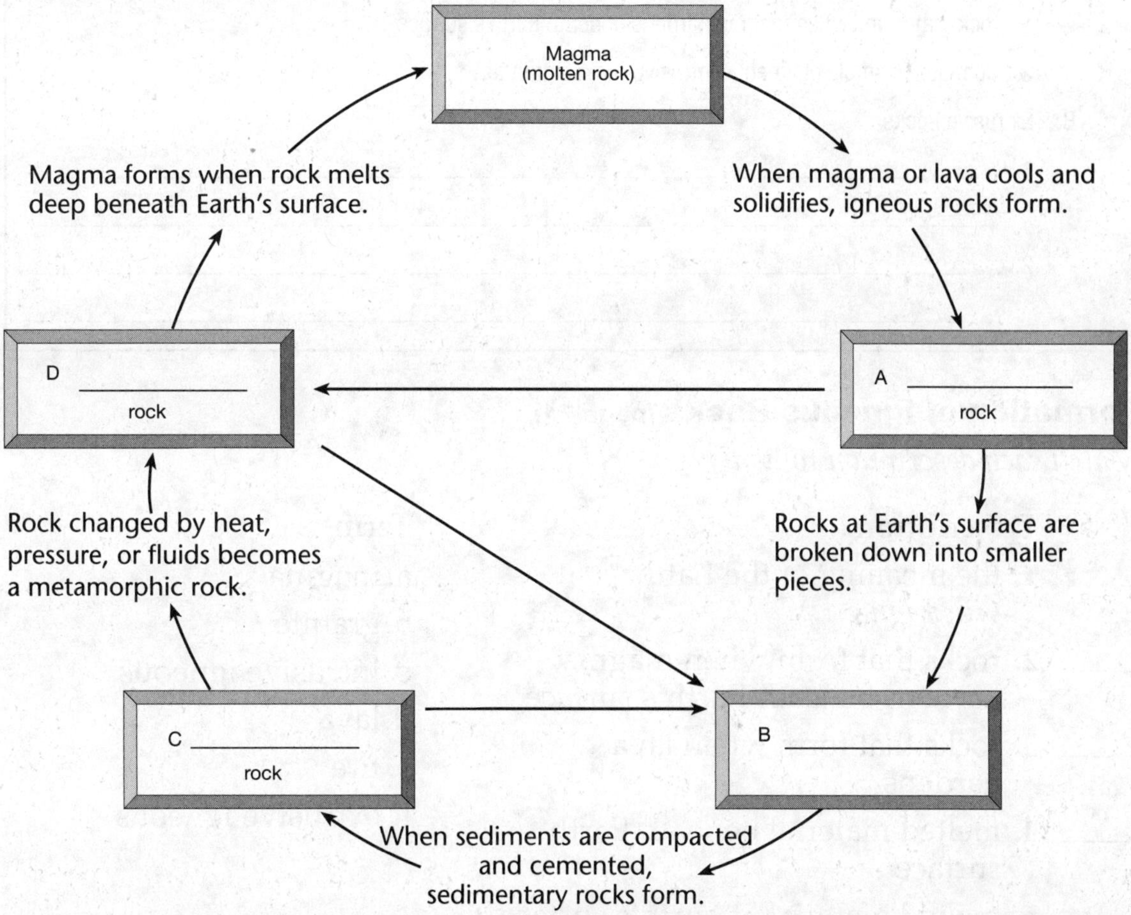

Magma (molten rock)

Magma forms when rock melts deep beneath Earth's surface.

When magma or lava cools and solidifies, igneous rocks form.

D _____ rock

A _____ rock

Rock changed by heat, pressure, or fluids becomes a metamorphic rock.

Rocks at Earth's surface are broken down into smaller pieces.

C _____ rock

B _____

When sediments are compacted and cemented, sedimentary rocks form.

Alternate Paths (page 69)

6. Is the following sentence true or false? Strong forces and high temperatures can change igneous rock into metamorphic rock.

_____

Chapter 3   Rocks

Section 3.2 Igneous Rocks
(pages 70–74)

This section discusses the characteristics of igneous rocks.

Reading Strategy (page 70)

Outlining Complete the outline as you read. Include points about how each of these rocks form, some of the characteristics of each rock type, and some examples of each. For more information on this Reading Strategy, see the **Reading and Study Skills** in the **Skills and Reference Handbook** at the end of your textbook.

I. Igneous Rocks

    A. Intrusive Rocks

        1. rock that forms when magma hardens beneath Earth's surface

        2. Common example of igneous intrusive rock is granite.

    B. Extrusive Rocks

        1. _____

           _____

        2. _____

           _____

Formation of Igneous Rocks (page 71)

Match each description to its term.

Description

_____ **1.** the meaning of the Latin word *ignis*

_____ **2.** rocks that form when magma hardens beneath Earth's surface

_____ **3.** rocks that form when lava hardens

_____ **4.** melted material beneath Earth's surface

_____ **5.** melted material at Earth's surface

_____ **6.** an intrusive igneous rock that forms when magma cools slowly beneath Earth's surface

Term

a. magma

b. granite

c. intrusive igneous

d. lava

e. fire

f. extrusive igneous

Chapter 3   Rocks

8. 👁 Both granite and rhyolite are types of igneous rock. Use the phrases in the box to complete the table.

| large interlocking crystals | intrusive igneous rock |
| small mineral grains | extrusive igneous rock |

Granite	Rhyolite
forms from slow cooling magma	forms from rapid cooling lava

Classification of Igneous Rocks (pages 72–74)

9. 👁 Two characteristics used to classify igneous rocks are

texture and _____.

10. Is the following sentence true or false? Igneous rocks that are composed primarily of quartz and feldspar have a granitic composition.

_____

11. Use one of the following terms below to fill in the blank.

basaltic composition
andesitic composition
granitic composition

Rocks that contain dark silicate minerals and plagioclase feldspar have

a(n) _____.

12. Circle the letters of the minerals that are found in andesitic rocks.

a. amphibole   b. pyroxene   c. biotite

13. Peridotite is composed almost entirely of dark silicate minerals. Its

chemical composition is referred to as _____.

14. Is the following sentence true or false? Much of the upper mantle is

thought to be made of granite. _____

Chapter 3   Rocks

Section 3.3 Sedimentary Rocks
(pages 75–79)

This section discusses the formation and classification of sedimentary rocks.

Reading Strategy (page 75)

Outlining This outline is a continuation of the outline from Section 3.2. Complete this outline as you read. Include points about how each of these rocks forms, some of the characteristics of each rock type, and some examples of each. For more information on this Reading Strategy, see the **Reading and Study Skills** in the **Skills and Reference Handbook** at the end of your textbook.

II. Sedimentary Rocks

    A. Clastic Rocks

        1. _____

           _____

        2. Common example of clastic sedimentary rock is shale._____

    B. Chemical Rocks

        1. rock that forms when dissolved minerals precipitate from water_

        2. _____

           _____

Formation of Sedimentary Rocks (page 76)

Match each description to its term.

Description	Term
_____ **1.** a process that squeezes, or compacts, sediments	a. cementation
_____ **2.** involves weathering and the removal of rock	b. deposition
_____ **3.** takes place when dissolved minerals are deposited in the tiny spaces among the sediments	c. compaction
_____ **4.** when sediments are dropped by water, wind, ice, or gravity	d. erosion

5. Is the following sentence true or false? Sedimentary rocks form when

solids settle out of a fluid such as water or air. _____

Chapter 3   Rocks

6. Circle the letters of the statements that are true of the formation of sedimentary rocks.

    a. Weathering is the first step in the formation of sedimentary rocks.

    b. Weathered sediments don't usually remain in place.

    c. Small sediments often are carried large distances before being deposited.

Classification of Sedimentary Rocks (pages 77–78)

7. ● Complete the chart below about the two main groups of sedimentary rocks. Use the terms in the box.

chemical	clastic	sandstone	rock salt

Type of Rock	Forms from	Examples
	weathered bits of rocks and minerals	shale,
	dissolved minerals that precipitate from water solution	limestone,

Features of Some Sedimentary Rocks (pages 78–79)

8. Is the following sentence true or false? In undisturbed sedimentary rocks, the oldest layers are found on the bottom. _____

9. Ripple marks in a sedimentary rock may indicate that the rock formed along a(n) _____ or stream bed.

10. Number the four major processes that form sedimentary rocks to place them in the correct order.

    _____ deposition

    _____ erosion

    _____ compaction and cementation

    _____ weathering

Section 3.4 Metamorphic Rocks
(pages 80–84)

This section discusses the formation and classification of metamorphic rocks.

Reading Strategy (page 80)

Outlining This outline is a continuation of the outline from Section 3.3. Complete it as you read. Include points about how each of these rocks forms, some of the characteristics of each rock type, and some examples of each. For more information on this Reading Strategy, see the **Reading and Study Skills** in the **Skills and Reference Handbook** at the end of your textbook.

III. Metamorphic Rocks

    A. Foliated Rocks

       1. _____

       _____

       2. Common example of foliated metamorphic rock is slate.

       _____

    B. Nonfoliated Rocks

       1. rock that does not have a banded (or "foliated") texture

       _____

       2. _____

       _____

1. Is the following sentence true or false? *Metamorphism* means "a change in form." _____

Formation of Metamorphic Rocks (pages 80–81)

Match each description to its term. The terms will be used more than once.

Description	Term
_____ **2.** takes place when magma intrudes rock	a. contact metamorphism
_____ **3.** produces high-grade metamorphism	b. regional metamorphism
_____ **4.** produces low-grade metamorphism	
_____ **5.** changes in rock are minor	
_____ **6.** results in large-scale deformation	

Chapter 3   Rocks

Agents of Metamorphism (pages 81–83)

9. ● The agents of metamorphism are _____, pressure, and hydrothermal solutions.

10. Is the following sentence true or false? During metamorphism, rocks are usually subjected to one agent at a time. _____

11. Complete the table below by using the terms in the box.

heat	reactions in solutions	pressure

Agents of Metamorphism	
Cause	**Effect**
	causes minerals to recrystallize; causes new minerals to form
	causes spaces between mineral grains to close; may cause minerals to recrystallize or to form new minerals; causes mineral grains to flatten and elongate
	solutions aid in recrystallization of minerals; promotes recrystallization by dissolving original minerals and depositing new ones

Classification of Metamorphic Rocks (pages 83–84)

12. Circle the letter of each sentence that is true about foliated metamorphic rocks.

    a. It is rock with a layered or banded appearance.

    b. Pressure can form it.

    c. Gneiss and marble are examples of it.

13. Circle the letter of each sentence that is true about nonfoliated metamorphic rocks.

    a. It is a metamorphic rock that does not have a banded texture.

    b. Most of it contains several different types of minerals.

    c. Marble is an example of it.

Name _____ Class _____ Date _____

Chapter 4 Earth's Resources

Summary

4.1 Energy and Mineral Resources

☞ A renewable resource can be replenished over fairly short time spans such as months, years, or decades.

☞ By contrast, a nonrenewable resource takes millions of years to form and accumulate.

- Population growth and a higher standard of living are depleting existing resources.

☞ Fossil fuels include coal, oil, and natural gas.

- A **fossil fuel** is any hydrocarbon used as a source of energy.

☞ Some energy experts believe that fuels derived from tar sands and oil shales could become good substitutes for dwindling petroleum supplies.

- Mining tar sand has significant environmental drawbacks.
- Oil shale has less heat energy than crude oil and is costly to process.

☞ Some of the most important mineral deposits form through igneous processes and from hydrothermal solutions.

- **Ore** is a useful metallic mineral that can be mined at a profit.
- Gold, silver, copper, mercury, lead, platinum, and nickel are examples of metallic minerals produced by igneous processes.
- Most hydrothermal deposits are formed by hot, metal-rich fluids left by magma.
- Placer deposits are formed when eroded heavy minerals settle quickly from moving water.

☞ Nonmetallic mineral resources are extracted and processed either for the nonmetallic elements they contain or for their physical and chemical properties.

- Nonmetallic mineral resources are useful for building materials, industrial minerals, and manufacturing chemicals and fertilizers.

4.2 Alternate Energy Sources

☞ Solar energy has two advantages: the "fuel" is free, and it's nonpolluting.

☞ In nuclear fission, the nuclei of heavy atoms such as uranium-235 are bombarded with neutrons. The uranium nuclei then split into smaller nuclei and emit neutrons and heat energy.

- About 7% of U.S. energy needs are met by nuclear power.

- Although it was once believed that nuclear power would be a safe and clean energy source, cost and safety are obstacles to expanded nuclear power.
- Fears about radioactive materials were realized in 1986, when a reactor at Chernobyl caused two explosions.

◖ **Some experts estimate that in the next 50 to 60 years, wind power could meet between 5 to 10 percent of the country's demand for electricity.**

- Wind energy is a promising source of energy, but technological advances are needed to fully realize its potential.

◖ **The water held in a reservoir behind a dam is a form of stored energy that can be released through the dam to produce electric power.**

- **Hydroelectric power**, which is generated by falling water, drives turbines that produce electricity.
- About 5% of the country's electricity comes from hydroelectric power.
- Limited usable sites and the finite lifetime of hydroelectric dams are both obstacles to further expansion.

◖ **Hot water is used directly for heating and to turn turbines to generate electric power.**

- **Geothermal energy** is harnessed by tapping natural underground reservoirs of steam and hot water.
- Geothermal power is nonpolluting but reservoirs are easily depleted.

◖ **Tidal power is harnessed by constructing a dam across the mouth of a bay or an estuary in coastal areas with a large tidal range. The strong in-and-out flow that results drives turbines and electric generators.**

4.3 Water, Air, and Land Resources

◖ **Each day, people use fresh water for drinking, cooking, bathing, and growing food.**

- Less than one percent of Earth's water is usable fresh water.
- **Point source pollution** is pollution that comes from a known and specific location.
- **Nonpoint source pollution** is pollution that does not have a specific point of origin.
- **Runoff** is the water that flows over the land rather than seeping into the ground. It often carries nonpoint pollution.
- Water pollution can have serious health effects for humans.

◖ **The chemical composition of the atmosphere helps maintain life on Earth.**

Chapter 4   Earth's Resources

- Pollution can change the chemical composition of the atmosphere and disrupt its natural cycles and functions.
- **Global warming**, caused by increased carbon dioxide in the atmosphere, is the unnatural warming of the lower atmosphere.

Earth's land provides soil and forests, as well as mineral and energy resources.

- Removing and using resources from Earth's crust can damage the environment.

4.4 Protecting Resources

Starting in the 1970s, the federal government passed several laws to prevent or decrease pollution and protect resources.

- Although they comprise only 6% of the world's population, Americans use about one third of the world's resources.
- **Conservation** is the careful use of resources.

In 1970, Congress passed the Clean Air Act, the nation's most important air pollution law.

- The Clean Air Act limited the amount of pollutants allowed in the air, resulting in improved air quality.

Protecting land resources involves preventing pollution and managing land resources wisely.

- Farmers are using new soil conservation practices to prevent the loss of topsoil.
- Some farmers and gardeners use fewer pesticides and inorganic fertilizers.
- **Compost** is partly decomposed organic material that is used as fertilizer.
- Better landfill management and disposal techniques prevent waste seepage.
- **Recycling** is the collecting and processing of used items so they can be made into new products.

Chapter 4   Earth's Resources

Section 4.1 Energy and Mineral Resources
(pages 94–101)

This section discusses different types of resources, including renewable, nonrenewable, energy, and mineral resources.

Reading Strategy (page 94)

Monitoring Your Understanding List what you know about energy and mineral resources in the first column and what you'd like to know in the second column. After you read, list what you have learned in the last column. For more information on this Reading Strategy, see the **Reading and Study Skills** in the **Skills and Reference Handbook** at the end of your textbook.

Energy and Mineral Resources		
What I Know	**What I Would Like to Know**	**What I Learned**
a.	c.	e.
b.	d.	f.

Renewable and Nonrenewable Resources (pages 94–95)

1. ☉ Is the following sentence true or false? Renewable resources can be replenished over fairly short time spans. _____

2. ☉ A(n) _____ resource takes millions of years to form and accumulate.

3. Circle the letter of the nonrenewable resource.

   a. trees   b. sunlight   c. natural gas

Fossil Fuels (pages 95–96)

4. ☉ Three examples of fossil fuels are coal, oil, and _____

5. Circle the letter of the last stage of coal development.

   a. anthracite   b. bituminous   c. lignite

6. Is the following sentence true or false? Natural gas forms from the buried remains of animals and plants. _____

Chapter 4   Earth's Resources

Tar Sands and Oil Shale (pages 97–98)

Match each description with its fuel source.

	Description	Fuel Source
_____ 7. ☛ World supplies are expected to dwindle in the future.		a. petroleum
_____ 8. mixture of bitumen, water, clay, and sand		b. oil shale
_____ 9. rock containing kerogen		c. tar sands

Formation of Mineral Deposits (pages 98–100)

10. ☛ Complete the table below by filling in the type of mineral deposit.

> hydrothermal vein deposit
>
> magma deposit
>
> placer deposit

Mineral Deposits		
Type	**How Forms**	**Mineral Examples**
	By igneous processes; A large magma body cools, and heavy minerals crystallize and settle to the bottom.	chromite, platinum
	Mineral-rich hot water seeps into rock fractures, cools, and leaves behind deposits.	gold, silver, mercury
	Eroded heavy minerals settle from moving water.	gold

Nonmetallic Mineral Resources (pages 100–101)

11. Circle the letter of the nonmetallic mineral resource.

   a. limestone   b. gold   c. chromite

12. ☛ Is the following sentence true or false? Nonmetallic mineral

   resources are used as a source of energy. _____

Chapter 4   Earth's Resources

Section 4.2 Alternate Energy Sources
(pages 102–107)

This section discusses solar, nuclear, wind, hydroelectric, geothermal, and tidal energy.

Reading Strategy (page 102)

Previewing Skim the section and complete the concept map for the various alternate energy sources. For more information on this Reading Strategy, see the **Reading and Study Skills** in the **Skills and Reference Handbook** at the end of your textbook.

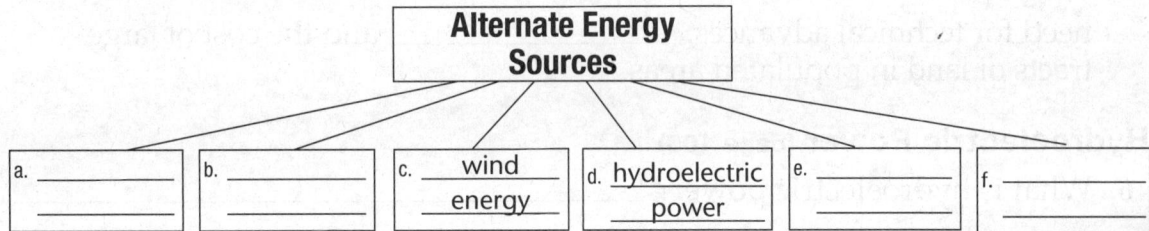

Solar Energy (page 102–103)

1. What is solar energy? _____

   _____

2. 🔵 Complete the table below.

Solar Energy	
Advantages	Disadvantages
a.	a.
b.	b.

Chapter 4   Earth's Resources

Nuclear Energy (pages 103–104)

3. Is the following sentence true or false? Uranium nuclei split during

nuclear fission. _____

Wind Energy (page 104)

4. Is the following sentence true or false? Experts estimate that 15 to 25
percent of the United States' electricity demand can be met by wind

power in the next 50 to 60 years. _____

5. Three obstacles to the development of future use of wind power are the

need for technical advances, _____ and the cost of large
tracts of land in populated areas.

Hydroelectric Power (page 105)

6. What is hydroelectric power? _____

_____

_____

7. Use one of the terms below to fill in the blank. At a hydroelectric

power plant, water is held in a(n) _____ behind a dam.

turbine	reservoir	generator

Geothermal Energy (pages 105–106)

8. Circle the letter of the geothermal energy source that is used for
heating and for turning turbines.

   a. hot water   b. sunlight   c. wind

9. Is the following sentence true or false? The fuel used in geothermal

energy is found above Earth's surface. _____

Tidal Power (pages 106–107)

10. Tidal power is harnessed by constructing a(n) _____
across the mouth of an estuary or a bay.

11. What drives the turbines and electric generators at a tidal

power plant? _____

_____

Chapter 4   Earth's Resources

Section 4.3 Water, Air, and Land Resources
(pages 108–112)

This section explains the importance of water, air, and land resources.

Reading Strategy (page 108)

Building Vocabulary As you read, add definitions and examples to complete the table. For more information on this Reading Strategy, see the **Reading and Study Skills** in the **Skills and Reference Handbook** at the end of your textbook.

Definition	Example
point source pollution: pollution that can be traced to a location	factory pipes, sewer pipes
nonpoint source pollution: a.	b.
runoff: c.	d. waste oil from streets, pesticides from farm fields
greenhouse gas: e.	f.

The Water Planet (pages 108–109)

1. Four ways people use fresh water are for drinking, cooking, bathing, and _____.

Match each description with its term.

Description

_____ 2. often carries nonpoint source pollution

_____ 3. chemicals from a factory pipe

_____ 4. pollution without a specific point of origin

Term

a. runoff
b. point source pollution
c. nonpoint source pollution

Chapter 4   Earth's Resources

Earth's Blanket of Air (pages 110–111)

5. 👁 The _____ of Earth's atmosphere helps to maintain life on the planet.

6. Circle the letter of the gas in the atmosphere that people need to live.

   a. ozone   b. oxygen   c. nitrogen

7. What are gases such as carbon dioxide and methane called that help maintain the warm temperatures near the surface of Earth?

   _____

8. Fill in the blanks in the following flowchart.

Possible Effects of Global Warming

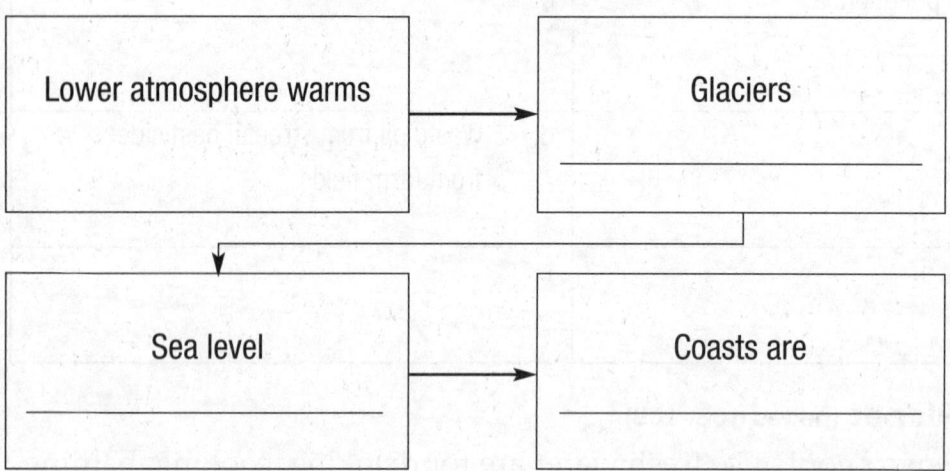

9. Use one of the terms below to fill in the blank. Burning fossil fuels is Earth's major source of _____.

   | oxygen | air pollution | nuclear energy |

Land Resources (pages 111–112)

10. 👁 Four resources that Earth's land provides are _____, forests, minerals, and energy resources such as petroleum.

11. Is the following sentence true or false? Agriculture has only a positive impact on the land. _____

12. Is the following sentence true or false? Mineral mining can destroy vegetation and cause soil erosion. _____

Chapter 4   Earth's Resources

Section 4.4 Protecting Resources
(pages 113–116)

This section discusses laws passed to protect Earth's water, air, and land resources.

Reading Strategy (page 113)

Summarizing After reading this section, complete the concept map to organize what you know about the major laws that help keep water, air, and land resources clean. For more information on this Reading Strategy, see the **Reading and Study Skills** in the **Skills and Reference Handbook** at the end of your textbook.

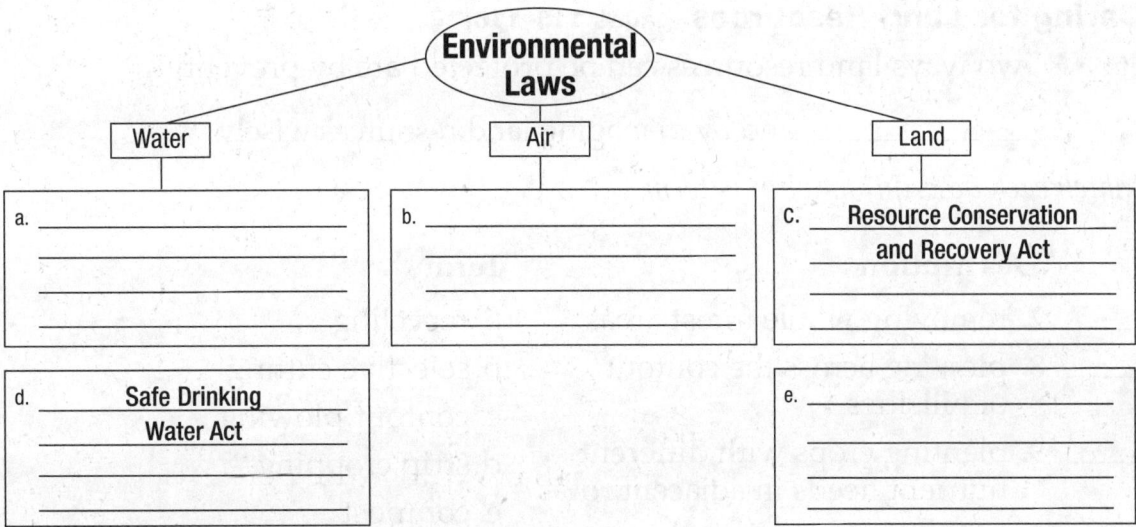

Keeping Water Clean and Safe (page 114)

1. Circle the letter of the term defined as "careful use of resources."

   a. recycling   b. composting   c. conservation

2. ◑ Circle the letter of the law that requires industries to reduce or stop point source pollution into surface waters.

   a. Safe Drinking Water Act

   b. Clean Water Act

   c. Resource Conservation and Recovery Act

3. ◑ Circle the letter of the law that sets maximum contaminant levels for water pollutants that could harm people's health.

   a. Safe Drinking Water Act

   b. Clean Water Act

   c. Resource Conservation and Recovery Act

Chapter 4   Earth's Resources

Protecting the Air (pages 114–115)

4. 👁 Is the following sentence true or false? The Clean Air Act is the United States' most important law for preventing air pollution.

_____

5. How could using less electricity help to reduce air pollution?

_____

_____

_____

Caring for Land Resources (pages 115–116)

6. 👁 Two ways land resources can be protected are by preventing

_____ and by managing land resources wisely.

Match each description with its term.

Description	Term
_____ **7.** removing whole forest areas	a. recycling
_____ **8.** plowing across the contour of hillsides	b. selective cutting
	c. contour plowing
_____ **9.** planting crops with different nutrient needs in adjacent rows	d. strip cropping
_____ **10.** fertilizer made of partly decomposed organic material	e. compost
	f. clear-cutting
_____ **11.** Only some trees in a forest are cut.	
_____ **12.** collecting and processing used items to make new products	

13. What law requires companies to store, transport, and dispose of their hazardous wastes according to guidelines? Circle the correct answer.

Safe Drinking Water Act   Clean Water Act   Resource Conservation and Recovery Act

Chapter 5 Weathering, Soil, and Mass Movements

Summary

5.1 Weathering

◉ **Mechanical weathering occurs when physical forces break rock into smaller and smaller pieces without changing the rock's mineral composition.**

◉ **In nature, three physical processes are especially important causes of mechanical weathering: frost wedging, unloading, and biological activity.**

- In nature, water finds its way into cracks in a rock. When the water freezes, it expands. This enlarges the cracks in the rock. Over time, the rock breaks into pieces. This is called **frost wedging**.
- Sections of rock that are wedged loose may tumble into large piles of rock debris called **talus**, which typically form at the base of steep, rocky cliffs.
- Unloading is when large masses of igneous rock are exposed through uplift and erosion, reducing the pressure on the igneous rock. Slabs of the outer rock separate like the layers of an onion and break loose in a process called **exfoliation**.
- Plants, animals, and humans all cause mechanical weathering.

◉ **Chemical weathering is the transformation of rock into one or more new compounds.**

- The most important agent of chemical weathering is water.
- Chemical weathering changes the properties of rock.
- Spheroidal weathering is a type of chemical weathering that changes the physical shape of the rock as well as its chemical composition.
- Mechanical weathering increases the rate of chemical weathering.

◉ **Two other factors that affect the rate of weathering are rock characteristics and climate.**

- Different rock types weather at different rates.
- Temperature and moisture both affect the rate of weathering.

5.2 Soil

◉ **Soil is the part of the regolith that supports the growth of plants.**

- **Regolith** is the layer of rocks and mineral fragments that covers nearly all of Earth's land surface.
- Composition, texture, and structure are three important characteristics of soil.

Chapter 5   Weathering, Soil, and Mass Movements

🜚 **Soil has four major components: mineral matter, or broken-down rock; organic matter, or humus, which is the decayed remains of organisms; water; and air.**

- The amount of these components in soil varies depending on the type of soil.
- Soil texture is the proportions of different particle sizes in soil. Texture strongly affects a soil's ability to support plant life.
- Plant cultivation, erosion, and water solubility are all affected by soil structure.

🜚 **The most important factors in soil formation are parent material, time, climate, organisms, and slope.**

- Parent material is the source of the mineral matter in soil.
- Temperature and precipitation, or climate, has the greatest effect on soil formation.
- In the nitrogen cycle, bacteria convert nitrogen gas into nitrogen compounds that plants can use.

🜚 **Soil varies in composition, texture, structure, and color at different depths.**

- These variations divide the soil into zones known as **soil horizons**.
- A vertical section through all of the soil horizons is called a **soil profile.**
- Mature soils often have three distinct soil horizons—the A horizon or topsoil, the B horizon or subsoil, and the C horizon, which contains partially weathered parent material.

🜚 **Three common types of soil are pedalfer, pedocal, and laterite.**

- **Pedalfers** usually form in temperate areas that receive more than 63 cm of rain each year. They contain large amounts of iron oxide and aluminum-rich clay.
- **Pedocals** are found in the drier western United States in areas that have grasses and brush vegetation. They contain abundant calcite and are a light gray-brown.
- **Laterites** form in hot, wet tropical areas where chemical weathering is intense. These are rich in iron oxide and aluminum oxide. Laterites contains almost no organic matter and few nutrients.

🜚 **Human activities that remove natural vegetation, such as farming, logging, and construction, have greatly accelerated soil erosion.**

- Soils are one of the most abused resources on Earth.
- Water, wind, and other forces such as climate, soil characteristics, and slope all affect the rate of erosion.
- Erosion can be controlled through planting windbreaks, terracing hillsides, plowing in contours, and rotating crops.

Chapter 5   Weathering, Soil, and Mass Movements

5.3 Mass Movements

◉ **The transfer of rock and soil downslope due to gravity is called mass movement.**

- Most landforms are caused by both weathering and mass movement.

◉ **Among the factors that commonly trigger mass movements are saturation of surface materials with water, oversteepening of slopes, removal of vegetation, and earthquakes.**

◉ **Geologists classify mass movements based on the kind of material that moves, how it moves, and the speed of movement.**

- A **rockfall** occurs when rocks or rock fragments fall freely through the air. This is common on steep slopes.
- In a slide, a block of material moves suddenly along a flat, inclined surface. Slides that include segments of bedrock are called **rockslides**.
- A **slump** is the downward movement of a block of material along a curved surface.
- A **mudflow** is a mass movement of soil and rock fragments containing a large amount of water, which moves quickly downslope.
- **Earthflows** are flows that move relatively slowly—from about a millimeter per day to several meters per day. They occur most often on hillsides in wet regions.
- The slowest type of mass movement is **creep**, which usually travels only a few millimeters or centimeters per year.

Chapter 5   Weathering, Soil, and Mass Movements

Section 5.1 Weathering
(pages 126–132)

This section describes different types of weathering in rocks.

Reading Strategy (page 126)

Building Vocabulary As you read the section, define each vocabulary term. For more information on this Reading Strategy, see the **Reading and Study Skills** in the **Skills and Reference Handbook** at the end of your textbook.

Vocabulary Term	Definition
Mechanical weathering	a. process in which physical forces break rock into pieces without changing the rock's mineral composition
Frost wedging	b.
Talus	c.
Exfoliation	d.
Chemical weathering	e.

Mechanical Weathering (pages 126–129)

1. Three types of mechanical weathering are frost wedging, unloading, and _____.

2. ⬛ Is the following sentence true or false? In nature, three physical processes are especially important causes of mechanical weathering: chemical reactions, spheroidal weathering, and the presence of water.

   _____

3. Circle the letter of each sentence that is true about mechanical weathering.

   a. Each piece of broken rock has the same characteristics as the original rock.

   b. In nature, three physical processes are especially important causes of mechanical weathering: frost wedging, unloading, and biological activity.

   c. When a rock is broken apart, less surface area is exposed to chemical weathering.

Chapter 5   Weathering, Soil, and Mass Movements

Chemical Weathering (pages 129–131)

4. Circle the letter of each sentence that is true about chemical weathering.

   a. Water is the most important agent in chemical weathering.

   b. Chemical weathering converts granite to clay minerals and quartz grains.

   c. Chemical weathering can change the shape of a rock and its chemical composition.

5. Use the term below to fill in the blank. The weathering process shown in the photograph is called_____.

   > spheroidal weathering
   > exfoliation
   > mechanical weathering

Rate of Weathering (pages 131–132)

6. Is the following sentence true or false? Factors that affect rate of weathering are surface area, rock characteristics, and climate.

   _____

7. Two characteristics that affect rate of weathering are number of cracks and _____.

8. How would an increase in the frequency of freezing and thawing affect the rate of weathering?

   a. decrease weathering

   b. increase weathering

   c. cause no change in weathering

Chapter 5   Weathering, Soil, and Mass Movements

Section 5.2 Soil
(pages 133–142)

This section describes the characteristics of soil.

Reading Strategy (page 133)

Comparing and Contrasting As you read this section, compare the three types of soils by completing the table. For more information on this Reading Strategy, see the **Reading and Study Skills** in the **Skills and Reference Handbook** at the end of your textbook.

Soil Type	Where It's Found
Pedalfer	a. temperate, forested areas that receive more than 63 cm of rain each year
Pedocal	b.
Laterite	c.

Characteristics of Soil (pages 133–135)

Match each description to its term.

	Description	Term
_____	**1.** layer of rock and mineral fragments	a. soil
_____	**2.** part of the regolith that supports growth of plants	b. humus
_____	**3.** decayed remains of organisms	c. regolith

4. 👁 Is the following sentence true or false? Soil has four major

components: mineral matter, humus, water, and air. _____

5. Humus is a source of plant nutrients, and it increases soil's ability

to _____.

6. Circle the letter of each sentence that is true about the functions that soil water serves in the soil.

a. Soil water provides the moisture needed for chemical reactions.

b. Soil water provides nutrients in a form that plants can use.

c. All soils contain the same amount of soil water.

Soil Formation (pages 135–137)

7. 👁 The most important factors in soil formation are parent materials,

time, climate, organisms, and _____.

Chapter 5   Weathering, Soil, and Mass Movements

The Soil Profile (page138)

8. Use the terms in the box to label each soil horizon shown in the figure.

| A   horizon | B   horizon | C   horizon |

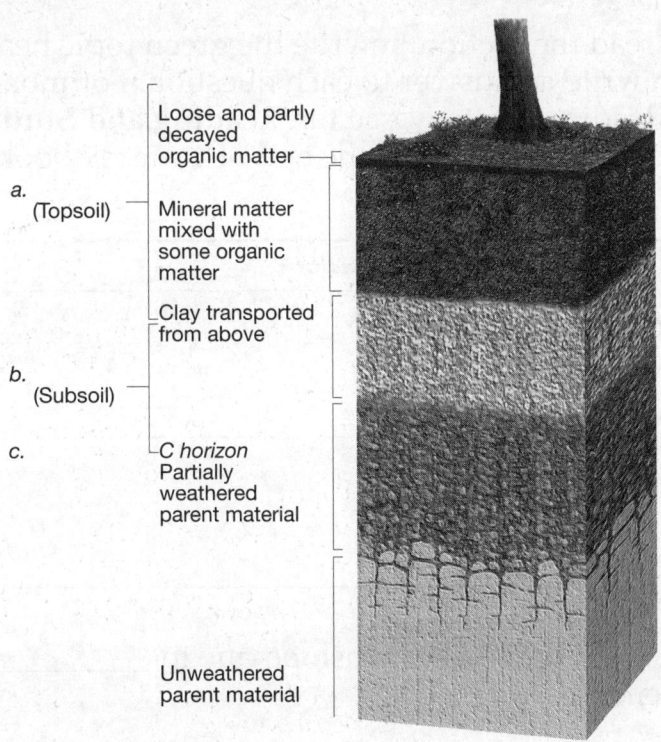

a.
(Topsoil)

Loose and partly decayed organic matter

Mineral matter mixed with some organic matter

Clay transported from above

b.
(Subsoil)

c.

C horizon
Partially weathered parent material

Unweathered parent material

Soil Types (pages 139–142)

9. ⬤ Three common types of soil are pedalfer, pedocal, and

_____.

Soil Erosion (pages 140–142)

10. ⬤ Is the following sentence true or false? Human activities, such as farming, logging, and construction, have slowed down the amount of

erosion that occurs today. _____

11. Is the following sentence true or false? In many regions of the world,

soil is eroding faster than it is being formed. _____

Section 5.3 Mass Movements
(pages 143–147)

This section describes situations in which large amounts of soil are moved naturally.

Reading Strategy (page 143)

Previewing As you read the section, rewrite the green topic headings as *what* questions. Then write an answer to each question. For more information on this Reading Strategy, see the **Reading and Study Skills** in the **Skills and Reference Handbook** at the end of your textbook.

Question	Answer
a. What triggers mass movements?	b.
c.	d.

1. 🔵 The transfer of rock and soil downslope due to _____ is called mass movement.

Triggers of Mass Movements (pages 144–145)

2. 🔵 The factors that commonly trigger mass movements are saturation of surface materials with water, oversteepening of slopes, removal of

vegetation, and _____.

3. Circle the letter of each sentence that is true about water triggering mass movements.

   a. Heavy rains and rapid melting of snow can trigger mass movements by saturating surface materials with water.

   b. When the pores in sediment become filled with water, the particles slide past one another more easily.

   c. If there is enough water, sand grains will ooze downhill.

4. Is the following sentence true or false? If the steepness of a slope exceeds

the stable angle, mass movements become more likely. _____

Chapter 5   Weathering, Soil, and Mass Movements

Types of Mass Movements (page 145–147)

Match each description with its term.

Description	Term
_____ **5.** a quickly moving mass of material that contains large amounts of water	a. rockfall
_____ **6.** when rock or rock fragments fall freely through the air	b. rockslide
_____ **7.** slides that include bedrock that move suddenly along a flat, inclined surface	c. mudflow

8. Identify each form of mass wasting shown below. Choose from these terms.

earthflow	slump	rockslide

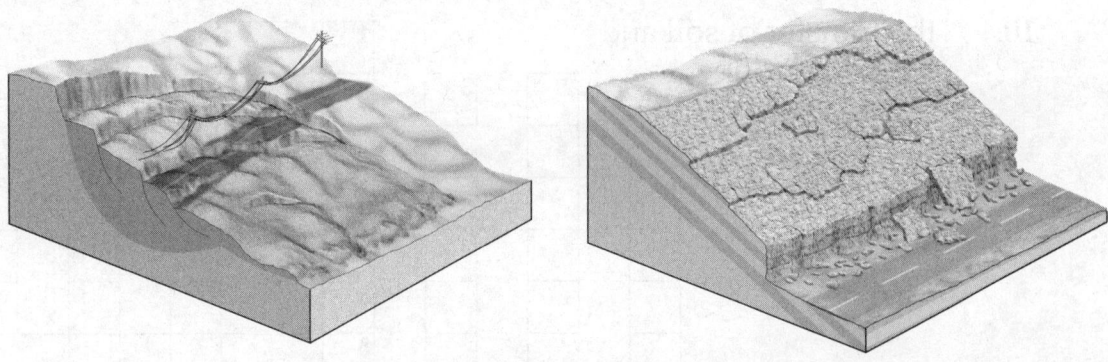

A. _____   B. _____

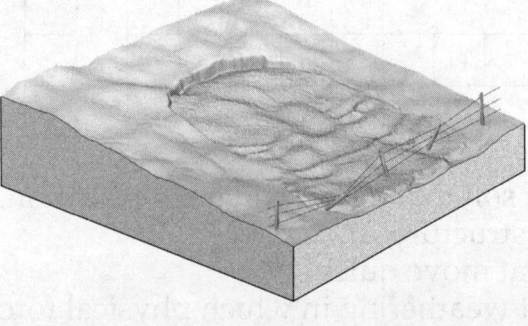

C. _____

Chapter 5   Weathering, Soil, and Mass Movements

WordWise

Use the vocabulary terms from Chapter 5 and the clues below to complete the crossword puzzle.

earthflow	mudflow	rockfall
laterite	pedalfer	rockslide
mass movement	pedocal	soil
mechanical	regolith	soil horizon

Clues across:

1. the part of the regolith that supports the growth of plants
6. soil usually found in drier western United States in areas that have grasses and brush vegetation
8. a layer of rock and mineral fragments produced by weathering
9. occurs when rocks or rock fragments fall freely through the air
10. the transfer of soil and rock downslope due to gravity

Clues down:

1. zones of soil that have similar composition, texture, structure, and color
2. flows that move quickly
3. a type of weathering in which physical forces break rock into smaller pieces without changing its composition
4. soil that forms in hot, wet tropical areas
5. flows that move relatively slowly
6. soil that usually forms in temperate areas
7. slide that include segments of bedrock

Chapter 6 Running Water and Groundwater

Summary

6.1 Running Water

Water constantly moves among the oceans, the atmosphere, the solid Earth, and the biosphere. This unending circulation of Earth's water supply is the water cycle.

- Energy from the sun and gravity power the water cycle.
- **Infiltration** is the movement of surface water into rock or soil through cracks and pore spaces.
- Plants also absorb water and release it into the atmosphere through transpiration.

Balance in the water cycle means the average annual precipitation over Earth equals the amount of water that evaporates.

The ability of a stream to erode and transport materials depends largely on its velocity.

- **Gradient** is the slope or steepness of a stream channel.
- A **stream channel** is the course the water in a stream follows.
- The **discharge** of a stream is the volume of water flowing past a certain point in a given unit of time.

While gradient decreases between a stream's headwaters and mouth, discharge increases.

- A **tributary** is a stream that empties into another stream.

Base level is the lowest point to which a stream can erode its channel.

- There are two types of base level—ultimate base level and temporary base level. Sea level is the ultimate base level. Temporary base levels include lakes and main streams that act as base level for their tributaries.
- A stream in a broad, flat-bottomed valley that is near its base level often develops a course with many bends called **meanders**.

6.2 The Work of Streams

Streams generally erode their channels lifting loose particles by abrasion, grinding, and by dissolving soluble material.

- Increased turbulence equals greater erosion.

Streams transport sediment in three ways.

1. in solution (dissolved load)
2. in suspension (suspended load)
3. scooting or rolling along the bottom (bed load)

Chapter 6   Running Water and Groundwater

- **Bed load** is the sediment that is carried by a stream along the bottom of its channel.
- The **capacity** of a stream is the maximum load it can carry.

◉ **Deposition occurs as streamflow drops below the critical settling velocity of a certain particle size. The sediment in that category begins to settle out.**

- The sorted material deposited by a stream is called **alluvium.**
- A **delta** is an accumulation of sediment formed where a stream enters a lake or ocean.
- A **natural levee** is a ridge made up mostly of coarse sediments that parallels some streams.

◉ **A narrow V-shaped valley shows that the stream's primary work has been downcutting toward base level.**

- A **floodplain** is the flat, low-lying portion of a stream valley subject to periodic flooding. It is caused by the side-to-side cutting of a stream close to base level.

◉ **Most floods are caused by rapid spring snow melt or storms that bring heavy rains over a large region.**

- A **flood** occurs when the discharge of a stream becomes so great that it exceeds the capacity of its channel and overflows its banks.

◉ **Measures to control flooding include artificial levees, flood control dams, and placing limits on floodplain development.**

◉ **A drainage basin is the land area that contributes water to a stream.**

- An imaginary line called a **divide** separates the drainage basins of one stream from another.

6.3 Water Beneath the Surface

◉ **Much of the water in soil seeps downward until it reaches the zone of saturation. The zone of saturation is the area where water fills all of the open spaces in sediment and rock. Groundwater is the water within this zone.**

- The upper limit of the zone of saturation is the **water table.**

◉ **Groundwater moves by twisting and turning through interconnected small openings. The groundwater moves more slowly when the pore spaces are smaller.**

- **Porosity** is the volume of open spaces in rock or soil.
- The **permeability** of a material is its ability to release a fluid.
- Permeable rock layers or sediments that transmit groundwater freely are **aquifers.** Aquifers are the source of well water.

Chapter 6   Running Water and Groundwater

A spring forms whenever the water table intersects the ground surface.

- A **spring** is a flow of groundwater that emerges naturally at the ground surface.
- A **geyser** is a hot spring in which a column of water shoots up with great force at various intervals.
- A **well** is a hole bored into the zone of saturation.
- In an **artesian well**, groundwater rises on its own under pressure.

Overuse and contamination threatens groundwater supplies in some areas.

- Supplies of groundwater are finite.

Groundwater erosion forms most caverns at or below the water table in the zone of saturation.

- A **cavern** is a naturally formed underground chamber.
- **Travertine** is a type of limestone formed over great spans of time from dripping water containing calcium carbonate. The resulting cave deposits are known as dripstone.

Karst areas typically have irregular terrain, with many depressions called sinkholes.

- **Karst topography** an area that has been shaped largely by the dissolving power of groundwater, and has a land surface with numerous depressions called sinkholes.
- A **sinkhole** is a depression made in a region where groundwater has removed soluble rock.

Section 6.1 Running Water
(pages 158–163)

This section discusses the water cycle and how water flows in streams.

Reading Strategy (page 158)

Building Vocabulary As you read this section, define in your own words each vocabulary term listed in the table. For more information on this Reading Strategy, see the **Reading and Study Skills** in the **Skills and Reference Handbook** at the end of your textbook.

Vocabulary Term	Definition
Water cycle	unending circulation of Earth's water supply
Infiltration	
Transpiration	

The Water Cycle (pages 158–159)

1. ⬤ Circle the letter of the term used to describe the unending circulation of Earth's water supply.

   a. water balance   b. water cycle   c. base level

2. Select the correct letter in the figure that shows each of the following processes in the water cycle.

   _____ runoff   _____ precipitation
   _____ infiltration

Chapter 6   Running Water and Groundwater

Earth's Water Balance (page 159)

3. 👄 Earth's water cycle is balanced in that each year the average amount of precipitation that occurs over Earth is equal to the amount of water that _____. Circle the correct answer.

discharges   evaporates   erodes

Streamflow (pages 160–161)

4. 👄 A stream's ability to erode and move material depends largely on its

_____.

Match each definition with its term.

Definition	Term
_____ 5. course that water in a stream follows	a. gradient
_____ 6. volume of water flowing past a certain point in a given unit of time	b. discharge
_____ 7. steepness of a stream channel	c. velocity
_____ 8. distance that water travels in a period of time	d. stream channel

Changes From Upstream to Downstream (page 162)

9. 👄 Is the following sentence true or false? A stream's discharge increases between the headwaters and mouth of the stream. _____

10. 👄 Is the following sentence true or false? From its headwaters to its mouth, a stream's gradient increases. _____

Base Level (pages 162–163)

11. 👄 Circle the letter of the lowest point to which a stream can erode its channel.

a. mouth   b. headwaters   c. base level

12. 👄 Circle the letter of the name of a bend in a stream.

a. meander   b. tributary   c. mouth

Chapter 6   Running Water and Groundwater

Section 6.2 The Work of Streams
(pages 164–170)

This section discusses streams and explains how they help shape Earth's surface.

Reading Strategy (page 164)

Comparing and Contrasting Preview the Key Concepts, topic headings, vocabulary, and figures in this section. List things you expect to learn about each. After reading, state what you learned about each item you listed. For more information on this Reading Strategy, see the **Reading and Study Skills** in the **Skills and Reference Handbook** at the end of your textbook.

What I Expect to Learn	What I Learned

Erosion (page 164)

1. ☞ Streams erode their channels by abrasion, _____, and dissolving soluble material.

Sediment Transport (page 165)

2. ☞ Circle the letter of the name for the material a stream carries in solution.

   a. bed load   b. dissolved load   c. mineral load

3. ☞ Circle the letter of what the large, solid material a stream carries along its bed is called.

   a. bed load   b. dissolved load   c. maximum load

4. Is the following sentence true or false? Most streams carry the largest part of their load in suspension. _____

5. Is the following sentence true or false? As a stream's velocity decreases, its competence increases. _____

6. A stream's _____ is the maximum load it can carry. Circle the correct answer.

   capacity   suspension   velocity

Chapter 6   Running Water and Groundwater

Deposition (pages 166–167)

7. 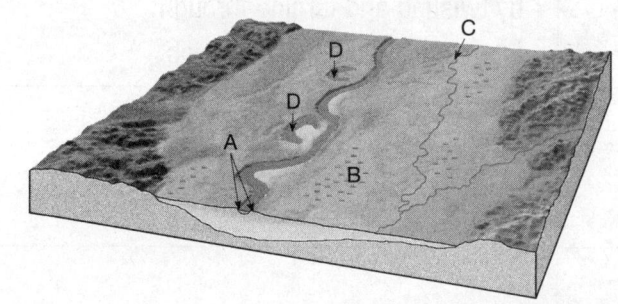 When stream flow drops below the critical settling velocity of a

   certain size particle, _____ occurs. Circle the correct answer.

   suspension   deposition   erosion

8. When a stream enters the still waters of an ocean or a lake, its velocity

   decreases and sediment is deposited to form a _____.

Stream Valleys (pages 167–168)

9. Circle the letter that represents an oxbow lake in the figure below.

   a. A   b. B   c. D

Floods and Flood Control (pages 168–169)

Match each description with its term.

	Description	Term
_____	10. 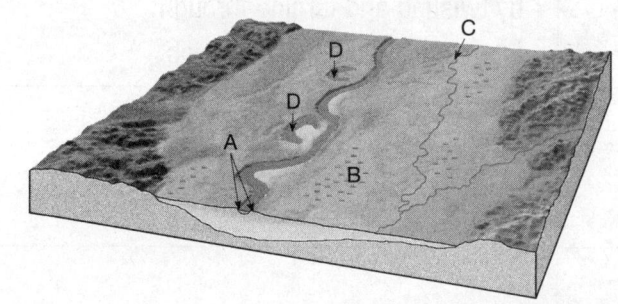 earthen mounds built on river banks	a. artificial levees
_____	11. 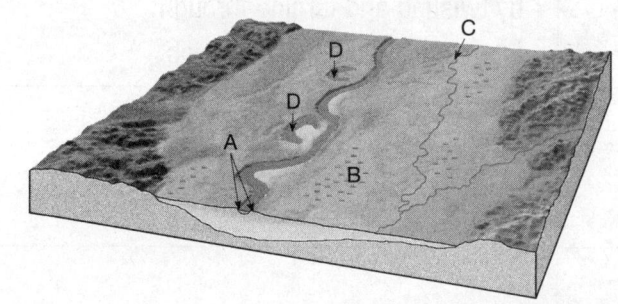 structures that store floodwater and let it out slowly	b. floods
_____	12. 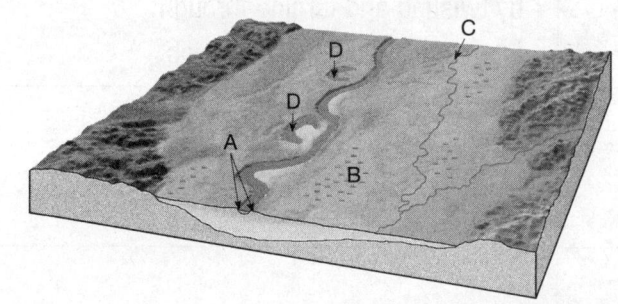 mostly caused by rapid snowmelt and storms	c. flood-control dams

Drainage Basins (page 170)

13. 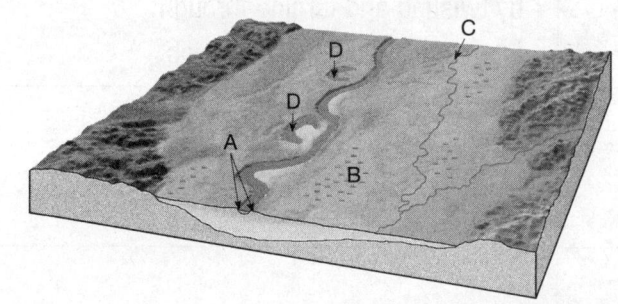 The land area that contributes water to a stream is known as a(n)

   _____. Circle the correct answer.

   drainage basin   artifical levee   stream valley

Section 6.3 Water Beneath the Surface
(pages 171–179)

This section discusses groundwater, including the environmental threats posed to it and landforms associated with it.

Reading Strategy (page 171)

Comparing and Contrasting Before you read the section, rewrite the green topic headings as *how*, *why*, and *what* questions. As you read, write an answer to each question. For more information on this Reading Strategy, see the **Reading and Study Skills** in the **Skills and Reference Handbook** at the end of your textbook.

Question	Answer
How does water move underground?	by twisting and turning through interconnected small openings
What are some environmental problems associated with groundwater?	

Distribution and Movement of Water Underground (pages 171–172)

1. ⬤ Select the appropriate letter in the figure that identifies each of the following groundwater features.

   _____ zone of saturation
   _____ aquitard
   _____ spring
   _____ water table
   _____ zone of aeration

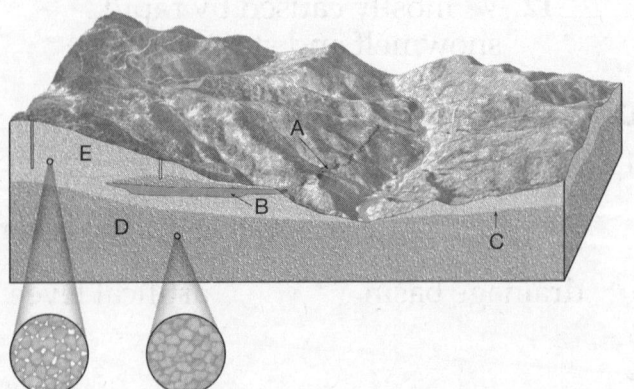

Chapter 6   Running Water and Groundwater

Springs (pages 172–173)

2. Circle the letter of the following that forms whenever the ground surface and water table intersect.

a. aquifer   b. spring   c. well

3. A type of spring called a(n) _____ is a column of water that shoots up intermittently with great force.

Wells (page 174)

4. Circle the letter of the location a well must be drilled to provide a continuous water supply.

a. in the zone of aeration

b. far below the water table

c above the zone of saturation

5. Is the following sentence true or false? In an artesian well, groundwater

rises on its own pressure. _____

Environmental Problems Associated With Groundwater (pages 175–176)

6. Two things that threaten groundwater supplies are overuse and

_____.

Caverns (pages 177–178)

Match each description with its groundwater feature.

Description

_____ 7. dripstone feature that forms on a cavern ceiling

_____ 8. type of limestone deposited in caverns by dripping water

_____ 9. natural process that forms caverns

_____ 10. naturally formed underground chamber

Groundwater Feature

a. cavern

b. travertine

c. stalactite

d. erosion

Karst Topography (pages 178–179)

11. Karst areas typically have irregular terrain and depressions called

_____.

Chapter 6   Running Water and Groundwater

WordWise

Use the vocabulary terms in the box and clues below. Write the terms, putting one letter in each blank. Use the circled letters to find the hidden word.

aquifer	gradient	permeablity
capacity	groundwater	porosity
delta	infiltration	transportation

Clues

1. how plants release water into the atmosphere
2. a stream's slope
3. the movement of surface water into rock or soil through cracks and pore spaces
4. a sediment's ability to release a fluid
5. a permeable rock layer that transmits groundwater freely
6. a triangular shaped sediment accumulation
7. the maximum load a stream can carry
8. the water within the zone of saturation
9. the percentage of a rock that is occupied by pore spaces

Vocabulary Terms

1. _ _ _ _ _ _ _ _ Ⓞ _ _ _
2. _ Ⓞ _ _ _ _ _ _ _
3. Ⓞ _ _ _ _ _ _ _ _ _ _
4. _ _ _ _ _ _ Ⓞ _ _ _ _ _
5. _ _ Ⓞ _ _ _ _
6. _ _ _ Ⓞ _
7. _ _ _ Ⓞ _ _ _ _
8. _ Ⓞ _ _ _ _ _ _ _ _
9. _ _ _ _ _ _ Ⓞ _

Hidden Word: _ _ _ _ _ _ _ _

Definition:

_____

_____

Chapter 7 Glaciers, Deserts, and Wind

Summary

7.1 Glaciers

🌊 **A valley glacier is a stream of ice that flows between steep rock walls from a place near the top of the mountain valley.**

- An **ice age** is a period of time when much of Earth's land is covered in glaciers.
- A **glacier** is a thick ice mass that moves slowly over the land surface.
- The **snowline** is the lowest elevation in a particular area that remains covered in snow all year.
- **Valley glaciers** are ice masses that slowly advance down valleys that were originally occupied by streams.

🌊 **Ice sheets are sometimes called continental ice sheets because they cover large regions where the climate is extremely cold. They are huge compared to valley glaciers.**

- **Ice sheets** are enormous ice masses that flow in all directions and cover everything but the highest land.
- The Antarctic Ice Sheet holds nearly two-thirds of Earth's fresh water.

🌊 **The movement of glaciers is referred to as flow. Glacial flow happens two ways: plastic flow and basal slip.**

- Plastic flow occurs when brittle ice begins to distort and change shape.
- Gravity causes basal slip, where the ice mass slips and slides downhill.

🌊 **The glacial budget is the balance or lack of balance between accumulation at the upper end of a glacier and loss, or wastage, at the lower end.**

- When a glacier loses ice faster than it gains ice, it retreats.
- When a glacier gains ice faster than it loses ice, it advances.

🌊 **Many landscapes were changed by the widespread glaciers of the recent ice age.**

- Glaciers erode the land by plucking and abrasion.

🌊 **Glaciers are responsible for a variety of erosional landscape features, such as glacial troughs, hanging valleys, cirques, arêtes, and horns.**

- After glaciation, alpine valleys are no longer narrow.
- As a glacier moves down a valley once occupied by a stream, the glacier widens, deepens, and straightens the valley. The once narrow V-shaped valley is changed into a U-shaped **glacial trough**.
- A glacier carves cirques, arêtes, and horns by plucking and removing rocks.

Chapter 7   Glaciers, Deserts, and Wind

☞ **Glacial drift applies to all sediments of glacial origin, no matter how, where, or in what form they were deposited. There are two types of glacial drift: till and stratified drift.**

- **Till** is the material deposited directly by the glacier. It is deposited as the glacier melts and drops its load of rock debris.
- **Stratified drift** is sediment laid down by glacial meltwater.

☞ **Glaciers are responsible for a variety of depositional features, including moraines, outwash plains, kettles, drumlins, and eskers.**

- When glaciers melt, they leave layers or ridges of till called **moraines**.
- During the recent ice age, glaciers covered almost 30 percent of Earth's land. The ice sheets significantly changed drainage patterns over large regions, creating lakes and changing the directions of rivers.

7.2 Deserts

☞ **Much of the weathered debris in deserts has resulted from mechanical weathering.**

☞ **Though mechanical weathering is more significant in deserts, chemical weathering is not completely absent. Over long time spans, clays and thin soils do form.**

☞ **In the desert, most streams are ephemeral—they only carry water after it rains.**

- Ephemeral streams, also known as washes or arroyos, may flow for only a few hours or a few days.
- Because they are found in areas that lack much vegetation, ephemeral streams are susceptible to dangerous flash floods.

☞ **Most desert streams dry up long before long before they ever reach the ocean. The streams are quickly depleted by evaporation and soil infiltration.**

- An **alluvial fan** is a cone of debris left when an intermittent stream flows out of a canyon, loses speed, and quickly dumps its sediment.
- After heavy rain or snowmelt in the mountains, streams may flow across the alluvial fans to the center of the basin, converting the basin floor into a shallow **playa lake**. Playa lakes last only a few days or weeks.

☞ **Most desert erosion results from running water. Although wind erosion is more significant in deserts than elsewhere, water does most of the erosional work in deserts.**

- Although running water in the desert is infrequent, it is an important geological force.

Chapter 7   Glaciers, Deserts, and Wind

7.3 Landscapes Shaped by Wind

Wind erodes in the desert in two ways: deflation and abrasion.

- Strong winds transport and deposit sediment.
- **Deflation** is the lifting and removal of loose particles such as clay and silt.
- Deflation creates a stony surface layer called **desert pavement** when it removes all the sand and silt and leaves only coarser particles.
- Abrasion happens when wind-blown sand cuts and polishes exposed rock surfaces.

The wind can create landforms when it deposits its sediments, especially in deserts and along coasts. Both layers of loess and sand dunes are landscape features deposited by wind.

- Loess is windblown silt that blankets the landscape.

Unlike deposits of loess, which form blanket-like layers over broad areas, winds commonly deposit sand in mounds or ridges called dunes.

- Whenever wind encounters an obstruction, no matter how small, dunes may form.

What form sand dunes assume depends on the wind direction and speed, how much sand is available, and the amount of vegetation.

- Barchan dunes are solitary sand dunes shaped like crescents.
- Transverse dunes form in long ridges that are perpendicular to the direction of the wind.
- Barchanoid dunes form at right angles to the wind and look like several barchan dunes placed side by side.
- Longitudinal dunes form parallel to the wind.
- Parabolic dunes look like backwards barchan dunes. They often form along coasts and where there is some vegetation.
- Star dunes have three or four sharp ridges, and their bases look like stars.

Chapter 7 Glaciers, Deserts, and Wind

Section 7.1 Glaciers
(pages 188–198)

This section discusses the characteristics of different types of glaciers.

Reading Strategy (page 188)

Building Vocabulary As you read this section, define each vocabulary term in your own words. For more information on this Reading Strategy, see the **Reading and Study Skills** in the **Skills and Reference Handbook** at the end of your textbook.

Vocabulary Term	Definition
Ice age	a. a period of time when much of Earth was covered by glaciers
Glacier	b.
Snowline	c.
Valley glacier	d.
Ice sheet	e. an enormous ice mass that flows in all directions from one or more centers and covers everything but the highest land
Glacial trough	f.
Till	g.
Stratified drift	h. sediment laid down by glacial meltwater
Moraine	i.

Types of Glaciers (pages 188–189)

1. 🖰 A _____ is a stream of ice that flows between steep rock walls from a place near the top of a mountain valley.

2. 🖰 _____ cover large regions where the climate is extremely cold.

How Glaciers Move (pages 190–191)

3. 🖰 Is the following sentence true or false? Glacial flow happens in two ways: plastic flow and basal slip. _____

Chapter 7   Glaciers, Deserts, and Wind

Glacial Erosion (page 192)

4. The two types of glacial erosion are plucking and _____.

Landforms Created by Glacial Erosion (pages 193–194)

5. The figure shows an area affected by glaciation. Select the correct letter in the figure that identifies each of the following features.

_____ cirque

_____ glacial trough

_____ hanging valley

_____ horn

_____ arête

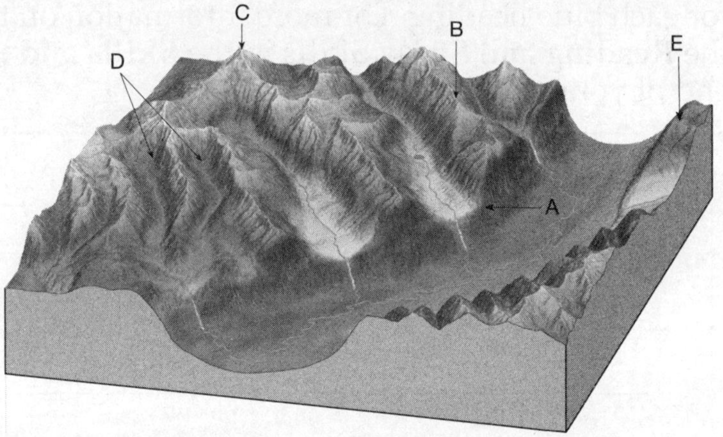

Glacial Deposits (pages 194–195)

6. ⬤ _____ applies to all sediments of glacial origin, no matter how, where, or in what form they were deposited.

7. ⬤ The two types of glacial drift are _____ and stratified drift.

Moraines, Outwash Plains, and Kettles (pages 195–197)

Match each description to its term.

	Description	Term
_____	8. layers or ridges of till	a. end moraine
_____	9. debris that forms at the end of a stationary glacier	b. kettle
_____	10. formed when blocks of stagnant ice become buried in drift	c. moraine

Glaciers of the Ice Age (pages 197–198)

11. Is the following sentence true or false? During the recent ice age, the Northern Hemisphere had twice as much ice as the Southern Hemisphere.

_____

Chapter 7   Glaciers, Deserts, and Wind

Section 7.2 Deserts
(pages 199–202)

This section explains the weathering and erosion processes that occur in the desert.

Reading Strategy (page 199)

Summarizing As you read this section, write a brief summary of the text for each blue heading. For more information on this Reading Strategy, see the **Reading and Study Skills** in the **Skills and Reference Handbook** at the end of your textbook.

Weathering
_____
_____
_____
The Role of Water
_____
_____
_____

Geological Processes in Arid Climates (pages 199–201)

1. ◉ Much of the weathered debris in deserts is a result of

    _____.

2. Why is rock weathering of any type greatly reduced in a desert climate?

    _____

    _____

    _____

3. Circle the letter of each sentence that is true about weathering and desert landscapes.

    a. Most weathering debris consists of rocks and minerals that remain unchanged.

    b. The rust-colored tint of some desert landscapes is due to iron-bearing silicate materials.

    c. Most of the weathering in desert climates is chemical.

4. ◉ Is the following sentence true or false? In the desert most streams are

    ephemeral—they only carry water after it rains. _____

Chapter 7   Glaciers, Deserts, and Wind

Basin and Range: A Desert Landscape (pages 201–202)

Match each description to its term.

Description	Term
_____ **5.** sediment that is carried down mountain canyons and deposited on the gentle slopes at the base of the mountains	a. alluvial fan
	b. playa lake
	c. running water
_____ **6.** formed when flat area in a desert receives abundant rainfall	
_____ **7.** the source of most desert erosion	

8. Complete the following concept map. Choose from these terms.

mechanical weathering   water   chemical weathering

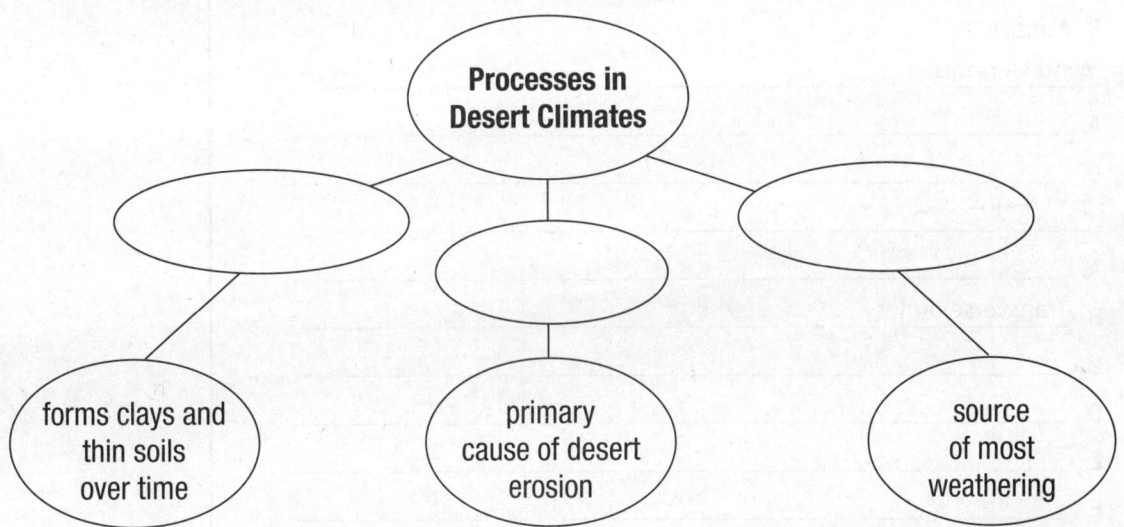

9. Circle the letter of each sentence that is true about a desert landscape.

a. Arid regions typically have interior drainage.

b. A dry, flat lakebed that was formerly a playa lake is called a playa.

c. The Nile River is an example of a permanent stream that crosses an arid region.

Chapter 7   Glaciers, Deserts, and Wind

Section 7.3 Landscapes Shaped by Wind
(pages 203–207)

This section describes how winds shape various landforms.

Reading Strategy (page 203)

Outlining As you read, make an outline of this section. Use the green headings as the main topics and the blue headings as subtopics. Add supporting details to the outline. For more information on this Reading Strategy, see the **Reading and Study Skills** in the **Skills and Reference Handbook** at the end of your textbook.

Landscapes Shaped by Wind
I. Wind Erosion
A. Deflation
B. Abrasion
II. Wind Deposits _____
A. _____
B. _____
III. _____
A. _____
B. Transverse dunes _____
C. _____
D. _____
E. _____
F. _____

Wind Erosion (pages 203–204)

Match each description to its term.

Description	Term
_____ **1.** shallow depressions caused by deflation	a. deflation
_____ **2.** a stony surface caused by deflation	b. abrasion
_____ **3.** the cutting and polishing of exposed rock surfaces by windblown sand	c. blowouts
_____ **4.** the lifting and removal of loose particles such as clay and silt	d. desert pavement

Chapter 7   Glaciers, Deserts, and Wind

5. Circle the letter of each statement that is true about wind erosion.

a. Wind erodes the desert in two ways: deflation and abrasion.

b. All blowouts caused by deflation are about the same size.

c. Sand rarely travels more than a meter above the surface, so the wind's sandblasting effect is limited in the vertical direction.

Wind Deposits (pages 204–205)

6. Is the following sentence true or false? Layers of loess and sand dunes

are landscaping features deposited by water. _____

7. _____ is windblown silt that blankets the landscape.

8. Circle the letter of each statement that is true about wind deposits.

a. The thickest and most extensive deposits of loess on Earth occur in western and northern China.

b. Winds commonly deposit sand in mounds or ridges called dunes.

c. Dunes occur on unobstructed flat ground.

Types of Sand Dunes (pages 206–207)

9. Write the type of each dune illustrated in the figures below. Choose from the terms in the box.

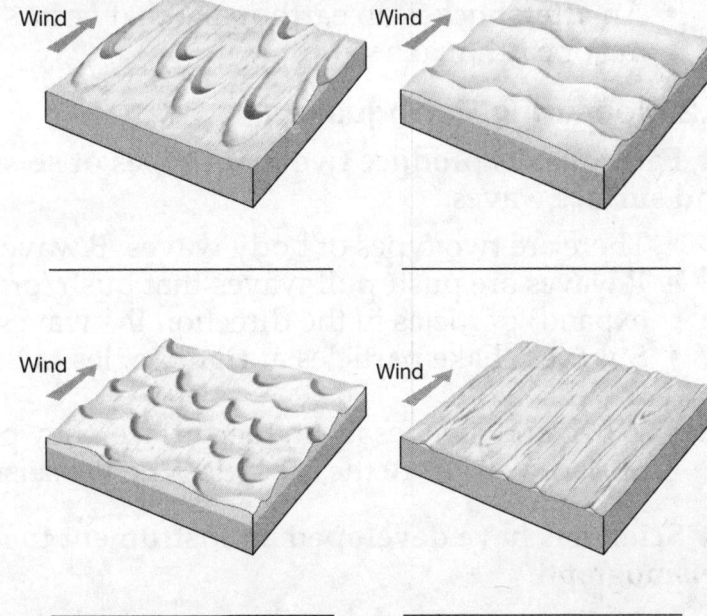

barchan
barchanoid
longitudinal
transverse

Chapter 8 Earthquakes and Earth's Interior

Summary

8.1 What Is an Earthquake?

◉ **Faults are fractures in Earth where movement has occurred.**

- An **earthquake** is the vibration of Earth produced by the rapid release of energy within the lithosphere.
- Earthquakes are caused by slippage along a break in the lithosphere, called a **fault**.
- The point within Earth where an earthquake starts is called the **focus**.
- The energy released by an earthquake travels in all directions from the focus in the form of **seismic waves**.
- The movement that occurs along faults during earthquakes is a major factor in changing Earth's surface.
- The **epicenter** is the location on the surface directly above the focus.

◉ **According to the elastic rebound hypothesis, most earthquakes are produced by the rapid release of energy stored in rock that has been subjected to great forces. When the strength of the rock is exceeded, it suddenly breaks, releasing some of its stored energy as seismic waves.**

- Forces inside Earth slowly deform the rock that makes up Earth's crust, causing rock to bend.
- **Elastic rebound** is the tendency for the deformed rock along a fault to spring back after an earthquake.
- An **aftershock** is an earthquake that occurs sometime soon after a major earthquake.

8.2 Measuring Earthquakes

◉ **Earthquakes produce two main types of seismic waves—body waves and surface waves.**

- There are two types of body waves: P waves and S waves.
- **P waves** are push-pull waves that push (or compress) and pull (or expand) particles in the direction the waves travel.
- **S waves** shake particles at right angles to the waves' direction of travel.
- When body waves reach the surface, they produce **surface waves**. Surface waves are the most destructive seismic waves.

◉ **Scientists have developed an instrument to record seismic waves—the seismograph.**

- A seismograph produces a time record of ground motion during an earthquake called a **seismogram**. A seismogram shows all three types of seismic waves.

⬤ **The Richter scale and the moment magnitude scale measure earthquake magnitude. The Modified Mercalli scale is based on earthquake intensity.**

- The **moment magnitude** is derived from the amount of displacement that occurs along a fault. Scientists today use the moment magnitude scale to measure earthquakes.

⬤ **A travel-time graph, data from seismograms made at three or more locations, and a globe can be used to determine an earthquake's epicenter.**

8.3 Earthquake Hazards

⬤ **Earthquake-related hazards include seismic shaking, liquefaction, landslides and mudflows, and tsunamis.**

- The ground vibrations caused by seismic waves are called seismic shaking.
- **Liquefaction** is a process earthquakes can cause in which soil and rock saturated with water turn into liquid and can no longer support buildings.
- A **tsunami** is a wave formed when the ocean floor shifts suddenly during an earthquake.
- Earthquakes can cause landslides and mudflows, two destructive events that can quickly bury entire towns under debris.

⬤ **Earthquake damage and loss of life can be reduced by determining the earthquake risk for an area, building earthquake-resistant structures, and following earthquake safety precautions.**

- A **seismic gap** is an area along a fault where there has not been any earthquake activity for a long period of time.

8.4 Earth's Layered Structure

⬤ **Earth's interior consists of three major layers defined by their chemical composition—the crust, mantle, and core.**

- The **crust**, the thin, rocky outer layer of Earth, is divided into oceanic and continental crust.
- Under the crust is the **mantle**—a solid, rocky shell that extends to a depth of 2890 kilometers.
- The **core** is a the innermost layer of Earth. The core is divided into an outer core and an inner core.

⬤ **Earth can be divided into layers based on physical properties—the lithosphere, the asthenosphere, the lower mantle, the outer core, and the inner core.**

- Earth's outermost layer consists of the crust and uppermost mantle and forms a relatively cool, rigid shell called the **lithosphere**.

Chapter 8   Earthquakes and Earth's Interior

- Beneath the lithosphere lies a soft, comparatively weak layer known as the **asthenosphere**.
- Near the base of the mantel lies a more rigid layer called the lower mantle.
- The **outer core** is a liquid layer beneath the mantle that is 2260 kilometers thick. The outer core generates Earth's magnetic field.
- The **inner core** is the solid innermost layer of Earth, which has a radius of 1220 kilometers.

◑ During the twentieth century, studies of the paths of P and S waves through Earth helped scientists identify the boundaries of Earth's layers and determine that the outer core is liquid.

- The boundary that separates the crust from the underlying mantle is known as the **Moho**.

◑ To determine the composition of Earth's layers, scientists studied seismic data, rock samples from the crust and mantle, meteorites, and high-pressure experiments on Earth materials.

Chapter 8   Earthquakes and Earth's Interior

Section 8.1 What Is an Earthquake?
(pages 218–221)

This section explains what earthquakes and faults are and what causes earthquakes.

Reading Strategy (page 218)

Building Vocabulary As you read this section, write a definition for each vocabulary term in your own words. For more information on this Reading Strategy, see the **Reading and Study Skills** in the **Skills and Reference Handbook** at the end of your textbook.

Vocabulary	Definition
earthquake	a.
fault	b. fracture in Earth where movement has occurred
focus	c.
epicenter	d.

1. Circle the letter of the approximate number of major earthquakes that take place each year.

   a. about 50   b. about 100   c. about 3000

Earthquakes (pages 218–219)

Match each description with its earthquake feature.

Description	Earthquake Feature
_____ 2. energy that travels in all directions from the earthquake origin	a. epicenter
_____ 3. ● fracture where movement has occurred	b. focus
_____ 4. surface location directly above where an earthquake originates	c. seismic wave
_____ 5. point within Earth where an earthquake starts	d. fault

Chapter 8   Earthquakes and Earth's Interior

The Cause of Earthquakes (pages 219–221)

6. Is the following sentence true or false? It was not until after the 1906 San Francisco earthquake was studied that the actual cause of earthquakes

was understood. _____

7. Complete the flowchart to show the sequence of events that occur when rocks are deformed along a fault.

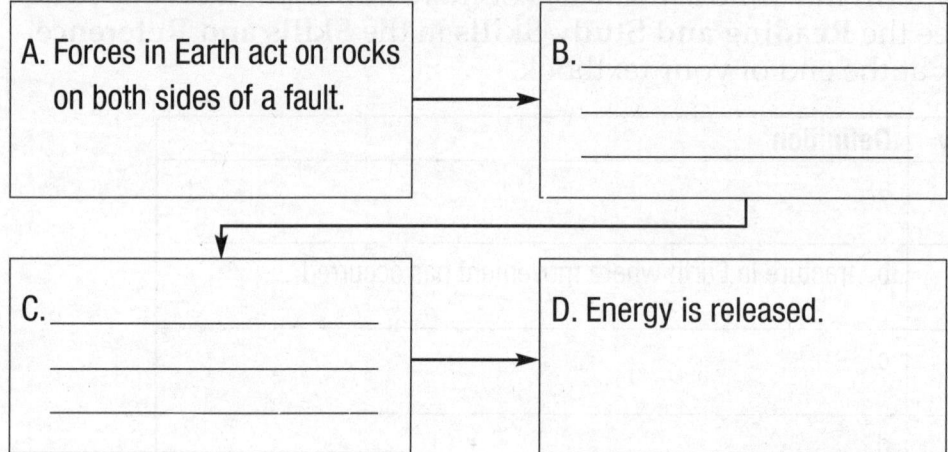

A. Forces in Earth act on rocks on both sides of a fault.

B. _____
_____
_____

C. _____
_____
_____

D. Energy is released.

8. The _____ hypothesis states that when rocks are deformed, they bend and then break, releasing stored energy.

9. Is the following sentence true or false? Most earthquakes occur along

existing faults. _____

10. Circle the letter of small Earth movements that occur following a major earthquake.

   a. foreshocks   b. slippage   c. aftershocks

11. What is fault creep? _____

_____

Section 8.2 Measuring Earthquakes
(pages 222–227)

This section discusses types of seismic waves and how earthquakes are located and measured.

Reading Strategy (page 222)

Outlining As you read, fill in the outline with the important ideas in this section. Use the green headings as the main topics and the blue headings as subtopics. For more information on this Reading Strategy, see the **Reading and Study Skills** in the **Skills and Reference Handbook** at the end of your textbook.

Measuring Earthquakes
I. Seismic Waves
A. P Waves
B. _____
C. _____
II. _____
A. _____
B. Seismograms
III. _____
A. Richter Scale
B. _____
C. _____
IV. _____

Seismic Waves (page 222–223)

1. ◉ Earthquakes produce two main types of seismic waves—body waves

   and _____ waves.

2. The figure shows a typical recording of an earthquake. Select the correct letter in the figure that identifies each of the following types of seismic waves.

   _____ surface wave

   _____ S wave

   _____ P wave

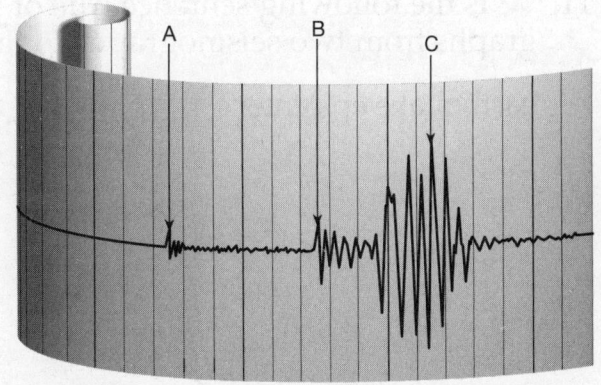

3. ◉ Circle the letter of the name of the recording of the three types of seismic waves in the figure on page 81.

   a. seismograph   b. seismogram   c. seismic wave

Measuring Earthquakes (pages 225–226)

4. ◉ Two types of measurements scientists use to describe the size of

   earthquakes are intensity and _____.

Match each description with its term related to earthquake measurement.

Description	Term
_____ 5. magnitude scale that estimates the energy released by earthquakes	a. intensity
_____ 6. outdated scale for measuring magnitude of earthquakes	b. magnitude
	c. Richter scale
	d. moment magnitude scale
_____ 7. ◉ measure of the size of seismic waves or amount of energy released at the earthquake source	
_____ 8. ◉ measure of the amount of earthquake shaking at a location based on damage	

9. ◉ What measurement do scientists today use for earthquakes? Circle the correct answer.

   a. Richter scale   b. moment magnitude   c. modified Mercalli
                            scale   scale

Locating an Earthquake (pages 226–227)

10. Is the following sentence true or false? On a seismogram, the greater the interval is between the arrival of the first P wave and the first S wave,

    the greater the distance to the earthquake source. _____

11. ◉ Is the following sentence true or false? You can use travel-time graphs from two seismographs to find the exact location of an

    earthquake epicenter. _____

Chapter 8   Earthquakes and Earth's Interior

Section 8.3 Earthquake Hazards
(pages 228–232)

This section discusses damage caused by earthquakes and explains how earthquakes are predicted.

Reading Strategy (page 228)

Monitoring Your Understanding Preview the Key Concepts, topic headings, vocabulary, and figures in this section. List two things you expect to learn. After reading, state what you learned about each item you listed. For more information on this Reading Strategy, see the **Reading and Study Skills** in the **Skills and Reference Handbook** at the end of your textbook.

What I Expect to Learn	What I Learned
a.	b.
c.	d.

Causes of Earthquake Damage (pages 228–230)

1. Define liquefaction.

_____

_____

2. Is the following sentence true or false? Most earthquakes generate

tsunamis. _____

3. The ground vibrations caused by seismic waves are called

_____ .

4. 🔵 During an earthquake, violent shaking can cause soil and rock on

slopes to move, resulting in _____ . Circle the correct answer.

waves   tsunamis   landslides

Chapter 8   Earthquakes and Earth's Interior

5. Complete the table about tsunamis.

Tsunamis		
Definition	**Causes**	**Areas Protected from Tsunamis by Warning System**
	a.	a.
	b. can also be triggered by underwater landslides or volcanic eruptions	b. after deadly 2004 tsunami, a similar system planned for Indian and Atlantic oceans

Reducing Earthquake Damage (pages 231–232)

6. Three factors that affect the degree of damage that occurs to

structures as a result of earthquakes are _____, nature of the material on which the structure is built, and design of the structure.

7. Circle the letter of the structure that is least likely to be damaged in a major earthquake.

   a. reinforced steel-frame building

   b. nonflexible wood-frame building

   c. unreinforced stone building

8. Is the following sentence true or false? Scientists are able to make accurate long-term earthquake predictions based on their understanding

of how earthquakes occur. _____

9. What do scientists call an area along a fault where no earthquake

activity has occurred for a long time? _____

Chapter 8   Earthquakes and Earth's Interior

Section 8.4 Earth's Layered Structure
(pages 233–237)

This section describes Earth's layers and their composition.

Reading Strategy (page 233)

Sequencing After you read, complete the sequence of layers in Earth's interior. For more information on this Reading Strategy, see the **Reading and Study Skills** in the **Skills and Reference Handbook** at the end of your textbook.

Earth's Internal Structure

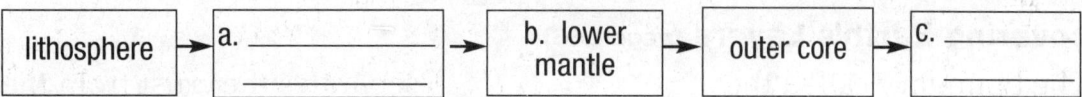

| lithosphere | → | a. _____ | → | b. lower mantle | → | outer core | → | c. _____ |

Layers Defined by Composition (pages 233–234)

1. ⬤ Label the three major layers of Earth's interior. Choose from the following terms.

| core | crust | mantle |

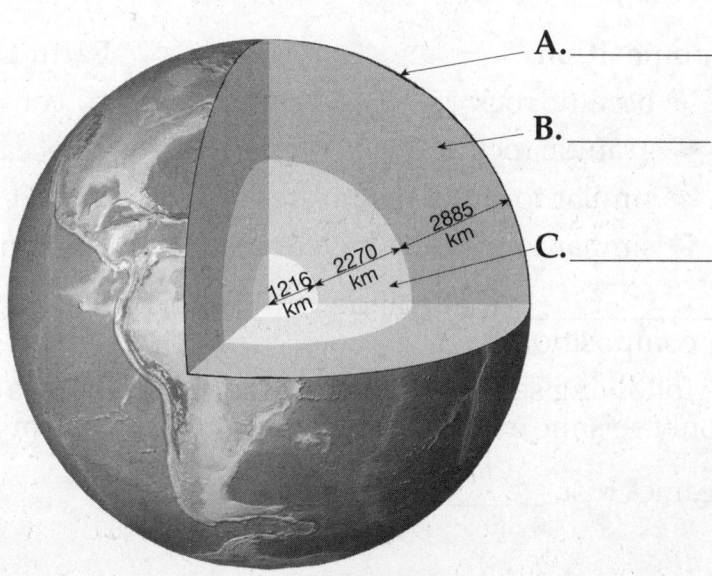

A. _____

B. _____

2885 km   2270 km   1216 km

C. _____

Chapter 8   Earthquakes and Earth's Interior

Layers Defined by Physical Properties (pages 234–235)

2. 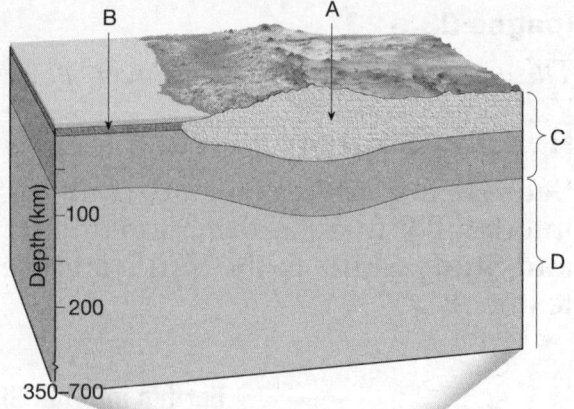 Use the figure of Earth's
   structure to write the letter(s) that
   represents each of the following
   layers.

   asthenosphere _____

   continental crust _____

   oceanic crust _____

   lithosphere _____

Discovering Earth's Layers (page 236)

3. The boundary called the _____ separates the crust from the
   mantle. Circle the correct answer.

   Lithosphere   Moho   Asthenosphere

4. Is the following sentence true or false? Geologists concluded that the
   outer core was liquid because P waves could not travel through it.

   _____

Discovering Earth's Composition (page 237)

Match each composition with its Earth layer.

	Composition	Earth Layer
_____	5. ◔ basaltic rock	a. continental crust
_____	6. ◔ granitic rock	b. oceanic crust
_____	7. ◔ similar to stony meteorites	c. core
_____	8. ◔ similar to metallic meteorites	d. mantle

9. _____ that collide with Earth provide evidence of Earth's
   inner composition.

10. Is the following sentence true or false? Until the late 1960s, scientists
    had only seismic evidence they could use to determine the composition

    of oceanic crust. _____

Name _____ Class _____ · Date _____

Chapter 9 Plate Tectonics

Summary

9.1 Continental Drift

🌐 **According to Wegener's hypothesis of continental drift, the continents had once been joined to form a single supercontinent.**

- He called this supercontinent **Pangaea**, meaning *all land*.
- Wegener believed that about 200 million years ago Pangaea began breaking into smaller continents.

🌐 **Fossil evidence for continental drift includes several fossil organisms found on different landmasses.**

- The distribution of Mesosaurus fossils supported the argument that South America and Africa had once been joined.

🌐 **Matching types of rock in several mountain belts that today are separated by oceans provide evidence for continental drift.**

🌐 **Wegener found glacial deposits showing that between 220 million and 300 million years ago, ice sheets covered large areas of the Southern Hemisphere. Deposits of glacial till occurred at latitudes that today have temperate or even tropical climates: southern Africa, South America, India, and Australia.**

🌐 **The main objection to Wegener's hypothesis was that he could not describe a mechanism capable of moving the continents.**

- The theory of plate tectonics proved that Wegener was correct.

9.2 Sea-Floor Spreading

🌐 **Earth's mid-ocean ridge system forms the longest features on Earth's surface. The system winds more than 7,000 kilometers through all the major ocean basins like the seam on a baseball.**

- **Sonar**, which stands for **so**und **na**vigation and **r**anging, is a system that uses sound waves to calculate the distance to an object.
- As scientists mapped the ocean floor using sonar, they found long, curved valleys along the edges of some ocean basins called **deep-ocean trenches**.
- The **mid-ocean ridge** is a long chain of mountains extending the length of the ocean.
- A **rift valley** is a deep, central valley that runs down the center of a ridge.

🌐 **In the process of sea-floor spreading, new ocean floor forms along Earth's mid-ocean ridges, moves slowly outward across ocean basins, and finally sinks back into the mantle beneath deep-ocean trenches.**

- In the process of **subduction**, ocean floor returns to the mantle as it sinks beneath a deep-ocean trench.

Earth Science Guided Reading and Study Workbook · **87**

© Pearson Education, Inc., publishing as Pearson Prentice Hall. All rights reserved.

Chapter 9   Plate Tectonics

👄 **Evidence for sea-floor spreading included magnetic stripes in ocean-floor rock, earthquake patterns, and measurements of the ages of ocean floor rocks.**

- Earth's magnetic field occasionally reverses polarity. As certain rocks form, they acquire the polarity that Earth's magnetic field has at the time.
- **Paleomagnetism** is the study of changes in Earth's magnetic field, as shown by patterns of magnetism in rocks that have formed over time.

9.3 Theory of Plate Tectonics

👄 **In the theory of plate tectonics, Earth's lithospheric plates move slowly relative to each other, driven by convection currents in the mantle.**

- The lithosphere is broken into several huge pieces, called plates.
- Deep faults separate the different plates.
- There are three types of plate boundaries. Each plate contains a combination of each of the three types.
- **Divergent boundaries** are found where two of Earth's plates move apart.
- **Convergent boundaries** form where two plates move together.
- **Transform fault boundaries** occur where two plates grind past each other.

👄 **Most divergent boundaries are spreading centers located along the crests of mid-ocean ridges. Some spreading centers, however, occur on the continents.**

👄 **At convergent boundaries, plates collide and interact, producing features including trenches, volcanoes, and mountain ranges.**

- A **continental volcanic arc** is a range of volcanic mountains produced in part by the subduction of oceanic lithosphere.
- When two oceanic slabs converge, the resulting volcanic activity can build a chain of islands called a **volcanic island arc**.
- When two pieces of continental lithosphere collide, the two continents eventually merge, creating complex mountains.

👄 **At a transform fault boundary, plates grind past each other without destroying the lithosphere.**

Chapter 9   Plate Tectonics

9.4 Mechanisms of Plate Motions

☁ **Convection currents in the mantle provide the basic driving forces for plate motions.**

- A **convection current** is the continuous flow that occurs in a fluid because of differences in density.
- The hot, but solid rock of the mantle behaves in a plastic way—that is, it can flow slowly over geologic times.
- The heat sources for mantle convection include energy released by radioactive isotopes in the mantle and heat from the core itself.
- In the process called *whole mantle convection*, rock rises from the lower mantle toward the top of the mantle, then sinks back down. This process takes millions of years.

☁ **The sinking of cold ocean lithosphere directly drives the motions of mantle convection through slab-pull and ridge-push. Some scientists think mantle plumes are involved in the upward flow of rock in the mantle.**

- In **slab-pull**, the force of gravity pulls old ocean lithosphere, which is relatively cold and dense, down into the deep mantle.
- In **ridge push**, the stiff ocean lithosphere slides down the asthenosphere that is elevated near mid-ocean ridges.
- A **mantle plume** is a rising column of hot, solid mantle rock at a hot spot.

Chapter 9   Plate Tectonics

Section 9.1 Continental Drift
(pages 248–253)

This section explains the hypothesis of continental drift and the evidence supporting it.

Reading Strategy (page 248)

Summarizing Fill in the table as you read to summarize the evidence of continental drift. For more information on this Reading Strategy, see the **Reading and Study Skills** in the **Skills and Reference Handbook.**

Hypothesis	Evidence
Continental Drift	a. continental puzzle
	b.
	c.
	d.

The Continental Puzzle (page 248)

1. Wegener called Earth's ancient supercontinent _____.

Evidence for Continental Drift (pages 249–251)

Match each example of continental drift with the type of evidence it is.

Example

_____ 2. ◉ Similar mountain chains run through eastern North America and the British Isles.

_____ 3. Land areas that show evidence of ancient glaciation are now located near the equator.

_____ 4. The Atlantic coastlines of South America and Africa fit together.

_____ 5. ◉ Remains of Mesosaurus are limited to eastern South America and southern Africa.

Evidence for Continental Drift

a. rock types and structures
b. matching fossils
c. continental puzzle
d. ancient climates

6. ◉ _____ evidence for continental drift includes several fossil organisms found on different landmasses.

7. Is the following sentence true or false? If the continents were once part of Pangaea, rocks found on one continent should closely match those on

the adjacent parts of another continent. _____

Name _____ Class _____ Date _____

Chapter 9   Plate Tectonics

8. 🗨 The figure shows Earth's ancient supercontinent as it appeared about 300 million years ago, according to Alfred Wegener. Write the letter that represents each of the following present-day continents.

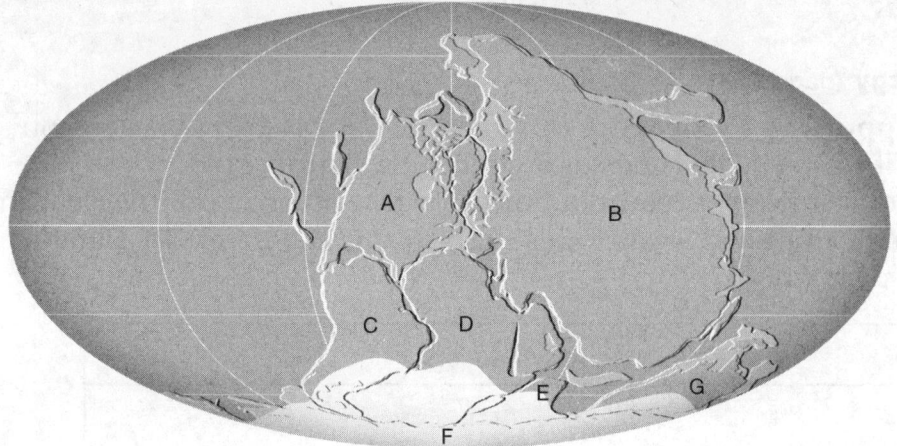

_____ Antarctica　　　　　_____ North America
_____ Europe and Asia　　_____ Africa
_____ South America　　　_____ Australia
_____ India

Rejection of Wegener's Hypothesis (page 252)

9. Circle the letter of an example of one objection that critics had about Wegener's continental drift hypothesis.

   a. Wegener could not provide any evidence to support continental drift.
   b. Wegener's idea of the mechanism capable of moving the continents was physically impossible.
   c. Wegener's fossil evidence was not accurate.

10. Is the following sentence true or false? Wegener proposed that during continental drift, larger continents broke through the oceanic crust.

   _____

11. By 1968, data collected about the ocean floor, earthquake activity, and

   the magnetic field led to a new theory called _____.

Section 9.2 Sea-Floor Spreading
(pages 254–260)

This section discusses sea-floor spreading and subduction zones, and evidence for sea-floor spreading.

Reading Strategy (page 254)

Identifying Supporting Evidence Copy the graphic organizer. After you read, complete it to show the types of evidence that supported the hypothesis of sea-floor spreading. For more information on this Reading Strategy, see the **Reading and Study Skills** in the **Skills and Reference Handbook** at the end of your textbook.

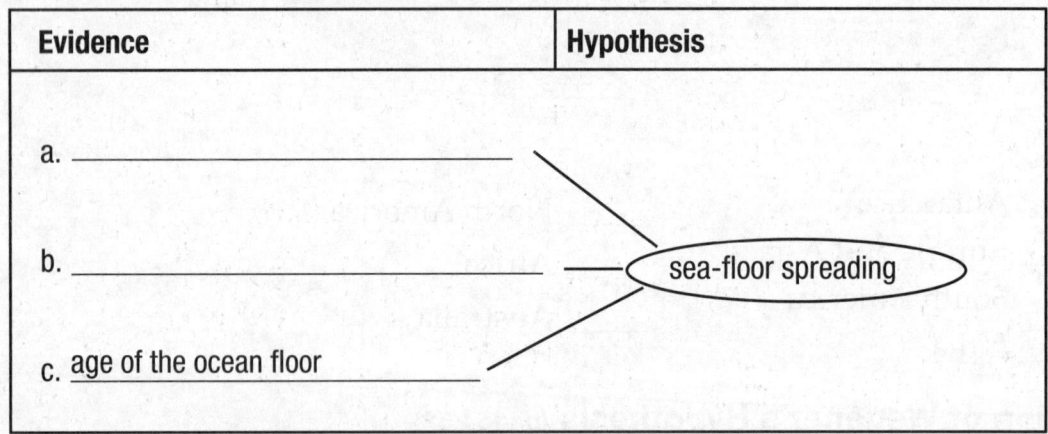

Evidence	Hypothesis
a. _____	
b. _____	sea-floor spreading
c. age of the ocean floor	

Exploring the Ocean Floor (page 254–255)

Match each definition with its term.

Definition

_____ **1.** system that uses sound waves to calculate the distance to an object

_____ **2.** deep faulted structure found along a divergent boundary

_____ **3.** a long chain of mountains extending through Earth's oceans

Term

a. sonar

b. rift valley

c. mid-ocean ridge

The Process of Sea-Floor Spreading (pages 256–257)

4. Circle the letter of the description of a subduction zone.

a. where an oceanic plate is forced beneath a second plate

b. where an oceanic plate grinds past a second plate

c. where an oceanic plate moves away from a second plate

Chapter 9   Plate Tectonics

Evidence for Sea-Floor Spreading (pages 257–260)

5. _____ has occurred when rocks formed millions of years ago show the location of the magnetic poles at the time of their formation.

6. 👁 Circle the letters of each statement that provides evidence for sea-floor spreading.

   a. magnetic stripes in ocean-floor rock
   b. earthquake patterns
   c. measurements of the ages of ocean-floor rock

7. Circle the letter of the definition of reverse polarity.

   a. the loss of magnetism by iron-rich mineral grains when heated
   b. the gain of magnetism by iron-rich mineral grains when cooled
   c. magnetism opposite to that of Earth's present magnetic field

8. Is the following sentence true or false? Deep-focus earthquakes occur away from ocean trenches within the slab of lithosphere descending into the mantle. _____

9. Where do shallow-focus earthquakes occur relative to ocean trenches?

   _____

   _____

10. 👁 Circle the letter of the location of the oldest oceanic crust, according to ocean drilling data.

    a. near the edges of continents
    b. at the ridge crest
    c. between the continental margins and ridge crest

11. 👁 Circle the letter of the location of the youngest oceanic crust, according to ocean drilling data.

    a. at the continental margins
    b. at mid-ocean ridges
    c. between the continental margins and ridge crest

Chapter 9   Plate Tectonics

Section 9.3 Theory of Plate Tectonics
(pages 261–268)

This section discusses plate tectonics, including lithospheric plates and types of plate boundaries.

Reading Strategy (page 261)

Comparing and Contrasting After you read, compare the three types of plate boundaries by completing the table. For more information on this Reading Strategy, see the **Reading and Study Skills** in the **Skills and Reference Handbook** at the end of your textbook.

Boundary Type	Relative Plate Motion
convergent	a.
divergent	b. plates move apart
transform fault	c.

Earth's Moving Plates (pages 261–263)

1. Label each type of plate boundary shown in the figure.

   Choose from the terms.

convergent	divergent	transform fault

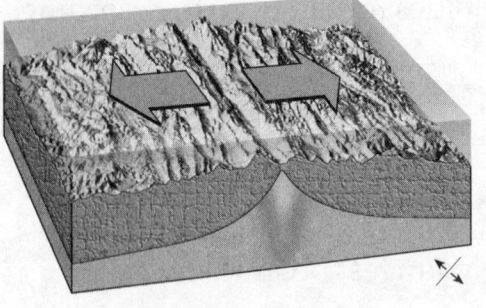

A. _____

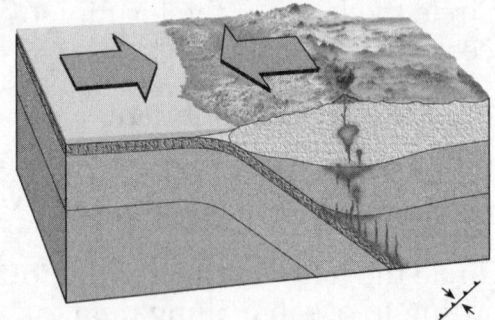

B. _____

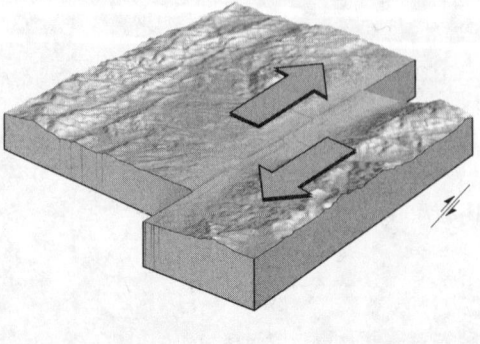

C. _____

Earth Science Guided Reading and Study Workbook ▪ **94**

Chapter 9   Plate Tectonics

2. Is the following sentence true or false? The lithospheric plates move at

   about 5 km per year. _____

Divergent Boundaries (page 264)

3. Is the following sentence true or false? Along divergent boundaries,

   plates move apart. _____

4. Is the following sentence true or false? Divergent boundaries only occur

   on the ocean floor. _____

Convergent Boundaries (pages 265–267)

5. 🖙 At convergent boundaries, plates _____ and interact.

6. Select the appropriate letter in the figure that identifies each of the
   following features.

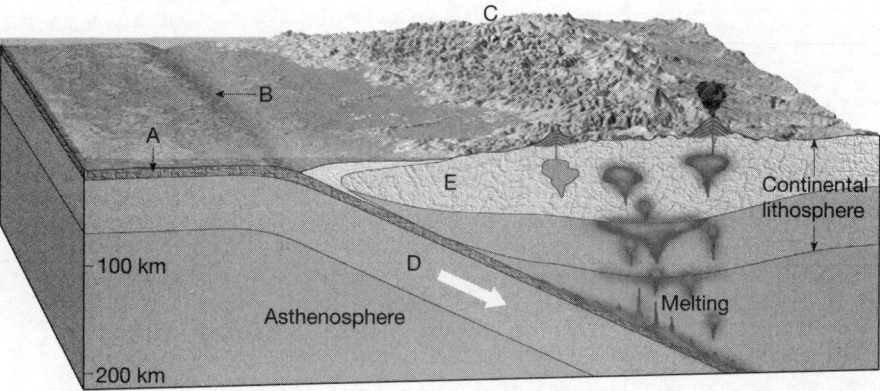

   _____ Subducting oceanic lithosphere
   _____ Oceanic crust
   _____ Trench
   _____ Continental volcanic arc
   _____ Continental crust

7. Newly formed land consisting of an arc-shaped island chain is called

   a(n) _____.

8. Is the following sentence true or false? Mountains form as a result of a

   collision between two continental plates. _____

Transform Fault Boundaries (page 268)

9. 🖙 Plates grind past each other without destroying the lithosphere at a

   _____ boundary.

Section 9.4 Mechanisms of Plate Motions
(pages 270–271)

This section explains what causes plate motion and the role played by unequal distribution of heat within Earth.

Reading Strategy

Identifying Main Ideas As you read, write the main ideas for each topic. For more information on this Reading Strategy, see the **Reading and Study Skills** in the **Skills and Reference Handbook** at the end of your textbook.

Topic	Main Idea
Slab-pull	a.
Ridge-push	b. mechanism of plate motion in which the force of new crust formed at the high ridges pushes on the plate
Mantle convection	c.

What Causes Plate Motions? (page 270)

1. Circle the letter of the basic force that drives plate tectonics.

   a. Earth's magnetic field

   b. convection currents in the mantle

   c. tidal influence of the moon

2. During convection, warm, less dense material rises and cooler, denser

   material _____.

3. A _____ is the continuous flow that occurs in a heated fluid because of differences of temperature and density.

Chapter 9   Plate Tectonics

Plate Motion Mechanisms (page 271)

4. ⬤ Is the following sentence true or false? The mechanism called ridge-push causes oceanic lithosphere to slide down the sides of the oceanic

   ridge. _____

5. ⬤ The mechanism that is the main downward component of mantle

   convection is _____.

6. Is the following sentence true or false? A mantle plume is a rising

   column of hot rock. _____

7. The feature in the diagram where rock is coolest and most dense is the

   a. lower mantle.
   b. descending oceanic plate.
   c. rising plume.

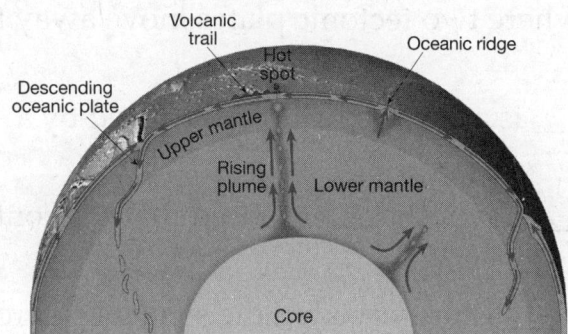

8. Circle the letter of the statement that best describes the whole-mantle convection model.

   a. Rock magnetism changes as rock layers melt under heat and pressure.

   b. Hot oceanic lithosphere descends into the mantle, and cold mantle plumes move heat toward the surface.

   c. Hot mantle plumes move heat toward the surface.

9. ⬤ Thermal convection in the mantle is caused by differences in

   temperature and _____ within Earth.

Chapter 9   Plate Tectonics

WordWise

Complete each sentence by using one of the vocabulary terms below.

continental drift   paleomagnetism
convergent boundaries   Pangaea
divergent boundaries   plates
oceanic ridges   subduction zones
                                            trench

Destructive plate margins called _____ are where one oceanic plate is forced down into the mantle beneath a second plate.

Where two plates collide, _____ occur.

Wegener proposed that in the past, the continents were joined to form a

supercontinent he named _____.

_____ occur where two tectonic plates move away from each other.

An ocean _____ is a surface feature produced by a descending plate.

Wegener's _____ hypothesis proposed that the continents changed position on Earth's surface.

A record of _____ is preserved in the sequence of rock strips at oceanic ridges.

Earth's lithosphere is divided into _____ that move and change shape.

Elevated areas of the seafloor called _____ occur along well-developed divergent plate boundaries.

Chapter 10 Volcanoes and Other Igneous Activity

Summary

10.1 Volcanoes and Plate Tectonics

👄 **Magma forms in the crust and upper mantle when solid rock partially melts. The formation of magma depends on several factors, including heat, pressure, and water content.**

- When hot yet solid mantle rock is less dense than the surrounding rock, it rises, decreasing the pressure on the rock. This lowers the rock's melting point, allowing **decompression melting** to occur.

👄 **Most volcanoes form along divergent and convergent plate boundaries. Some volcanoes form far from plate boundaries above "hot spots" in the crust.**

- At divergent boundaries, volcanic activity occurs where the plates pull apart.
- The **Ring of Fire** is the long belt of volcanoes that circles much of the Pacific Ocean.
- Volcanic activity within a plate is called **intraplate volcanism**.
- A small volcanic region a few hundred kilometers across that forms above a mantle plume is called a **hot spot**.

10.2 The Nature of Volcanic Eruptions

👄 **The primary factors that determine whether a volcano erupts explosively or quietly include characteristics of the magma and the amount of dissolved gases in the magma.**

- **Viscosity** is a substance's resistance to flow.
- A **vent** is an opening to the Earth's surface. During explosive eruptions, the gases trapped in magma push the magma out.

👄 **Depending on the type of eruption, volcanoes may produce lava flows or eject pyroclastic materials, or both. All volcanic eruptions also emit large amounts of gases.**

- Particles from volcanic eruptions are called **pyroclastic materials**.
- The fragments ejected during eruptions range in size from very fine dust and ash to pieces that weigh several tons.

👄 **The three main volcanic types are shield volcanoes, cinder cones, and composite cones.**

- Repeated eruptions of lava or pyroclastic material eventually build a mountain called a **volcano**.

Chapter 10   Volcanoes and Other Igneous Activity

- Located at the summit of many volcanoes is a steep-walled depression called a **crater**.
- **Shield volcanoes** are produced by the accumulation of fluid basaltic lavas and have the shape of a broad, slightly domed structure.
- A **cinder cone** is a small volcano built primarily of pyroclastic material ejected from a single vent.
- A **composite cone** is a large, nearly symmetrical volcanic mountain composed of layers of both lava and pyroclastic deposits.

◉ **Volcanic landforms also include calderas, volcanic rocks, and lava plateaus.**

- A **caldera** is a depression in a volcanic mountain.
- A **volcanic neck** is a landform made of magma that hardened in a volcano's pipe and later was exposed by eruption.
- A **lava plateau** is a volcanic landform produced by repeated eruptions of very fluid, basaltic lava. Instead of building a core, the lava spreads out over a wide area.

◉ **Volcano hazards include lava flows, volcanic ash, pyroclastic flows, and mudflows.**

- A **lahar** occurs when water-soaked volcanic ash and rock slide rapidly downhill.

10.3 Intrusive Igneous Activity

◉ **Types of plutons include sills, laccoliths, and dikes. Geologists classify plutons and other bodies of intrusive igneous rock according to their size, shape, and relationship to surrounding rock layers.**

- The structures that result from the cooling and hardening of magma beneath Earth's surface are called **plutons**. Uplift and erosion can expose plutons at the surface.
- A **sill** is a pluton that forms where magma flows between parallel layers of sedimentary rock.
- A **laccolith** is a lens-shaped pluton that has pushed the overlying rock layers upward.
- A **dike** is a pluton that forms when magma moves into fractures that cut across rock layers.

◉ **A batholith is a body of intrusive rock that has a surface exposure of more than 100 square kilometers.**

- Batholiths are the largest bodies of intrusive igneous rocks.

Chapter 10   Volcanoes and Other Igneous Activity

Section 10.1 Volcanoes and Plate Tectonics
(pages 280–285)

This section explains how magma forms and discusses the relationship between plate boundaries and igneous activity.

Reading Strategy (pages 280)

Outlining After you read, complete the outline of the most important ideas in the section. For more information on this Reading Strategy, see the **Reading and Study Skills** in the **Skills and Reference Handbook** at the end of your textbook.

I. Origin of Magma

    A. Heat

    B. _____

    C. _____

II. Volcanoes and Plate Boundaries

    A. _____

    B. Convergent Boundary Volcanism

    C. _____

Origin of Magma (pages 280–281)

1. Is the following sentence true or false? Magma forms when solid rock in the crust and upper mantle partially melts. _____

2. How is decompression melting of rocks triggered? _____

    _____

3. Does increasing the water content of a rock lower or raise the rock's melting point? _____

Volcanoes and Plate Boundaries (pages 281–285)

4. Most volcanoes form along divergent and _____ plate boundaries.

5. Circle the letters of the changes that allow rock melting to begin at convergent plate boundaries.

    a. decreasing pressure   b. decreasing temperature

            c. water reducing the melting point

6. What landforms develop as a result of the volcanic activity that occurs where one oceanic plate descends beneath another oceanic

   plate? _____

   _____

7. What depth must a sinking slab reach in order for water to reduce the melting point of hot mantle rock low enough for melting to begin?

   a. 100 to 150 km.
   b. 500 to 550 km.
   c. 700 to 750 km.

8. Complete the concept map showing where intraplate volcanism occurs.

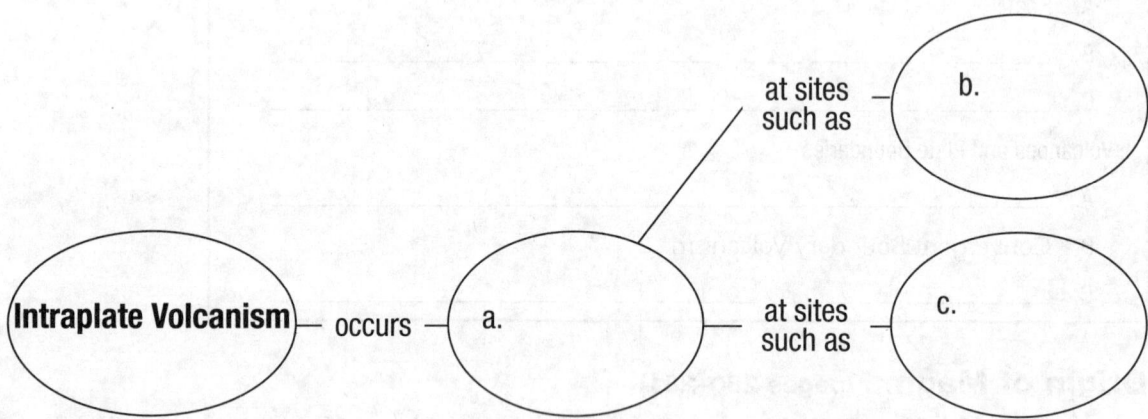

9. 🔵 Circle the letter of the time in which most intraplate volcanism occurs.

   a. when oceanic crust sinks into the mantle and melts
   b. when a mantle plume rises to the surface
   c. when oceanic plates separate and magma rises to fill the rift

10. The result of a magma plume rising and decompression melting occurring

   may be the formation of a small volcanic region called a(n) _____.

11. Circle the letter of the number of years most hot spots have lasted.

   a. hundreds of years
   b. thousands of years
   c. millions of years

Chapter 10   Volcanoes and Other Igneous Activity

Section 10.2 The Nature of Volcanic Eruptions
(pages 286–294)

This section discusses volcanic eruptions, types of volcanoes, and other volcanic landforms.

Reading Strategy (page 286)

Previewing Before you read the section, rewrite the green topic headings as questions. As you read, write the answers to the questions. For more information on this Reading Strategy, see the **Reading and Study Skills** in the **Skills and Reference Handbook** at the end of your textbook.

The Nature of Volcanic Eruptions	
What factors affect an eruption?	a. viscosity and dissolved gases
What are the types of volcanoes?	

Factors Affecting Eruptions (pages 286–287)

1. ◉ What are the factors that determine how violently or quietly a volcano erupts? _____

   _____

2. Circle the letter of the term that describes lava's resistance to flow.

   a. temperature   b. eruption   c. viscosity

3. Magma's viscosity is determined by its chemical composition and

   _____ .

Volcanic Material (pages 288–289)

4. ◉ During a volcanic eruption, particles called _____, ranging from very fine dust to pieces weighing several tons, are ejected.

Chapter 10 Volcanoes and Other Igneous Activity

Types of Volcanoes (pages 289–292)

5. ◔ Label each type of volcano.

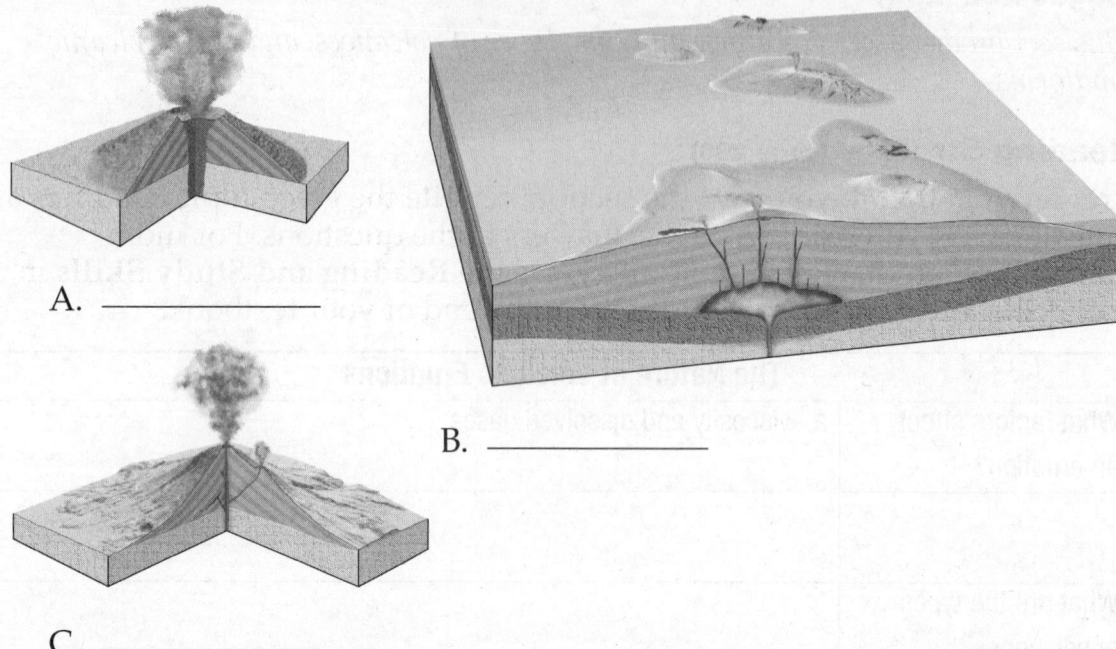

A. _____

B. _____

C. _____

6. The steep-walled depression known as a(n) _____ is located at the summit of many volcanoes. Circle the correct answer.

caldera   cone   crater

Other Volcanic Landforms (pages 292–293)

Match each description with its volcanic landform or feature.

Description	Volcanic Landform or Feature
_____ 7. wide area that forms when low-viscosity basaltic lava erupts through fissures	a. caldera
_____ 8. rock that remains when the surrounding cone has been eroded	b. lava plateau
_____ 9. ◔ depression formed by the collapse of the top of a volcano	c. volcanic neck

Volcanic Hazards (page 294)

11. Is the following sentence true or false? Cinder cones are the most dangerous volcanoes. _____

Section 10.3 Intrusive Igneous Activity
(pages 295–297)

This section explains how to classify intrusive igneous features.

Reading Strategy (page 295)

Comparing and Contrasting After you read, compare the types of intrusive igneous features by completing the table. For more information on this Reading Strategy, see the **Reading and Study Skills** in the **Skills and Reference Handbook** at the end of your textbook.

Types of Plutons	Description
Sill	a. pluton formed parallel with sedimentary rocks, commonly horizontal
Laccolith	b.
Dike	c.
Batholith	d.

Classifying Plutons (pages 295–296)

1. Structures that result from the cooling and hardening of magma beneath Earth's surface are called

   _____.

2. ◉ Select the appropriate letter in the diagram that identifies each of the following igneous intrusive features.

   _____ sill
   _____ laccolith
   _____ dike

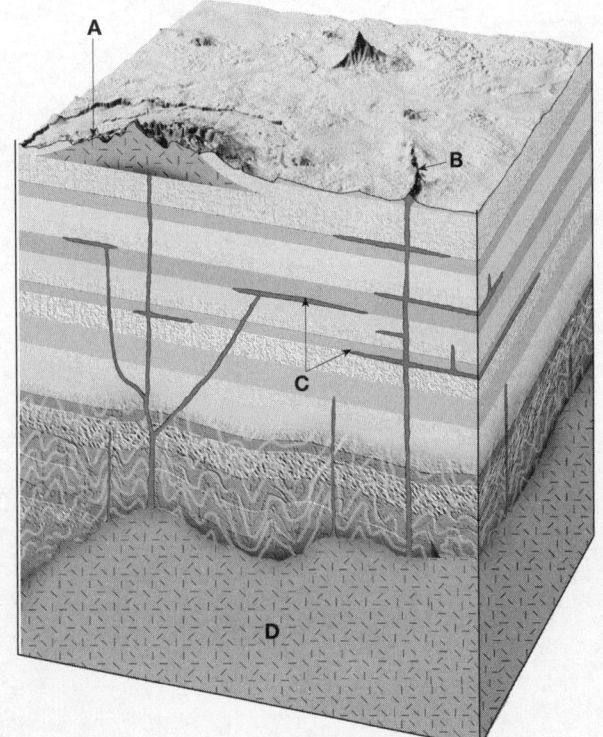

Chapter 10   Volcanoes and Other Igneous Activity

3. 👁 Three characteristics used to classify intrusive igneous bodies are

_____ and relationship to the surrounding rock layers.

Match each way plutons formed with the pluton type.

How Formed	Pluton
_____ 4. 👁 when magma from a large magma chamber invades fractures in the surrounding rocks	a. sill
_____ 5. 👁 when magma is injected between sedimentary layers close to Earth's surface and collects as a lens-shaped mass	b. laccolith
_____ 6. 👁 when magma is injected along sedimentary layers close to Earth's surface	c. dike

Batholiths (page 297)

7. A large intrusive igneous body with an area greater than 100 km^2

exposed at the surface is called a _____.

Chapter 11 Mountain Building

Summary

11.1 Forces in Earth's Crust

- The factors that affect the deformation of rock include temperature, pressure, rock type, and time.
  - **Deformation** is any change in the original shape and/or size of a rock body.
  - **Stress** is the force per unit area acting on a solid. When rocks are under stresses greater than their own strength, they begin to deform.
  - The change in shape or volume of a body of rock as a result of stress is called a strain.

- The three types of stress that cause deformation of rocks are tensional stress, compressional stress, and shear stress.
  - When rocks are squeezed or shortened, the stress is compressional.
  - When rocks are pulled in opposite directions, the stress is tensional.
  - When a body of rock is distorted, the stress is shear.

- Because of isostasy, deformed and thickened crust will undergo regional uplift both during mountain building and for a long period afterward.
  - The concept of a floating crust in gravitational balance is called **isostasy**.
  - The process of establishing a new level of gravitational balance is called **isostatic adjustment**.

11.2 Folds, Faults, and Mountains

- The three main types of folds are anticlines, synclines, and monoclines.
  - An **anticline** is formed by the upfolding, or arching, of rock layers.
  - Often found in association with anticlines are downfolds, or troughs, called **synclines**.
  - **Monoclines** are large, step-like folds in sedimentary strata.

- The major types of faults are normal faults, reverse faults, thrust faults, and strike-slip faults.
  - The rock surface just above the fault is called the hanging wall, and the rock surface below the fault is called the footwall.
  - In a **normal fault,** the hanging wall moves down relative to the footwall.
  - In a **reverse fault,** the hanging wall moves up relative to the footwall.
  - **Thrust faults** are reverse faults with dips of less than 45°.
  - Faults in which the movement is horizontal and parallel to the trend, of the fault surface are called **strike-slip faults.**

Chapter 11   Mountain Building

🔹 **The major types of mountains include volcanic mountains, folded mountains, fault-block mountains, and dome mountains.**

- Geologists refer to the collection of processes involved in mountain building as **orogenesis.**
- Mountains that are formed primarily by compressional stresses, which create folds in the rock layers are called **folded mountains.**
- Compressional stress is the major factor that forms **folded mountains**.
- **Fault-block mountains** form as large blocks of crust are uplifted and tilted along normal faults.
- As the crust is stretched along a normal fault, a block called a **graben**, which is bounded by normal faults, drops down.
- Grabens produce an elongated valley bordered by relatively uplifted structures called **horsts**.

🔹 **Up-and-down movements of the crust can produce a variety of landforms, including plateaus, domes, and basins.**

11.3 Mountains and Plates

🔹 **The convergence of two oceanic plates mainly produces volcanic mountains.**

- The result of this collision is the formation of a volcanic island arc.

🔹 **The convergence of an oceanic plate and a continental plate produces volcanic mountains and folded mountains.**

- During subduction, sediment is scraped from the subducting plate. The sediment forms a large mass called an **accretionary wedge**, which becomes attached to the overriding crustal block.

🔹 **At a convergent boundary, a collision between two plates carrying continental crust will form folded mountains. This happens because the continental crust is not dense enough to be subducted.**

🔹 **The mountains that form along ocean ridges at divergent plate boundaries are fault-block mountains made of volcanic rock.**

- These mountains are elevated because of isostasy.

🔹 **Volcanic mountains at hot spots, as well as some upwarped mountains and fault-block mountains, can form far from plate boundaries.**

🔹 **The process of accretion enlarges continental landmasses and forms mountains along the edges of continents.**

- When fragments of crust collide with a continental plate they become stuck to or embedded into the continent through **accretion**.
- A **terrane** is any crustal fragment with a distinct geologic history.

Chapter 11   Mountain Building

Section 11.1 Forces in Earth's Crust
(pages 308–311)

This section explains how rocks are deformed.

Reading Strategy (page 308)

Previewing Before you read, rewrite the green topic headings as how, why, and what questions. As you read, write an answer to each question. For more information on this Reading Strategy, see the **Reading and Study Skills** in the **Skills and Reference Handbook** at the end of your textbook.

Forces in Earth's Crust	
What causes deformation of rock?	
What are the types of stress?	
What is the principle of isostasy?	the thicker the crust, the higher it "floats" on the mantle below.

Deformation of Rock (pages 308–309)

Match each definition to its term.

Definition

_____ 1. the force per unit area acting on a solid

_____ 2. the change in shape or volume of a body of rock as a result of stress

_____ 3. a general term that refers to all changes in the original shape and/or size of a body of rock

Term

a. deformation

b. stress

c. strain

4. ● Four factors that influence the strength of a rock and how it will

deform are _____, _____, rock type and time.

5. ● Two ways rocks permanently deform are brittle deformation, and

_____ deformation.

Chapter 11   Mountain Building

6. Circle the letters of the statements that are true about rock deformation.

   a. Ductile deformation is strongly aided by high temperature and high confining pressure.

   b. Small stresses applied over time play an important role in rock deformation.

   c. The mineral composition and texture of a rock affect how it will deform.

Types of Stress (page 309)

7. ● Use the terms in the box to label the diagram with the three types of stress that cause deformation of rocks.

compressional stress	shear stress	tensional stress

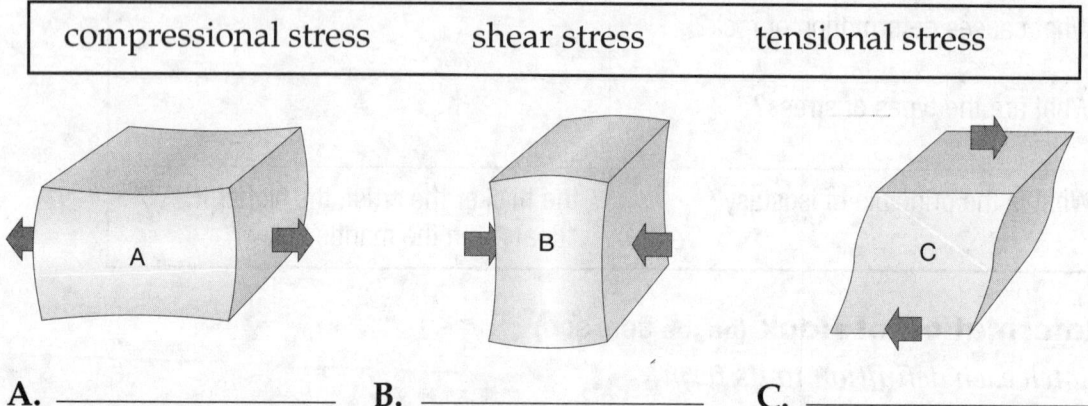

A. _____   B. _____   C. _____

Principle of Isostasy (pages 310–311)

8. Isostasy is the idea that Earth's crust is floating in gravitational balance on the denser rocks of the _____.

9. Use the terms below to fill in the blank.

isostasy	isostatic adjustment	deformation

   The process of establishing a new level of gravitational balance after weight is removed from or added to the crust is called

   _____.

Section 11.2 Folds, Faults, and Mountains
(pages 312–319)

This section explains the characteristics of various types of mountains.

Reading Strategy (page 312)

Comparing and Contrasting As you read this section, compare types of faults by completing the table below.

Types of Fault	Description
Normal fault	a.
b.	c. a hanging wall block moves up relative to the footwall block; high angle fault
d.	e.
f. Strike-slip fault	g.

Folds (pages 312–313)

Match each definition to its term.

Definition
_____ **1.** large, step-like folds in otherwise horizontal sedimentary strata

_____ **2.** upfolding, or arching, of rock layers

_____ **3.** downfolds or troughs

Term
a. anticlines
b. synclines
c. monoclines

Faults (pages 314–315)

4. ⬤ Which type of stress occurs in each type of fault? Choose from these terms. One term will be used twice.

compression	shear	tensional

Reverse fault: _____

Strike-slip fault: _____

Normal fault: _____

Thrust fault: _____

Name _____   Class _____   Date _____

Chapter 11   Mountain Building

Types of Mountains (pages 316–317)

Match each definition to its term.

	Definition	**Term**
_____ 5.	🔹 mountains formed primarily by folding	a. orogenesis
_____ 6.	the collection of processes that produce a mountain belt	b. folded mountains
_____ 7.	the major force that forms folded mountains	c. compressional forces

8. _____ is also important in the formation of folded mountains, which are often called fold-and-thrust belts.

9. Circle the letter of the mountain ranges that are examples of folded mountains.

   a. Appalachian Mountains

   b. northern Rocky Mountains

   c. Teton Range in Wyoming

10. Select the letter from the figure that identifies each formation.

    _____ graben

    _____ horst

11. Which type of fault is illustrated in the figure? _____

12. Circle the letter of each true statement about fault-block mountains.

    a. Normal faulting occurs where tensional stresses cause the crust to be stretched.

    b. Grabens produce an elongated valley bordered by horsts.

    c. The Basin and Range region of Nevada, Utah, and California is made of fault-block mountains separated by grabens.

Plateaus, Domes, and Basins (pages 318–319)

13. 🔹 When upwarping produces a circular or an elongated structure, the

    feature is called a(n) _____. Circle the correct answer.

    basin   dome   plateau

14. Is the following sentence true or false? The Black Hills of South Dakota contain exposed igneous and metamorphic rock in the center of a dome.

    _____

Earth Science Guided Reading and Study Workbook • **112**

© Pearson Education, Inc., publishing as Pearson Prentice Hall. All rights reserved.

Chapter 11   Mountian Building

Section 11.3 Mountains and Plates
(pages 320–325)

This section explains how mountains are formed at plate boundaries.

Reading Strategy (page 320)

Outlining As you read, make an outline of the important ideas in this section. Use the green topic headings as the main topics and the blue headings as subtopics. For more information on this Reading Strategy, see the **Reading and Study Skills** in the **Skills and Reference Handbook** at the end of your textbook.

I. Mountains and Plates

  A. Convergent Boundary Mountains

    1. Ocean-Ocean Convergence

    2. _____

    3. _____

  B. Divergent Boundary Mountains

  C. _____

  D. _____

    1. Terranes

    2. _____

Convergent Boundary Mountains (pages 320–323)

1. Is the following sentence true or false? Most mountain building occurs at convergent plate boundaries. _____

2. Use the terms below to fill in the blank.

Colliding plates	Grabens	Divergent boundaries

_____ provide the compressional forces that fold, fault, and metamorphose the thick layers of sediment deposited at the edges of landmasses.

3. ⬤ Is the following sentence true or false? The types of mountains formed by ocean-continental convergence are volcanic mountains and folded mountains. _____

Chapter 11   Mountain Building

4. The figure illustrates mountain building along an Andean-type subduction zone. Select the appropriate letter in the figure that identifies each of the following features.

_____ ocean trench

_____ asthenosphere

_____ continental volcanic arc

_____ accretionary wedge

_____ subducting oceanic lithosphere

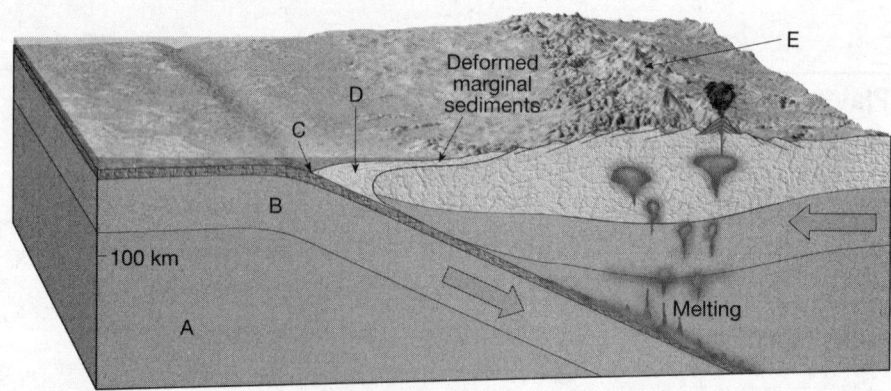

5. Is the following sentence true or false? At a convergent boundary, a collision between two plates carrying continental crust will result in the formation of folded mountains. _____

Divergent Boundary Mountains (page 323)

6. _____ mountains are formed along ocean ridges at divergent plate boundaries.

Non-Boundary Mountains (page 323)

7. Use the terms below to fill in the blank.

ocean ridge	hot spot	normal fault

The Hawaiian Islands are volcanic mountains that formed far from plate boundaries at a _____.

Continental Accretion (pages 324–325)

8. When crustal fragments called _____ collide with a continental plate, they become stuck to or embedded into the continent in a process called accretion. Circle the correct answer.

plates   terranes   ridges

Chapter 11   Mountain Building

WordWise

Use the clues to determine which vocabulary terms from the list below are hidden in the puzzle. Then find and circle the terms in the puzzle. The terms may occur vertically, horizontally, diagonally, or backwards.

accretion	fault-block	strain
anticline	monocline	stress
deformation	orogenesis	syncline

```
Q A C C R E T I O N D S C A M A
K L W O A U A V J E T N Q T K H
D C I Z Y D O W F R N I A R T S
E V O B I F D O E E Q N F P V G
N I P L Z M R S N K E H Y E N G
I C D X B M S I S E N E G O R O
L R K M A T L Y G X E I R R Z B
C J T T O C L J N N F H E Z B M
I P I N O P Q U E C Y Y A X M W
T O V N P Q U I A R L A F G H X
N E O M R S W B H F C I A J Z S
A M P A X M U D S R W D N D L R
Q Z B S H F C M K P X J E E F K
```

Clues	**Hidden Words**
The general term that refers to all changes in the shape or size of a rock body	_____
Force per unit area acting on a solid	_____
The change in shape or volume of a body of rock as a result of stress	_____
Commonly formed by the upfolding, or arching, of rock layers	_____
A trough associated with anticlines	_____
A large, step-like fold in otherwise horizontal sedimentary strata	_____
The collection of processes that produce a mountain belt	_____
Mountains formed as large blocks of crust are uplifted and tilted along normal faults	_____
The process in which fragments become embedded or stuck to a continental plate	_____

Chapter 12 Geologic Time

Summary

12.1 Discovering Earth's History

In studying Earth's history, geologists make use of three main ideas:
- the rock record provides evidence of geological events and life forms of the past;
- processes observed on Earth in the present also acted in the past;
- Earth is very old and has changed over geologic time.
- The principle of **uniformitarianism** states that the physical, chemical, and biological laws that operate today have also operated in the geologic past.

In relative dating, geologists follow several principles: the law of superposition, the principle of original horizontality, and the principle of cross-cutting relationships.
- The method that geologists use to place rocks in chronological order is called **relative dating**.
- The **law of superposition** states that in an undeformed sequence of sedimentary rocks, each layer is older than the one above it and younger than the one below it.
- The **principle of original horizontality** states that layers of sediment are generally deposited in a horizontal position.
- The **principle of cross-cutting relationships** states that when a fault cuts through rock layers, or when magma intrudes other rocks and hardens, then the fault or intrusion is younger than the rocks around it.

Methods that geologists use to interpret the rock record include the study of inclusions and unconformities. Geologists also correlate rock layers at different locations.
- Inclusions are pieces of one rock unit that are contained within another.
- A surface that represents a break in the rock record is termed an **unconformity**.
- Geologists use **correlation** to match rocks of similar age in different locations.

12.2 Fossils: Evidence of Past Life

The different types of fossils include petrified fossils, molds and casts, carbon films, preserved remains, and trace fossils.
- An **extinct** organism is one that no longer exists on Earth.
- A **fossil** is the remains or traces of an organism preserved from the geologic past.

Chapter 12   Geologic Time

☛ **Two conditions that favor preservation of an organism as a fossil are rapid burial and the possession of hard parts.**

☛ **Two major scientific developments helped scientists explain the fossil record: the principle of fossil successions and the theory of evolution.**

- The **principle of fossil succession** states that fossil organisms succeed one another in a definite and determinable order.
- The **theory of evolution** states that life forms have changed over time, or evolved, from simpler to more complex forms.
- In **natural selection**, individuals that are better adapted to their environment are more likely to survive and reproduce than others of the same type.
- Organisms possess certain traits, called **adaptations**, that affect their ability to survive and reproduce.

☛ **Geologists used fossils to improve the correlation of rock layers and reconstruct past environments.**

- An **index fossil** is the fossil of an organism that was geographically widespread and abundant in the fossil record, but that existed for only a limited span of time.

12.3 Dating With Radioactivity

☛ **During radioactive decay, unstable atomic nuclei spontaneously break apart, or decay, releasing energy.**

- **Radioactivity** is the process by which atoms decay.
- A **half-life** is the amount of time necessary for one half of the nuclei in a sample to decay to its stable isotope.

☛ **In radiometric dating, scientists measure the ratio between the radioactive parent isotope and the daughter products in a sample to be dated. The older the sample, the more daughter product it contains.**

- **Radiometric dating** is a way of calculating the absolute ages of rocks and minerals that contain certain radioactive isotopes.
- **Radiocarbon dating** is a method to date organic materials using carbon-14.

☛ **When an organism dies, the amount of carbon-14 gradually decreases as it decays. By comparing the ratio of carbon-14 to carbon-12 in a sample, radiocarbon dates can be determined.**

☛ **To determine the age of sedimentary rock, geologists must relate the sedimentary rock to datable masses of igneous rock.**

12.4 The Geologic Time Scale

☛ **The geologic time scale is a record that includes both geologic events and major developments in the evolution of life.**

Chapter 12   Geologic Time

- The **geologic time** scale is a timeline that divide Earth's history into units representing specific intervals of time.

🖙 **Eons represent the longest intervals of geologic time. Eons are divided into eras. Each era is subdivided into periods. Finally, periods are divided into still smaller units called epochs.**

- Geologists divide Earth's history into four long units called **eons**.
- The first three eons when Earth formed, the atmosphere and oceans developed, and early life evolved are grouped together and called **Precambrian time**.
- There are three **eras** within the Phanerozoic eon: the Paleozoic, Mesozoic, and Cenozoic eras.
- Different geologic events, environmental conditions, and life forms characterize each **period**.
- We live in the Holocene epoch of the Quaternary (or Neogene) period.

Chapter 12   Geologic Time

Section 12.1 Discovering Earth's History
(pages 336–341)

This section explains how geologists use rocks to interpret Earth's history.

Reading Strategy (page 336)

Identifying Main Ideas As you read, fill in the first column of the table with a main idea and add details that support it in the second column. For more information on this Reading Strategy, see the **Reading and Study Skills** in the **Skills and Reference Handbook** at the end of your textbook.

Main Idea	Details
1. rock record	clues to geological events and changing life forms
2.	
3. relative dating	
4.	
5.	

Studying Earth's History (pages 336–337)

1. The rocks record provides evidence of _____ and life forms of the past.

2. The concept that the processes at work on Earth today were also at work long ago is known as the principle of _____. Circle the correct answer.

   original horizontality   supposition   uniformitarianism

Relative Dating—Key Principles (pages 337–339)

3. Is the following sentence true or false? Scientists use relative dating to tell how long ago events occurred on Earth. _____

4. Use the following figure to complete each sentence comparing the relative ages of the features.

a. Dike B is _____ than Fault B.

b. The shale is _____ than the sandstone.

c. Dike B is _____ than the batholith.

d. The sandstone is _____ than Dike A.

e. The conglomerate is _____ than the shale.

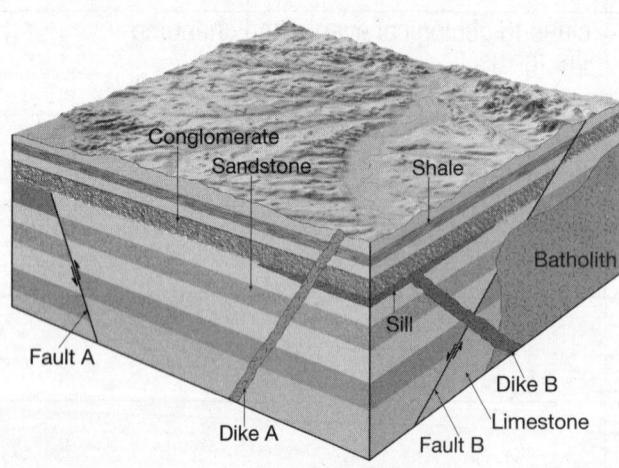

Reading the Rock Record (pages 339–341)

Match each description with its term.

Description	Term
_____ 5. represents a long period when deposition stopped, erosion occurred, and deposition resumed	a. angular unconformity
	b. disconformity
	c. unconformity
_____ 6. two sedimentary rock layers separated by an erosional surface	
_____ 7. represents a period when deformation and erosion occurred	

8. Circle the letter of the task of matching up rocks of similar age in different regions.

a. correlation   b. superposition   c. uniformitarianism

Chapter 12   Geologic Time

Section 12.2 Fossils: Evidence of Past Life
(pages 342–346)

This section discusses how fossils form and how they are used to correlate rock layers.

Reading Strategy (page 342)

Monitoring Your Understanding Complete the chart. After you finish this section, correct and add details as needed. For more information on this Reading Strategy, see the **Reading and Study Skills** in the **Skills and Reference Handbook** at the end of your textbook.

Fossils	How Fossils Form	How Fossils Are Used
a. Fossils are traces or remains of an organism preserved from the geologic past.	b.	c.

1. 🔵 Is the following sentence true or false? An extinct organism is one that is still found on Earth. _____

2. 🔵 What are fossils? _____

_____

Types of Fossils (pages 342–343)

3. Casts are a common type of _____.

4. Circle the letter of the type of fossil formed when an organism is buried in sediment and then dissolved by underground water.

   a. coprolite   b. trace fossil   c. mold

Chapter 12   Geologic Time

Match each example with its type of fossil. Some types will be used more than once.

	Example		Type of Fossil
_____	**5.** frozen mammoth	a.	preserved remains
_____	**6.** animal footprint	b.	trace fossil
_____	**7.** fly in amber		

Conditions for Fossilization (page 344)

8. Complete the following concept map showing conditions that favor the preservation of fossils.

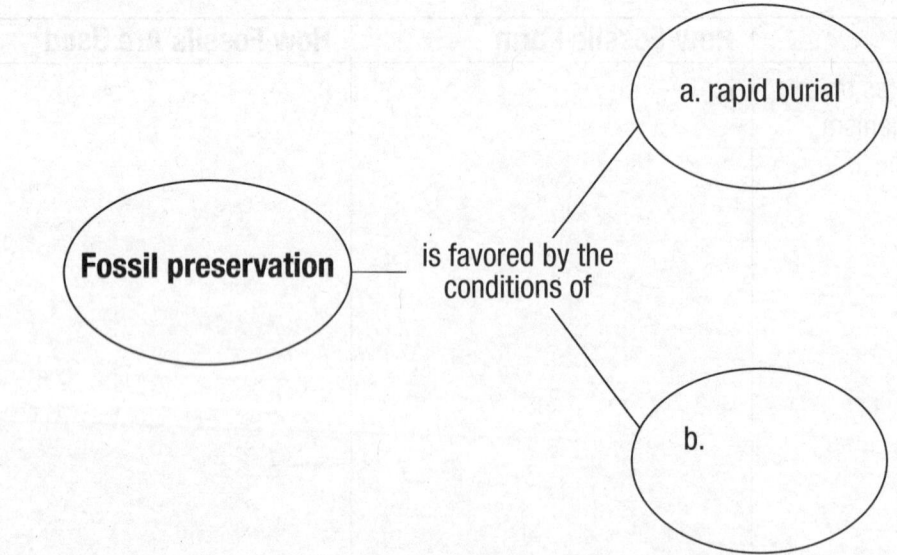

Fossils and the History of Life (pages 344–345)

9. Fossil organisms succeed each other in an order that is definite and

determinable according to the principle of _____. Circle the
correct answer.

fossil preservation   fossil succession   natural selection

10. According to Darwin's theory of evolution, one species can evolve into

another through the process of _____.

Interpreting the Fossil Record (pages 345–346)

11. What are index fossils? _____

_____

_____

12. Is the following sentence true or false? Scientists use fossils to

interpret and describe ancient environments. _____

Chapter 12   Geologic Time

Section 12.3 Dating With Radioactivity
(pages 347–351)

This section explains how radioactivity is used to determine the age of rocks.

Reading Strategy (page 347)

Monitoring Your Understanding Preview the key concepts, topics, headings, vocabulary, and figures in this section. List two things you expect to learn about each. After reading, state what you learned about each item you listed. For more information on this Reading Strategy, see the **Reading and Study Skills** in the **Skills and Reference Handbook** at the end of your textbook.

What I expect to learn	What I learned
1.	
2.	

What Is Radioactivity? (pages 347–348)

1. Is the following sentence true or false? Isotopes of the same element have different numbers of neutrons. _____

2. The process by which unstable nuclei spontaneously decay is known as _____.

3. Circle the letter of the final result of radioactive decay.

   a. parent element
   b. radioactive isotope
   c. stable daughter product

4. Circle the letter of what decays first during radioactive decay.

   a. parent element
   b. stable isotope
   c. stable daughter product

Chapter 12   Geologic Time

Use the graph to answer the following three questions.

5. After one half-life, what fraction of the parent element has decayed to a

daughter product? _____

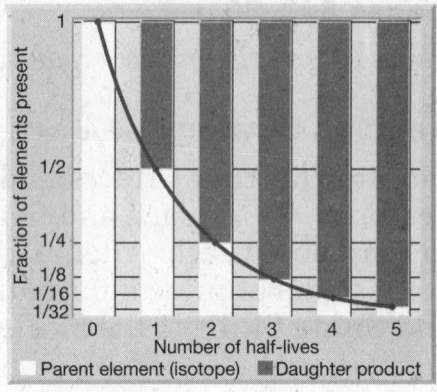

6. After three half-lives, what fraction of the daughter product has

formed? _____

7. How many half-lives must pass before only 1/32 of the parent element

remains undecayed to a daughter product? _____

Radiometric Dating (pages 348–349)

8. Use one of the terms below to fill in the blank. The procedure called

_____ provides a way to determine the ages of rocks that
contain certain radioactive isotopes.

radiometric dating	carbon dating	correlation

9. Is the following sentence true or false? A radioactive isotope

decays at a varying rate from the time it forms. _____

Dating With Carbon-14 (page 350)

10. ● Circle the letter of the ratio of two substances that is compared in a
sample of a dead organism during radiocarbon dating.

  a. carbon-12 to uranium 238   b. carbon-14 to carbon-12
  c. uranium-238 to lead-206

Radiometric Dating of Sedimentary Rock (pages 350–351)

11. Is the following sentence true or false? Radiometric dating is rarely used

to determine the age of sedimentary rocks. _____

Chapter 12   Geologic Time

Section 12.4 The Geologic Time Scale
(pages 353–355)

This section discusses the geologic time scale and difficulties with constructing it.

Reading Strategy (page 353)

Outlining As you read, complete the outline of the important ideas in this section. Use the green headings as the main topics and fill in details from the remainder of the text. For more information on this Reading Strategy, see the **Reading and Study Skills** in the **Skills and Reference Handbook** at the end of your textbook.

I. Structure of the Time Scale

   A. Eons

      a. geologic time scale: _____

      _____

      b. eon: _____

      c. Precambrian time: _____

   B. _____

      d. era: _____

   C. _____

      e. period: second-shortest unit of geologic time

      f. epoch: _____

Structure of the Time Scale (pages 353–355)

2. ⬤ Complete the following flowchart with the types of subdivisions of the geologic time scale, from longest to shortest expanse of time. Use the following terms.

eon   epoch   era   period

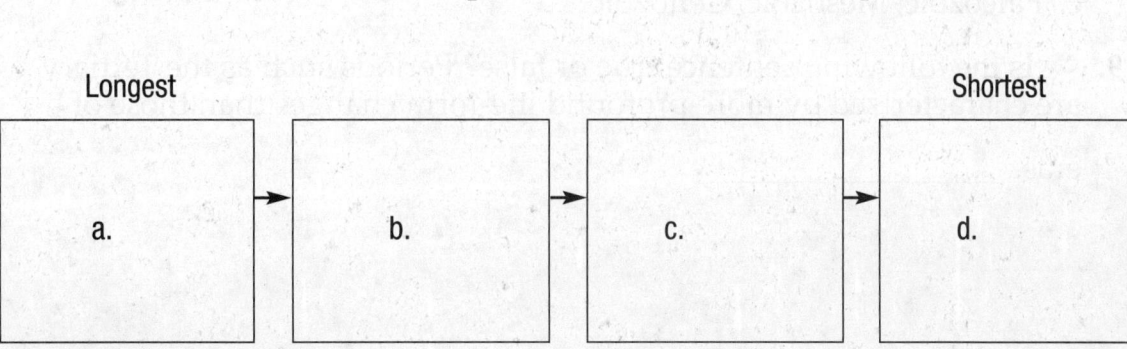

Longest   Shortest

| a. | b. | c. | d. |

Chapter 12   Geologic Time

3. Is the following sentence true or false? The Precambrian represents a much longer part of Earth's history than the Phanerozoic.

   _____

4. 👁 Circle the letter of the statements that tell why geologists know so little about Precambrian history.

   a. There were fewer life forms during this time.

   b. Fossils from this time are scarce.

   c. Precambrian rocks have been disturbed.

5. The Precambrian time starts at Earth's beginning and continues until the

   start of the _____ period over 4 billion years later. Circle the correct answer.

   Cambrian   Permian   Devonian

6. Circle the approximate percentage of the geologic time scale that Precambrian time comprises.

   a. 50 percent

   b. 73 percent

   c. 88 percent

7. The eon called the _____ began about 540 million years ago. Circle the correct answer.

   Proterozoic   Phanerozoic   Hadean

8. 👁 Circle the letter of the eras into which the Phanerozoic is divided.

   a. Proterozoic, Archean, Hadean

   b. Triassic, Jurassic, Cretaceous

   c. Paleozoic, Mesozoic, Cenozoic

9. 👁 Is the following sentence true or false? Periods such as the Tertiary are characterized by more profound life-form changes than those of

   eras. _____

Name _____ Class _____ Date _____

WordWise

Test your knowledge of vocabulary terms from Chapter 12 by completing this crossword puzzle. Use the terms and the clues below.

correlation	index fossil	radiocarbon
epoch	law of superposition	unconformity
era	period	uniformitarianism

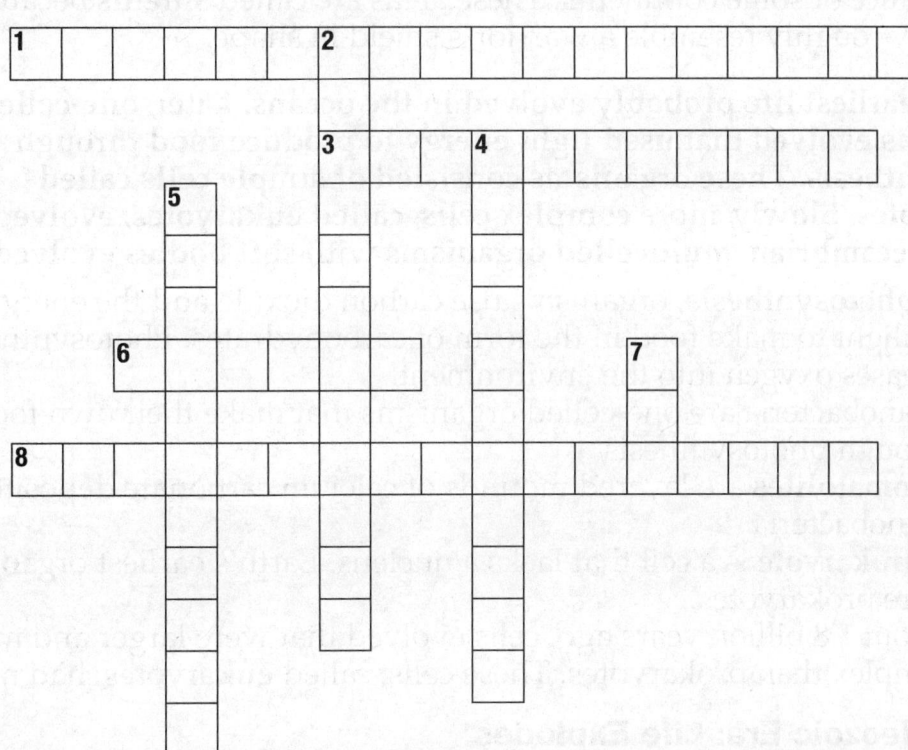

Clues across:

1. states that in an undeformed sequence of sedimentary rocks, each bed is older than the one above it

3. task of matching up rocks of similar age in different regions

6. subdivision of an era

7. shorter than a period on the geologic time scale

8. principle that states that the same physical, chemical, and biological laws operate today as in the past

Clues down:

2. represents a break in the rock record

4. _____ dating: method of using carbon-14 to find the age of dead organisms

5. time indicator that is a particularly useful means of correlating rocks of similar age in different regions

Chapter 13 Earth's History

Summary

13.1 Precambrian Time

🕑 **Earth formed about 4.56 billion years ago. During Precambrian time, the atmosphere and oceans formed and plate tectonics began to build up continental landmasses.**

- There are large core areas of Precambrian rocks that make up the surface of some continents. These areas are called **shields** because they roughly resemble a warrior's shield in shape.

🕑 **The earliest life probably evolved in the oceans. Later, one-celled organisms evolved that used light energy to produce food through photosynthesis. These organisms consisted of simple cells called prokaryotes. Slowly, more complex cells, called eukaryotes, evolved. Late in the Precambrian, multicelled organisms with soft bodies evolved.**

- In **photosynthesis**, organisms use carbon dioxide and the energy of sunlight to make food in the form of carbohydrates. Photosynthesis releases oxygen into the environment.
- Cyanobacteria are one-celled organisms that make their own food through photosynthesis.
- **Stromatolites** are layered mounds of calcium carbonate deposited by cyanobacteria.
- A **prokaryote** is a cell that lacks a nucleus. Earth's earliest organisms were prokaryotes.
- About 1.8 billion years ago, cells evolved that were larger and more complex than prokaryotes. These cells, called **eukaryotes**, had nuclei.

13.2 Paleozoic Era: Life Explodes

🕑 **Environmental changes that have affected the course of evolution on Earth include the formation and breakup of continents, mountain building, volcanic activity, changes in climate, and changes in sea level.**

- Rapid change can lead to the extinction of many groups of organisms in a relatively short time, in an event called **mass extinction**.

🕑 **Many new groups of organisms evolved in a relatively short time in an event called the "Cambrian Explosion."**

- The breakup of the supercontinent Rodinia created new environments, which contributed to the Cambrian Explosion.

Chapter 13   Earth's History

☞ **During the Ordovician period, more complex communities of organisms developed in the oceans. The first land-dwelling plants evolved.**

- **Gondwana** is a late Paleozoic continent that formed the southern portion of Pangea.
- Parts of five of today's continents make up Gondwana—South America, Africa, Australia, Antarctica, and parts of Asia.

☞ **The Silurian Period was a time of reef-building and continued evolution of the fishes in the seas. By the end of the period, plants and animals were becoming widespread on land.**

☞ **During the Devonian period, jawed fishes and sharks evolved in the seas. Plants continued to colonize the land, along with insects and other small arthropods. Later, amphibians evolved with adaptations for life on land.**

- During the Devonian period there were two large continents.
- To the north, continental landmasses collided to form a new large continent, called **Laurasia**.
- Toward the end of the Devonian period, amphibians evolved from fishes.
- An **amphibian** is a four-legged animal with lungs for breathing, that lives on land but lays its eggs in water.

☞ **The Carboniferous period saw the development of great "coal swamp forests" in wet, tropical regions. Amphibians and winged insects became common, and the first reptiles evolved.**

- **Reptiles** evolved from amphibians and are animals that lay leathery-shelled eggs that can survive out of water. They were among the first animals that evolved during the Carboniferous period.

☞ **As the Permian period began, Earth's continents were joined in the supercontinent Pangaea. The evolution of life during the period continued trends that began during the Carboniferous. But the Permian ended with the greatest mass extinction in geologic history.**

- Nearly 250 million years ago, the Permian period ended with a mass extinction that killed 96 percent of life on Earth.

Chapter 13   Earth's History

13.3 Mesozoic Era: Age of Reptiles

☙ **Pangaea continued as a single, large landmass through most of the Triassic period. After a slow recovery from the Permian extinction, many kinds of reptiles evolved. Late in the period, the first mammals appeared.**

- **Mammals** are warm-blooded animals that nourish their young with milk.
- **Gymnosperms** are a group of plants with seeds that lack a protective outer coat.

☙ **Pangaea continued to split apart during the Jurassic period. Many kinds of dinosaurs evolved and became widely distributed.**

☙ **A greater diversity of life forms evolved during the Cretaceous period. Dinosaurs, birds, flowering plants, and small mammals all flourished.**

- **Angiosperms** are plants that produce flowers and seeds with an outer covering.

☙ **Most scientists think that a large meteorite collided with Earth and caused the mass extinction at the end of the Cretaceous.**

13.4 Cenozoic Era: Age of Mammals

☙ **Mammals succeeded during the Cenozoic because of adaptations that enabled them to out-compete the surviving reptiles.**

☙ **During the Tertiary period, mountain building and climate changes accompanied the breakup of Pangaea. Mammals became widespread and diverse worldwide.**

☙ **Two factors have greatly affected life on Earth during the Quaternary period: the advance and retreat of continental glaciers, which have formed and melted about 30 times in the last 3 million years, and the migration of *Homo sapiens*—modern humans—to every corner of Earth.**

- In the 1940s, astronomer Milutin Milankovitch proposed that three different cycles, related to Earth's movements, were the main cause of ice ages. These cycles are called **Milankovitch cycles.**

Chapter 13   Earth's History

Section 13.1 Precambrian Time
(pages 364–368)

This section discusses Earth's history during the Precambrian time.

Reading Strategy (page 364)

Building Vocabulary As you read this section, use the information about the vocabulary terms to complete these phrases. For more information on this Reading Strategy, see the **Reading and Study Skills** in the **Skills and Reference Handbook** at the end of your textbook.

1. Shields are composed of a. _____; are evidence of the early continents; and are significant to Precambrian time because

    b. _____.

2. Stromatolites are composed of d. calcium carbonate; are evidence of

    c. _____; and are significant to Precambrian

    time because d. _____.

Precambrian Earth (pages 364–366)

1. Is the following sentence true or false? Little is know about Precambrian time because many rocks of this age have been disturbed in some way

    and contain few fossils. _____

Match each description to its term.

Description	Term
_____ **2.** large core areas of Precambrian rocks that make up the surface of some continents	a. shields
	b. ores
_____ **3.** source of information about Precambrian rocks	c. greenstone
_____ **4.** some of Earth's oldest rocks	

5. Write the letter of each step below about Earth's formation in the correct order in the flowchart.

A. High-velocity impact of rocks from space caused the planet to melt.

B. Less dense materials, such as silicates, formed layers that became the mantle and crust.

C. Gravity pulled together dust, rock, and ice in space.

D. Melting allowed dense materials, such as iron and nickel, to sink toward Earth's center.

Earth's Formation

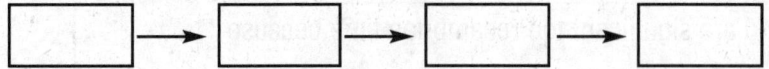

6. Is the following sentence true or false? There was no oxygen in Earth's original atmosphere. _____

7. The process that helped speed up the cooling of Earth's surface and eventually allowed the formation of the oceans was _____. Circle the correct answer.

condensation   evaporation   gravity

Precambrian Life (pages 367–368)

8. Circle the letter of each sentence that is true about Precambrian fossils.

a. Precambrian fossils made by cyanobacteria are stromatolites.

b. Prokaryotes evolved before eukaryotes.

c. Cyanobacteria are eukaryotes.

9. Is the following sentence true or false? Stromatolites are trace fossils.

_____

Section 13.2 Paleozoic Era: Life Explodes
(pages 369–376)

This section explains the changes that took place on Earth during the Paleozoic era.

Reading Strategy (page 369)

Identifying Details As you read this section, fill in the table below with notes. For more information on this Reading Strategy, see the **Reading and Study Skills** in the **Skills and Reference Handbook** at the end of your textbook.

Period	Geologic Developments	Developments in Life Forms
Cambrian	Breakup of Rodinia, warming trend	Cambrian explosion of animals in the oceans
Ordovician		
Silurian		
Devonian		
Carboniferous		
Permian		

1. What is a mass extinction?

   _____

   _____

Cambrian Period (pages 369–370)

2. What is the first period of the Paleozoic? Circle the correct answer.

   Cambrian   Devonian   Silurian

Ordovician Period (page 371)

3. ● During the Ordovician, the first _____ plants evolved.

Chapter 13   Earth's History

Silurian Period (page 372)

4. ⬤ Which of the following is a major difference between life in the Silurian period and the Ordovician period?

   a. The first animals with hard parts evolved.

   b. Plants and animals evolved that could live on land.

   c. Fishes evolved that did not require oxygen.

Devonian Period (pages 372–373)

5. Read the map below and decide if the following sentence is true or false. The continent of Laurasia was composed of the present-day continents of North America, Europe, and

   Australia. _____

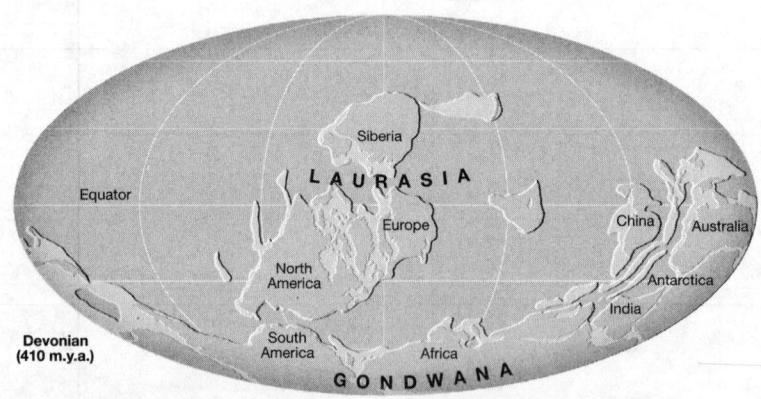

Carboniferous Period (pages 374–375)

6. Among the animals that evolved during the Carboniferous were the

   first _____. Circle the correct answer.

   mammals   birds   reptiles

Permian Period (pages 375–376)

7. ⬤ Is the following sentence true or false? As the Permian period began, all the continents had fused into the supercontinent of Pangaea.

   _____

8. Two hypotheses about the mass extinction of species that ended the Permian period are that volcanic eruptions led to climate change and that an

   _____ may have led to climate change.

Chapter 13   Earth's History

Section 13.3 Mesozoic Era: Age of Reptiles
(pages 377–381)

This section describes the changes that took place during the Mesozoic era.

Reading Strategy (page 377)

Summarizing As you read, write a brief summary of the text for each heading. For more information on this Reading Strategy, see the **Reading and Study Skills** in the **Skills and Reference Handbook** at the end of your textbook.

I. Triassic Period
- Supercontinent Pangaea forms.

- First dinosaurs evolve.

_____

_____

_____

_____

_____

- Flowering plants evolve.

_____

_____

1. What were the three periods that divided the Mesozoic era?

_____

Triassic Period (page 378)

2. Circle the letter of each sentence that is true about the Triassic period.

   a. When the Triassic began, much of the world's land was in one supercontinent.

   b. A major event of the Triassic was the formation of Pangaea.

   c. Toward the end of the Triassic, mammals evolved.

3. 👁 Is the following sentence true or false? Gymnosperms became common during the Triassic period. _____

Chapter 13   Earth's History

4. Complete the following table.

Changes During the Triassic Period	
Continental positions	The continent of Pangaea broke apart, and the present-day continents began to drift toward their current positions.
Plant life	
Animal life	

Jurassic Period (pages 379–380)

5. Many kinds of _____, such as *Diplodocus* and *Stegosaurus*, evolved and became widely distributed.

Cretaceous Period (page 380)

6. Is the following sentence true or false? All dinosaurs were large.

_____

7. Is the following sentence true or false? Angiosperms evolved during

the Cretaceous. _____

The Cretaceous Extinction (page 381)

8. Using the numbers 1–4, put in order the events that may have occurred if a large meteorite collided with Earth.

_____ Animals that ate the plant-eating animals died because the plant eaters were dead.

_____ Plants were unable to undergo photosynthesis because of lack of light, and they died.

_____ Huge quantities of dust block the light from the sun.

_____ Animals that ate plants died because of lack of plants to eat.

Section 13.4 Cenozoic Era: Age of Mammals
(pages 382–385)

This section describes the changes that took place during the Cenozoic era.

Reading Strategy (page 382)

Monitoring Your Understanding Preview the Key Concepts, topic headings, vocabulary, and figures in this section. List two things you expect to learn about each. After reading, state what you learned about each item listed. For more information on this Reading Strategy, see the **Reading and Study Skills** in the **Skills and Reference Handbook** at the end of your textbook.

What I Expect to Learn	What I Learned

The Age of Mammals (pages 382–383)

1. Circle the letter of the dominant land animals during the Cenozoic era.

    a. reptiles   b. mammals   c. amphibians

2. Complete the following chart.

Contrasting Mammals and Reptiles	
Mammals	Reptiles
a. have body hair	
b.	are cold-blooded
c. have adaptations to survive in cold regions	

Chapter 13   Earth's History

3. Is the following sentence true or false? The adaptations of mammals

allow them to lead more active lives than reptiles. _____

Tertiary Period (page 383)

4. ● Is the following sentence true or false? Plate interactions during the Tertiary caused many events including mountain building.

_____

5. Is the following sentence true or false? Grasses developed and spread

rapidly over the plains during the Tertiary. _____.

6. Circle the letter of each statement that is true about adaptations of teeth in mammals.

   a. sharp teeth for cutting and tearing

   b. self-sharpening front teeth for gnawing

   c. flat molars for chewing

Quaternary Period (pages 384–385)

7. Circle the letter of each sentence that is true about mammals during the Quaternary.

   a. Milankovitch cycles provide a partial explanation for recent ice ages.

   b. Many very large mammals evolved.

   c. Saber-toothed cats that evolved during this era can be found in some parts of Asia today.

8. Hunting by humans, disease, or _____ may have caused the extinction of large mammals at the end of the last ice age.

Chapter 14 The Ocean Floor

Summary

14.1 The Vast World Ocean

◉ **Nearly 70 percent of Earth's surface is covered by global ocean.**

- **Oceanography** is a science that draws on the methods and knowledge of geology, chemistry, physics, and biology to study all aspects of the world ocean.

◉ **The world ocean can be divided into four main ocean basins—the Pacific Ocean, the Atlantic Ocean, the Indian Ocean, and the Arctic Ocean.**

◉ **The topography of the ocean floor is as diverse as that of continents.**

- **Bathymetry** (*bathos* = depth, *metry* = measurement) is the measurement of ocean depths and the charting of the shape or topography of the ocean floor.

◉ **Today's technology—particularly sonar, satellites, and submersibles—allows scientists to study the ocean floor in a more efficient and precise manner than ever before.**

- **Sonar** is an acronym for **so**und **n**avigation **a**nd **r**anging. Sonar calculates ocean depth by recording the time it takes sound waves to reach the ocean floor and return.
- A **submersible** is a small underwater craft used for deep-sea research. Submersibles are used to collect data about areas of the ocean that were previously unreachable by humans.

14.2 Ocean Floor Features

◉ **The ocean floor regions are the continental margins, the ocean basin floor, and the mid-ocean ridge.**

- The zone of transition between a continent and the adjacent ocean basin floor is known as the **continental margin**.

◉ **In the Atlantic Ocean, thick layers of undisturbed sediment cover the continental margin, an area with very little volcanic or earthquake activity.**

◉ **In the Pacific Ocean, oceanic crust is plunging beneath continental crust. This force results in a narrow continental margin that experiences both volcanic activity and earthquakes.**

◉ **Continental shelves contain important mineral deposits, large reservoirs of oil and natural gas, and huge sand and gravel deposits.**

- The **continental shelf** is the gently sloping submerged surface extending from the shoreline.

Chapter 14   The Ocean Floor

- Marking the seaward edge of the continental shelf is the **continental slope**, a steep gradient that leads to the deep-ocean floor.
- Deep, steep-sided valleys known as **submarine canyons** are cut into the continental slope.
- **Turbidity currents** are occasional movements of dense, sediment-rich water down the continental slope.
- In regions where trenches do not exist, the steep continental slope merges into a more gradual incline known as the **continental rise.**
- Between the continental margin and the mid-ocean ridge lies the **ocean basin floor.** This region includes deep-ocean trenches, abyssal plains, seamounts, and guyots.

☞ **Trenches form at sites of plate convergence where one moving plate descends beneath another and plunges back into the mantle.**

- Deep-ocean trenches are long, narrow creases in the ocean floor that form the deepest parts of the ocean.

☞ **The sediments that make up abyssal plains are carried there by turbidity currents or deposited as a result of suspended sediments settling.**

- **Abyssal plains** are deep, extremely flat features. These regions are possibly the most level places on Earth.
- Submerged volcanic peaks on the ocean floor are **seamounts.**

☞ **New ocean floor is formed at mid-ocean ridges as magma rises between the diverging plates and cools.**

- The **mid-ocean ridge** is an interconnected system of mountains that have developed on newly formed crust. The rifts at the crest of ridges represent divergent plate boundaries.
- **Seafloor spreading** occurs at divergent plate boundaries where two lithospheric plates are moving apart.

14.3 Seafloor Sediments

☞ **Ocean-floor sediments can be classified according to their origin into three broad categories: terrigenous sediments, biogenous sediments, and hydrogenous sediments.**

☞ **Terrigenous sediments consist primarily of mineral grains that were eroded from continental rocks and transported to the ocean.**

- **Terrigenous sediment** is sediment that originates on land.

☞ **Biogenous sediments consist of shells and skeletons of marine animals and algae.**

- **Biogenous sediment** is sediment that is biological in origin.
- **Calcareous ooze** is the most common biogenous sediment, and is produced from the calcium carbonate shells of organisms.

Chapter 14   The Ocean Floor

- **Siliceous ooze** is composed primarily of the shells of diatoms—single-celled algae—and radiolarians—single-celled animals that have shells made out of silica.

- **Hydrogenous sediment consists of minerals that crystallize directly from ocean water through various chemical reactions.**

  - Hydrogenous sediments make up only a small portion of the overall sediment in the ocean.

14.4 Resources From the Seafloor

- **Oil and natural gas are the main energy products currently being obtained from the ocean floor.**

  - Oil and natural gas are the ancient remains of microscopic organisms.

- **Most oceanic gas hydrates are created when bacteria break down organic matter trapped in ocean-floor sediments.**

  - **Gas hydrates** are compact chemical structures made of water and natural gas.

- **Other major resources from the ocean floor include sand and gravel, evaporative salts, and manganese nodules.**

  - **Manganese nodules** are hard lumps of manganese and other metals that precipitate around a smaller object.

Chapter 14   The Ocean Floor

Section 14.1 The Vast World Ocean
(pages 394–400)

This section discusses how much of Earth is covered by water and how that water is studied.

Reading Strategy (page 394)

Building Vocabulary As you read the section, define each term in the table in your own words. For more information on this Reading Strategy, see the **Reading and Study Skills** in the **Skills and Reference Handbook** at the end of your textbook.

Vocabulary Term	Definition
oceanography	a.
bathymetry	b.
sonar	c. echo sounding to measure ocean depth
submersible	d.

The Blue Planet (page 394)

1. 🌐 Circle the letter of the percentage of Earth's surface covered by the global ocean.

   a. 11 percent   b. 29 percent   c. 71 percent

Geography of the Oceans (page 395)

Match each description with its ocean.

Description	Ocean
_____ 2. shallowest ocean	a. Pacific
_____ 3. located almost entirely in the Southern Hemisphere	b. Atlantic
_____ 4. about half the size of the Pacific	c. Indian
_____ 5. largest and deepest ocean	d. Arctic

Chapter 14   The Ocean Floor

6. 👄 Using the following map, list the names of Earth's four main ocean basins from smallest to largest.

   a. _____

   b. _____

   c. _____

   d. _____

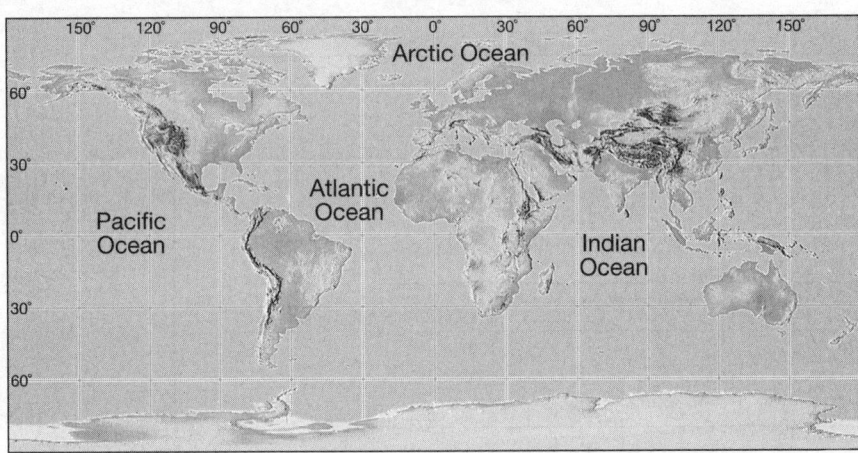

Mapping the Ocean Floor (pages 396–400)

7. 👄 Is the following sentence true or false? The ocean floor's topography is much less diverse than that of the continents. _____

8. What do scientists call the charting of the ocean floor and the measurement of its depths? Circle the correct answer.

   bathymetry   oceanography   topography

9. 👄 Electronic depth-sounding equipment called _____ allowed scientists in the 1920s and later to precisely measure ocean depth.

10. 👄 How are satellites used to measure ocean-surface height?

    _____

    _____

11. 👄 Is the following sentence true or false? Submersibles make it possible for scientists to collect data from areas of the ocean that were previously

    unreachable. _____

Chapter 14   The Ocean Floor

Section 14.2 Ocean Floor Features
(pages 401–405)

This section discusses the features found in the three main regions of Earth's ocean floor.

Reading Strategy (page 401)

Outlining In the outline, use the green headings as the main topics and the blue headings as subtopics. As you read, add supporting details. For more information on this Reading Strategy, see the **Reading and Study Skills** in the **Skills and Reference Handbook** at the end of your textbook.

I. Continental Margins

   A. Continental Shelf

   B. Continental Slope

   C. Continental Rise

II. _____

   A. _____

   _____

   _____

   _____

   _____

   _____

1. 　Three ocean floor regions that have their own unique characteristics are the continental margin, ocean basin floor, and _____.

Continental Margins (pages 402–403)

2. A(n) _____ can best be described as a transition zone between an ocean basin floor and a continent.

3. 　What covers the Atlantic Ocean's continental margin?

_____

_____

4. 　Is the following sentence true or false? The continental margin of the Pacific Ocean has very little volcanic or earthquake activity.

_____

5. Write the letter of each of the following features of the continental margin shown in the figure.

_____ submarine canyon

_____ continental slope

_____ continental shelf

_____ continental rise

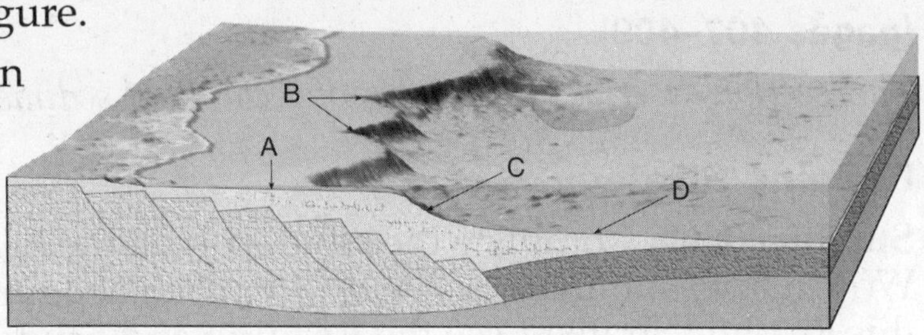

6. Circle the letter of occasional movements down the continental slope of dense water rich in sediment.

a. submarine flows   b. turbidity currents   c. continental rises

Ocean Basin Floor (page 404)

7. Is the following sentence true or false? The area covered by the ocean basin floor is comparable to the percentage of land on Earth's surface

that is above sea level. _____

Match each description with its ocean feature.

Description	Ocean Feature
_____ **8.** submerged volcanic peak	a. abyssal plain
_____ **9.** submerged, flat-topped peak	b. guyot
_____ **10.** crease in the ocean floor formed where one plate plunges beneath another	c. seamount
	d. trench
_____ **11.** flat feature formed when suspended sediments settle from turbidity currents	

Mid-Ocean Ridges (page 405)

13. Circle the letter of the location where a new ocean floor forms.

a. mid-ocean ridge   b. trench   c. continental shelf

14. _____ is the moving apart of two plates at divergent plate boundaries.

Chapter 14   The Ocean Floor

Section 14.3 Seafloor Sediments
(pages 407–409)

This section describes three types of ocean floor sediments.

Reading Strategy (page 407)

Summarizing Complete the table with all the headings for the section. Write a brief summary of the text for each heading. For more information on this Reading Strategy, see the **Reading and Study Skills** in the **Skills and Reference Handbook** at the end of your textbook.

Actions at Boundaries
I. Types of Seafloor Sediments
• Terrigenous sediments originated on land. _____ _____ _____ _____
• Biogenous sediments are biological in origin. _____ _____ _____ _____
• _____ _____ They are crystallized through chemical reactions. These sediments are composed of manganese nodules, calcium carbonates, and evaporites.

1. Is the following sentence true or false? In general, as you move from the continental shelf toward the deep-ocean floor, sediments become coarser. _____

2. Circle the letter of the usual amount of seafloor sediments in a given location.

   a. about 100 to 450 m   b. about 500 to 1000 m
   c. about 100 to 450 km

Chapter 14   The Ocean Floor

Types of Seafloor Sediments (pages 408–409)

Match how each sediment forms with its type of sediment.

How Sediment Forms	Type of Sediment
_____ 3. ⬭ crystallizes directly from ocean water through chemical reactions	a. hydrogenous
_____ 4. ⬭ accumulates on the ocean floor after erosion and transportation from land	b. terrigenous
_____ 5. ⬭ accumulates on the ocean floor when marine animals and algae die and their hard parts sink	c. biogenous

6. Is the following sentence true or false? Ocean-floor sediments are

   usually mixtures of the various sediment types. _____

7. Is the following sentence true or false? Biogenous sediment called siliceous ooze consists mostly of shells of radiolarians and diatoms.

   _____

8. Ocean sediment made up of the calcium carbonate shells of marine

   organisms is called _____.

9. Three types of hydrogenous sediment are manganese nodules, calcium

   carbonates, and _____. Circle the correct answer.

   silica   evaporites   diatoms

10. Circle the letter of a material that, when buried and hardened, becomes a type of limestone.

    a. evaporites   b. radiolarians   c. calcium carbonates

Section 14.4 Resources From the Seafloor
(pages 410–413)

This section discusses the energy and mineral resources obtained from Earth's seafloor.

Reading Strategy (page 410)

Identifying Details As you read, complete the concept map to identify details about resources from the ocean. For more information on this Reading Strategy, see the **Reading and Study Skills** in the **Skills and Reference Handbook** at the end of your textbook.

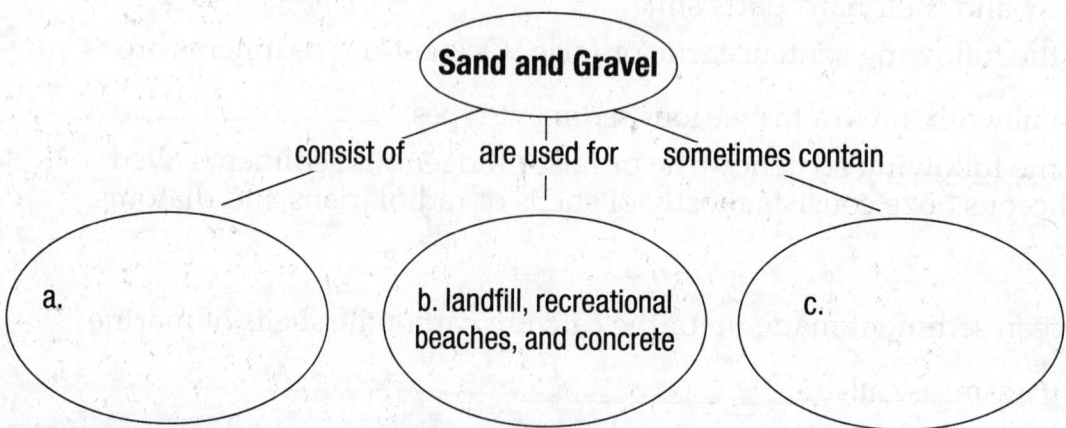

Energy Resources (pages 410–411)

1. ● Circle the letter of the main energy products currently being obtained from the seafloor.

   a. gas hydrates and salts

   b. coal and oil

   c. natural gas and oil

2. The source of today's natural gas and oil deposits is the ancient remains of microscopic _____.

3. Is the following sentence true or false? The majority of the world's oil is produced from ocean floor resources. _____

4. What is one environmental concern about offshore petroleum

   exploration? _____

   _____

   _____

Chapter 14   The Ocean Floor

5. Compact chemical structures made of water and natural gas under the ocean floor are called _____. Circle the correct answer.

   gas hydrates   calcium carbonates   water molecules

6. 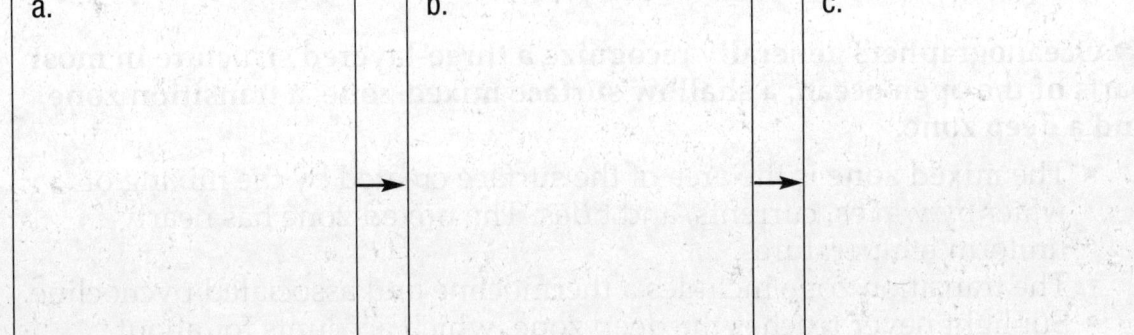 How do gas hydrates form? _____

   _____

   _____

7. Is the following sentence true or false? When brought up from the ocean floor to the ocean surface, gas hydrates rapidly break down. _____

Other Resources (pages 412–413)

8. Circle the letter of the method of obtaining sand and gravel from the ocean.

   a. drilling offshore
   b. mining with suction devices
   c. collecting with submersibles

9. How do manganese nodules form? _____

   _____

   _____

10. Use the statements below to complete the following flowchart to show how evaporative salts form.

   Salts precipitate out and form salt deposits.
   Salts in seawater increase in concentration.
   Seawater evaporates.

a.	b.	c.

Chapter 15 Ocean Water and Ocean Life

Summary

15.1 The Composition of Seawater

● Because the proportion of dissolved substances in seawater is such a small number, oceanographers typically express salinity in parts per thousand.

- **Salinity** (*salinus* = salt) is the total amount of solid material dissolved in water.

● Most of the salt in seawater is sodium chloride, common table salt.

● Chemical weathering of rocks on the continents is one source of elements found in seawater.

● The second major source of elements found in seawater is from Earth's interior.

- Some of the processes affecting the salinity of seawater are runoff and melting icebergs, which decrease salinity, and evaporation and the formation of sea ice, which increase salinity.

● The ocean's surface water temperature varies with the amount of solar radiation received, which is primarily a function of latitude.

- The **thermocline** (*thermo* = heat, *cline* = slope) is the layer of ocean water between about 300 meters and 1000 meters, where there is a rapid change of temperature with depth.

● Seawater density is influenced by two main factors: salinity and temperature.

- **Density** is defined as mass per unit volume. It can be thought of as a measure of how heavy something is for its size.
- The **pycnocline** (*pycno* = density, *cline* = slope) is the layer of ocean water between about 300 meters and 1000 meters where there is a rapid change of density with depth.

● Oceanographers generally recognize a three-layered structure in most parts of the open ocean: a shallow surface mixed zone, a transition zone, and a deep zone.

- The **mixed zone** is the area of the surface created by the mixing of water by waves, currents, and tides. The mixed zone has nearly uniform temperatures.
- The transition zone includes a thermocline and associated pycnocline.
- Sunlight never reaches the deep zone, which accounts for about 80 percent of ocean water.

- In high latitudes, the three-layered structure of the open ocean does not exist because there is no rapid change in temperature or density with depth.

15.2 The Diversity of Ocean Life

👄 Marine organisms can be classified according to where they live and how they move.

👄 Plankton (*planktos* = wandering) include all organisms—algae, animals, and bacteria—that drift with ocean currents.
- Among plankton, the algae that undergo photosynthesis are called **phytoplankton**.
- Animal plankton are called **zooplankton** and include the larval stages of many marine organisms.

👄 Nekton (*nektos* = swimming) include all animals capable of moving independently of the ocean currents, by swimming or other means of propulsion.

👄 The term *benthos* (*benthos* = bottom) describes organisms living on or in the ocean bottom.

👄 Three factors are used to divide the ocean into distinct marine life zones: the availability of sunlight, the distance from shore, and the water depth.
- The upper part of the ocean into which sunlight penetrates is called the **photic zone** (*photos* = light).
- The area where the land and ocean meet and overlap is the **intertidal zone**.
- Seaward from the low-tide line is the **neritic zone**, which covers the continental shelf.
- Beyond the continental shelf is the **oceanic zone**.
- Open ocean of any depth is called the **pelagic zone**.
- The **benthic zone** includes any sea-bottom surface regardless of its distance from shore and is mostly inhabited by benthos organisms.
- The **abyssal zone** is a subdivision of the benthic zone and includes the deep-ocean floor.
- At hydrothermal vents, super-heated and mineral-filled water escapes into the ocean through cracks in the crust. At some vents, high water temperatures support organisms found nowhere else in the world.

15.3 Oceanic Productivity

👄 Two factors influence a region's photosynthetic productivity: the availability of nutrients and the amount of solar radiation, or sunlight.
- **Primary productivity** is the production of organic compounds from inorganic substances through photosynthesis or chemosynthesis.

Chapter 15   Ocean Water and Ocean Life

- **Photosynthesis** is the use of light energy to convert water and carbon dioxide into energy-rich glucose molecules.
- **Chemosynthesis** is the process by which certain microorganisms create organic molecules from inorganic nutrients using chemical energy.

☁ The availability of solar energy is what limits photosynthetic productivity in polar areas.

☁ Photosynthetic productivity in tropical regions is limited by the lack of nutrients.

☁ In temperate regions, which are found at midlatitudes, a combination of two limiting factors, sunlight and nutrient supply, controls productivity.

☁ The transfer of energy between tropic levels is very inefficient.

- A **trophic level** is a feeding level in a food chain. Plants and algae make up the first level, followed by herbivores that eat the plants, and a series of carnivores that eat the herbivores.

☁ Animals that feed through a food web rather than a food chain are more likely to survive because they have alternative foods to eat should one of their food sources diminish or disappear.

- A **food chain** is a sequence of organisms through which energy is transferred, starting with the primary producer.
- A **food web** is a group of interrelated food chains.

Chapter 15   Ocean Water and Ocean Life

Section 15.1 The Composition of Seawater
(pages 422–427)

This section describes substances found in seawater, the temperature profiles of oceans, and the density profiles of oceans.

Reading Strategy (page 422)

Previewing Before you read, preview the figures in this section and add three more questions to the table. As you read, write the answers to your questions. For more information on this Reading Strategy, see the **Reading and Study Skills** in the **Skills and Reference Handbook** at the end of your textbook.

Questions About Seawater	Answers
What processes affect seawater salinity?	a. evaporation, runoff, ice formation, melting of ice
b.	c.
d.	e.
f.	g.

1. Circle the letter of each sentence that is true about seawater.

   a. Seawater contains dissolved substances that give it a salty taste.

   b. Sodium chloride, other salts, metals, and gases are dissolved in seawater.

   c. Seawater is suitable for drinking and irrigation of crops.

Salinity (pages 422–424)

2. Is the following sentence true or false? The average salinity of seawater is 35 percent. _____

3. ☛ Most of the salt in seawater is _____, or common table salt.

4. ☛ Two sources of dissolved substances in the ocean are chemical weathering of rocks on the continents and _____ interior.

Chapter 15   Ocean Water and Ocean Life

5. Four ways in which fresh water is naturally added to seawater are

decreasing its salinity, precipitation, _____,

_____, and sea ice melting.

6. Two natural processes that increase the salinity of seawater are

evaporation and the formation of _____.

Ocean Temperature Variation (pages 424–425)

7. ● The ocean's surface water temperature varies with the amount of
solar radiation received, which is primarily a function of

_____. Circle the correct answer.

    latitude   longitude   salinity

8. Using the following graph,
what temperature is
seawater below 1500 m
in the low latitudes?

    _____

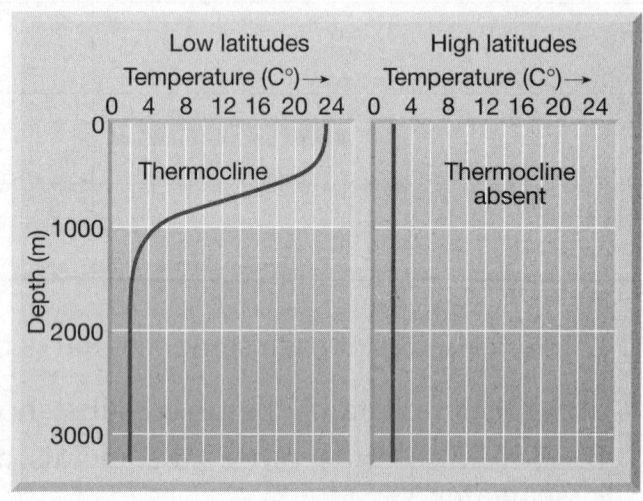

9. What is the temperature profile of seawater in the high latitudes,
according to the graph?

    _____

Ocean Density Variation (pages 425–426)

10. ● Circle the letters of the two main factors that influence density of
seawater.

    a. salinity   b. temperature   c. pycnocline

Ocean Layering (pages 426–427)

11. ● Oceanographers generally recognize a three-layered structure in
most parts of the open ocean: a shallow surface mixed zone, a transition

zone, and a _____ zone.

Section 15.2 The Diversity of Ocean Life
(pages 428–432)

This section describes the diversity of organisms found in the ocean.

Reading Strategy (page 428)

Building Vocabulary As you read, add definitions and examples to complete the table below. For more information on this Reading Strategy, see the **Reading and Study Skills** in the **Skills and Reference Handbook** at the end of your textbook.

Definitions	Examples
Plankton: organisms that drift with ocean currents	bacteria
Phytoplankton: a.	b.
Zooplankton: c.	d. larval fish
Nekton: e.	f.
Benthos: g.	h.

1. What organism directly or indirectly provides food for the majority of

   organisms? _____

Classification of Marine Organisms (page 428–429)

2. ● Marine organisms are classified according to where they live and

   how they _____.

Match each classification to its example.

	Classification	**Example**
_____	3. plankton	a. adult sea star
_____	4. nekton	b. diatom
_____	5. benthos	c. salmon

Chapter 15   Ocean Water and Ocean Life

Marine Life Zones (pages 430–431)

6. ● Three factors used to divide the ocean into distinct marine life zones are the availability of sunlight, the distance from shore, and the

_____ .

7. Circle the letter of each sentence that is true about life in the ocean.

   a. In the euphotic zone, phytoplankton use sunlight to produce food.

   b. Phytoplankton is the basis of most oceanic food webs.

   c. Photosynthesis occurs from the surface to deep into the abyssal zone of the ocean.

8. Using the figure, select the letter that identifies each of the following marine life zones.

   _____ euphotic zone   _____ abyssal zone

   _____ neritic zone   _____ photic zone

   _____ aphotic zone   _____ pelagic zone

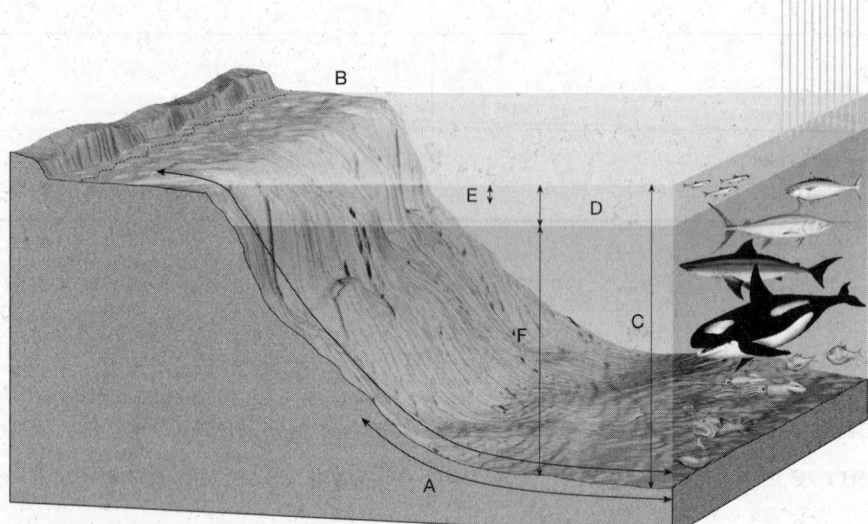

Hydrothermal Vents (page 432)

9. Is the following sentence true or false? A hydrothermal vent is a crack in Earth's crust where seawater seeps in and becomes superheated by

Earth's internal energy. _____

10. What is unusual about life and these hydrothermal vents?

   _____

   _____

   _____

Chapter 17   The Atmosphere: Structure and Temperature

Section 17.1 Atmosphere Characteristics
(pages 476–482)

This section describes the components and vertical structure of the atmosphere. It also explains how the relationship between Earth and the sun causes the seasons.

Reading Strategy (page 476)

Comparing and Contrasting As you read, complete the Venn diagram by comparing and contrasting summer and winter solstices. For more information on this Reading Strategy, see the **Reading and Study Skills** in the **Skills and Reference Handbook** at the end of your textbook.

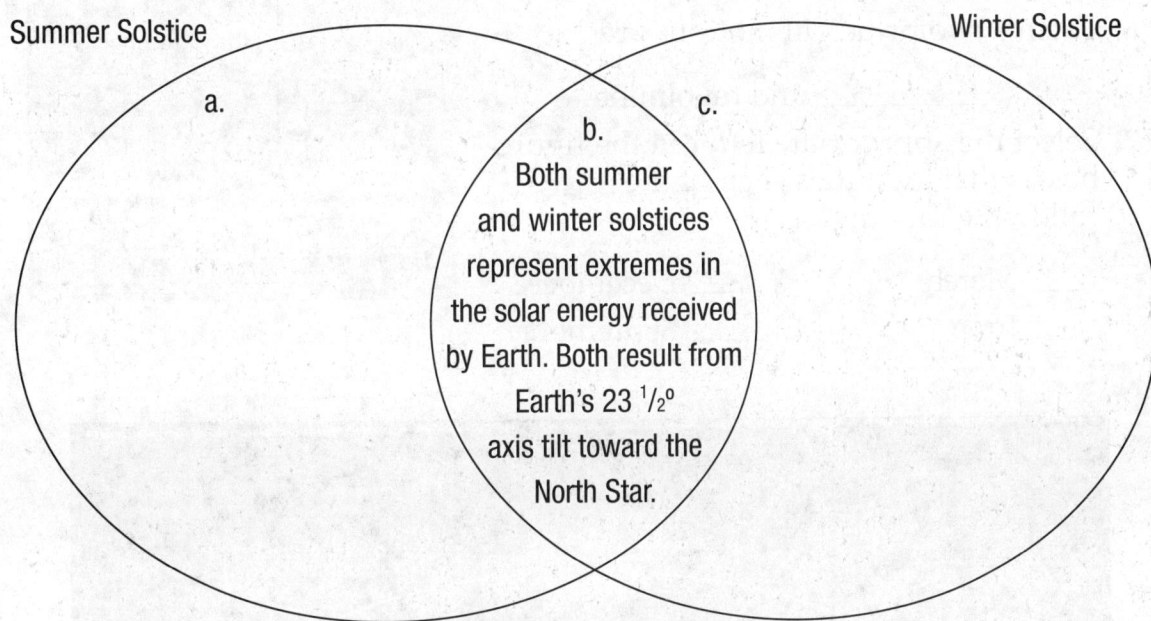

Summer Solstice

Winter Solstice

a.

c.

b.
Both summer and winter solstices represent extremes in the solar energy received by Earth. Both result from Earth's 23 ½° axis tilt toward the North Star.

Composition of the Atmosphere (pages 477–478)

1. Circle the letter of the gas that is the largest component of the atmosphere.

    a. oxygen   b. nitrogen   c. water vapor

2. 🖊 Is the following sentence true or false? The source of all clouds and

    precipitation is water vapor. _____

Height and Structure of the Atmosphere (pages 479–480)

3. Is the following sentence true or false? Atmospheric pressure increases

    with height. _____

Name _____ Class _____ Date _____

Chapter 17   The Atmosphere: Structure and Temperature

4. Select the letter in the figure that identifies the following layers of the atmosphere.

_____ mesosphere   _____ thermosphere

_____ troposphere   _____ stratosphere

5. ◔ In the figure, the atmosphere is divided vertically into four layers based

on _____.

Earth-Sun Relationships (pages 481–482)

6. Earth's two principal motions are

_____ and revolution.

7. Select the appropriate letter in the figure below that identifies each of the following months.

_____ March   _____ December
_____ June   _____ September

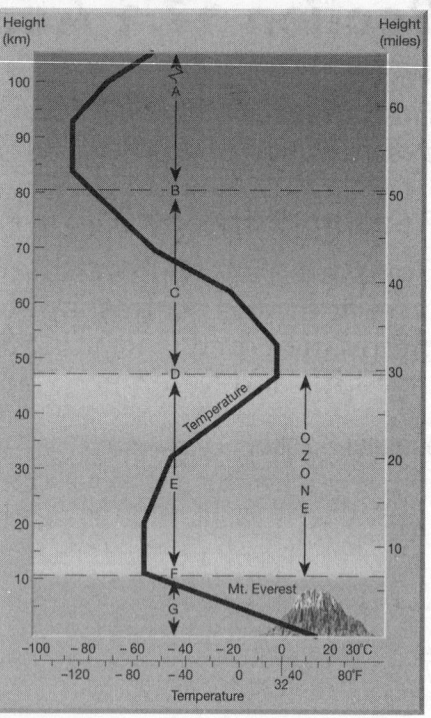

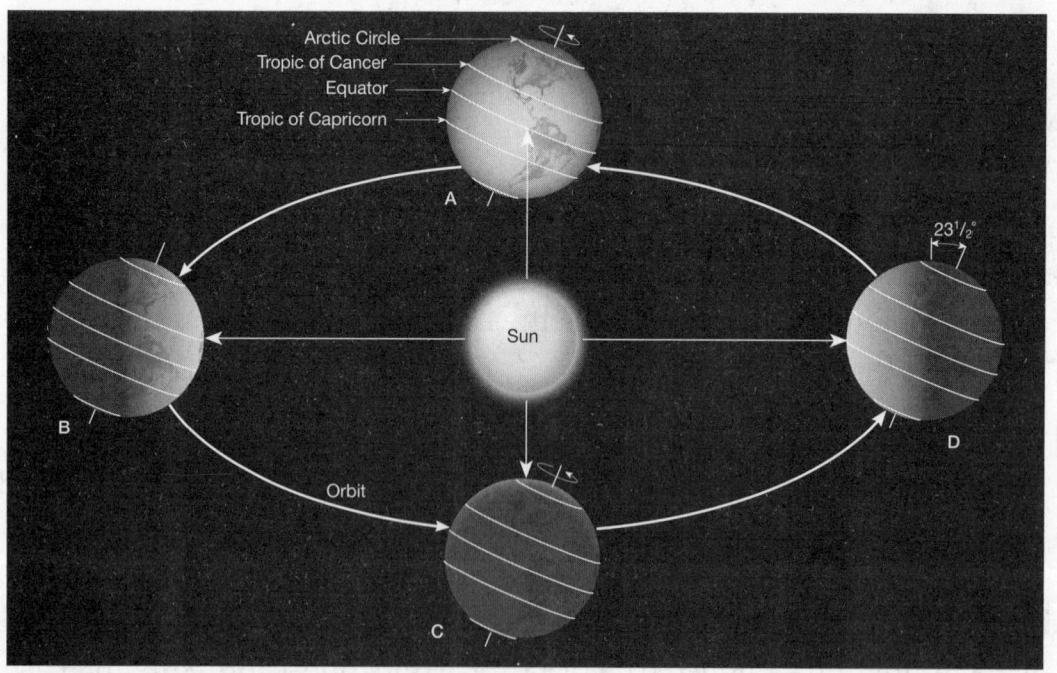

8. In the diagram above, the northern end of Earth's axis is tilted toward the sun. When Earth is in this position, what season is it in the northern hemisphere?

a. spring   b. summer   c. winter

Section 17.2 Heating the Atmosphere
(pages 483–487)

This section describes the three ways in which heat can be transferred. It also explains what happens to solar radiation that hits Earth's atmosphere and surface.

Reading Strategy (page 483)

Using Prior Knowledge Before you read, write your definition for each term. After you read, write the scientific definition of each term and compare it to your original definition. For more information on this Reading Strategy, see the **Reading and Study Skills** in the **Skills and Reference Handbook** at the end of your textbook.

Term	Your Definition	Scientific Definition
Heat		
Temperature		

Energy Transfer as Heat (pages 483–485)

Match each description with its mechanism of energy transfer.

Description

_____ **1.** transfer of heat by mass movement or circulation within a substance

_____ **2.** transfer of heat through matter by molecular activity

_____ **3.** ⬭ transfer of heat without requiring a medium to travel through

Mechanism of Energy Transfer

a. radiation

b. convection

c. conduction

4. Circle the letter of the act of light bouncing off an object.

a. absorption

b. scattering

c. reflection

Chapter 17   The Atmosphere: Structure and Temperature

5. Complete the chart below.

Mechanism of Energy Transfer		
Mechanism	Requires direct contact?	Requires a medium?
Conduction	yes	
Convection		
Radiation		no

6. 🔊 Is the following sentence true or false? All objects at any temperature emit radiant energy. _____

7. 🔊 Hotter objects emit _____ total energy per unit area than colder objects do.

8. 🔊 Is the following sentence true or false? The hotter a radiating body is, the longer the wavelengths of maximum radiation it will produce.

_____

9. 🔊 Objects that are good absorbers of radiation are also good

_____ of radiation.

What Happens to Solar Radiation? (pages 486–487)

10. 🔊 Three things that can happen when radiation strikes an object are energy may be absorbed by the object, energy may be transmitted by the

object, and energy may _____ the object.

11. Circle the letter of the process that produces rays that travel in all directions.

   a. absorption
   b. reflection
   c. scattering

12. What is the greenhouse effect? _____

_____

_____

_____

13. Is the following sentence true or false? Another term for the greenhouse

effect is global warming. _____

Chapter 17   The Atmosphere: Structure and Temperature

Section 17.3 Temperature Controls
(pages 488–493)

This section describes the factors that influence temperature and discusses worldwide temperature distribution.

Reading Strategy (page 488)

Previewing Before you read, use Figure 15 to describe the temperature variations for Vancouver and Winnipeg. For more information on this Reading Strategy, see the **Reading and Study Skills** in the **Skills and Reference Handbook** at the end of your textbook.

Temperature Variations	
Vancouver	
Winnipeg	

Why Temperatures Vary (page 488)

1. ● Five factors other than latitude that exert a strong influence on

   temperature are heating of land and water, _____, geographic

   position, _____, and ocean currents.

Match each location with its effect on temperature. You may use some effects more than once.

Location	Effect on Temperature
_____ 2. windward of a large body of water	a. lower temperatures
_____ 3. at a low altitude	b. higher temperatures
_____ 4. on a leeward coast	c. more moderate temperatures
_____ 5. behind a mountain range	d. less moderate temperatures
_____ 6. at a high altitude	

7. ● Circle the letter of the sentence that is true.

   a. Land heats more rapidly and cools more slowly than water.

   b. Land heats more rapidly and cools more rapidly than water.

   c. Land heats more slowly and cools more rapidly than water.

Chapter 17   The Atmosphere: Structure and Temperature

8. Is the following sentence true or false? The Southern Hemisphere has smaller annual temperature variations than the Northern Hemisphere because the South Hemisphere has much more water area and much less land area than the Northern Hemisphere. _____

9. Is the following sentence true or false? A location on a windward coast will have a more moderate climate than an inland location at the same latitude. _____

10. Mountains can affect temperatures by acting as _____.

11. Locations at higher altitudes will have _____ mean temperatures than locations at lower altitudes.

12. Circle the letter of the correct definition of *albedo*.

   a. line that connects points with the same temperature

   b. fraction of total radiation reflected by a surface

   c. trapping of heat in Earth's atmosphere

13. ☁ What effect do clouds have on incoming solar radiation? _____

_____

_____

_____

14. Is the following sentence true or false? Clouds have the same effect on temperatures during the night as they do during the day.

_____

World Distribution of Temperature (page 492)

15. Circle the letter of the lines on a map that connect points with the same temperature.

   a. albedos

   b. latitudes

   c. isotherms

16. A world isothermal map shows that temperatures _____ going from the tropics toward the poles. Circle the correct answer.

   increase   decrease   stay the same

Chapter 17   The Atmosphere: Structure and Temperature

WordWise

Complete the sentences by using the vocabulary terms below.

troposphere	isotherms	heat
spring equinox	autumnal equinox	mesosphere
thermosphere	conduction	ozone
summer solstice	stratosphere	scattering
radiation	convection	

The _____ is the bottom layer of the atmosphere.

Many clouds reflect a lot of sunlight because they have a high _____.

Temperatures decrease in the third layer of the atmosphere, the

_____.

The _____ contains only a tiny fraction of the atmosphere's mass.

The _____ is the first day of summer.

In the Northern Hemisphere, the _____ occurs on September 22 or 23.

_____ is a form of oxygen with three oxygen atoms in each molecule.

Solar energy reaches Earth by _____.

March 21 or 22 is the _____ in the Northern Hemisphere.

_____ is the energy transferred from one object to another due to a difference in their temperatures.

The average kinetic energy of the atoms or molecules in a substance is its

_____.

The ozone layer is found in the _____.

When you touch a hot metal spoon, you experience heat transferred by

_____.

The lines on a world isothermal map are called _____.

Water being heated in a pan circulates because of _____.

Light reaches areas that are not in direct light by means of _____.

Chapter 18 Moisture, Clouds, and Precipitation

Summary

18.1 Water in the Atmosphere

⬤ **When it comes to understanding atmospheric processes, water vapor is the most important gas in the atmosphere.**

- Water vapor is the source of all condensation and **precipitation**, which is any form of water that falls from a cloud.

⬤ **The process of changing state requires that energy is transferred in the form of heat.**

- **Latent heat** is the energy absorbed or released during a change in state. Latent heat does not produce a temperature change.
- The process of changing a liquid to a gas is called **evaporation**.
- The process of changing water vapor to the liquid state is called **condensation**.
- **Sublimation** is the conversion of a solid directly to a gas, without passing through the liquid state.
- **Deposition** is the conversion of a vapor directly to a solid.

⬤ **When saturated, warm air contains more water vapor than saturated cold air.**

- The general term for the amount of water vapor in air is **humidity**.
- **Saturated** is the state of air that contains the most water vapor that it can hold at any given temperature and pressure.

⬤ **Relative humidity is a ratio of the air's actual water-vapor content compared with the amount of water vapor air can hold at that temperature and pressure.**

- Relative humidity indicates how near the air is to saturation, rather than the actual amount of water vapor in the air.

⬤ **When the water-vapor content of air remains constant, lowering air temperature causes an increase in relative humidity, and raising air temperature causes a decrease in relative humidity.**

- The dew-point temperature or simply the **dew point** is the temperature to which a parcel of air would need to be cooled to reach saturation.
- Relative humidity is commonly measured by using a **hygrometer**.

Name _____ Class _____ Date _____

18.2 Cloud Formation

⬭ **When air is allowed to expand, it cools, and when it is compressed, it warms.**

- Temperature changes that happen even though heat isn't added or subtracted are called adiabatic temperature changes.
- The rate of adiabatic cooling or heating in unsaturated air and is called the **dry adiabatic rate**.
- The rate of adiabatic cooling in saturated air is called the **wet adiabatic rate** and it is always slower than the dry adiabatic rate.

⬭ **Four mechanisms that can cause air to rise are orographic lifting, frontal wedging, convergence, and localized convective lifting.**

- **Orographic lifting** of air occurs when elevated terrains, such as mountains, act as barriers to air flow, forcing the air to ascend.
- A **front** is the boundary between colliding masses of warm and cold air. Frontal wedging is a process that occurs at a front in which cold, dense air acts as a barrier over which warmer, less dense air rises.
- Convergence is the lifting of air that results from air in the lower atmosphere flowing together.
- Localized convection lifting occurs when unequal heating of Earth's surface warms a pocket of air more than the surrounding air, lowering the air pocket's density.

⬭ **Stable air tends to remain in its original position, while unstable air tends to rise.**

- The most stable conditions happen when air temperature actually increases with height, called a **temperature inversion**.

⬭ **For any form of condensation to occur, whether dew, fog, or clouds, the air must be saturated.**

- When condensation occurs in the air above the ground, tiny bits of particulate matter, called **condensation nuclei**, serve as surfaces for water-vapor condensation.

18.3 Cloud Types and Precipitation

⬭ **Clouds are classified on the basis of their form and height.**

- **Cirrus** (*cirrus* = a curl of hair) clouds are high, white, and thin. They can occur as patches or as delicate veil-like sheets or extended wispy fibers that often have a feathery appearance.
- **Cumulus** (*cumulus* = a pile) clouds consist of rounded individual cloud masses. Normally, they have a flat base and the appearance of rising domes or towers.

Chapter 18   Moisture, Clouds, and Precipitation

- **Stratus** (*stratum* = a layer) clouds are best described as sheets or layers that cover much or all of the sky. While there may be minor breaks, there are no distinct individual cloud units.

◗ **Fog is defined as a cloud with its base at or very near the ground.**

◗ **For precipitation to form, cloud droplets must grow in volume by roughly one million times.**

- The **Bergeron process** is a theory that relates the formation of precipitation to supercooled clouds, freezing nuclei, and the different saturation levels of ice and liquid water.
- Water in the liquid state below 0°C is said to be **supercooled**. Supercooled water will readily freeze if it touches a solid object.
- When air is saturated (100% relative humidity) with respect to water, it is **supersaturated** with respect to ice (greater than 100% humidity).
- The **collision-coalescence** process is a theory of raindrop formation in warm clouds in which large cloud droplets collide and join together with smaller droplets to form a raindrop.

◗ **The type of precipitation that reaches Earth's surface depends on the temperature profile in the lowest few kilometers of the atmosphere.**

- Rain, snow, sleet, glaze, and hail are all types of precipitation.

Chapter 18   Moisture, Clouds, and Precipitation

Section 18.1 Water in the Atmosphere
(pages 504–509)

This section describes how water changes from one state to another. It also explains humidity and relative humidity.

Reading Strategy (page 504)

In the table below, list what you know about water in the atmosphere and what you would like to learn. After you read, list what you have learned. For more information on this Reading Strategy, see the **Reading and Study Skills** in the **Skills and Reference Handbook** at the end of your textbook.

What I Know	What I Would Like to Learn	What I Have Learned
a.	b.	c.
d.	e.	f.

1. ◐ Circle the letter of the most important gas in atmospheric processes.

    a. oxygen   b. nitrogen   c. water vapor

Water's Changes of State (pages 504–506)

2. Select the appropriate letter in the figure that identifies each of the following changes of state.

_____ evaporation   _____ condensation   _____ melting

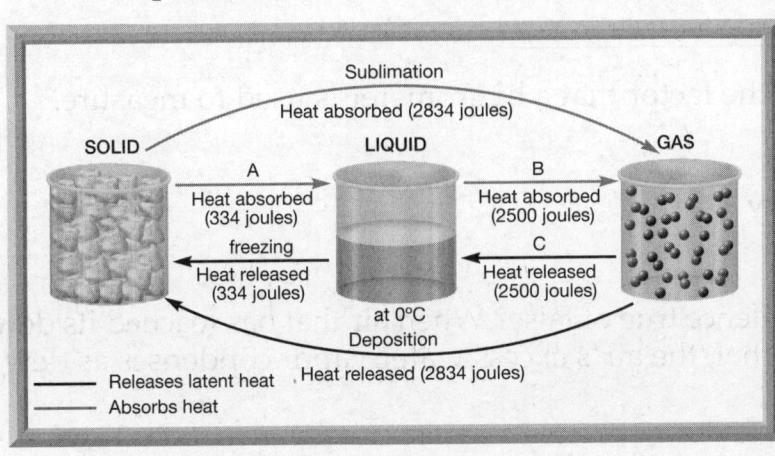

Chapter 18   Moisture, Clouds, and Precipitation

3. For each change of state, write the opposite change of state.

melting	evaporation	sublimation

   a. condensation: _____
   b. freezing: _____
   c. deposition: _____

4. The heat absorbed or released during a change of state is called

_____.

Humidity (pages 506–509)

5. ◎ Is the following sentence true or false? Saturated warm air contains

more water vapor than saturated cold air. _____

6. ◎ The difference between humidity and relative humidity is the amount

of _____ in air. Relative humidity is the ratio of the amount
of water vapor in air to the maximum amount that could be in air at that

_____ and pressure.

Match each situation to its change in relative humidity.

Situation	Change in Relative Humidity
_____ **7.** Water vapor is added.	a. increases
_____ **8.** ◎ Air temperature decreases.	b. no change
_____ **9.** Water vapor is removed.	c. decreases
_____ **10.** ◎ Air temperature increases.	

11. When a parcel of air is cooled to the temperature at which it is saturated,

   it has reached its _____.

12. Circle the letter of the factor that a hygrometer is used to measure.

   a. humidity
   b. relative humidity
   c. temperature

13. Is the following sentence true of false? When air that has reached its dew
point is cooled further, the air's excess water vapor condenses as dew,

   fog, or clouds. _____

Chapter 18   Moisture, Clouds, and Precipitation

Section 18.2 Cloud Formation
(pages 510–516)

This section explains what happens when air is compressed and expanded. It also describes processes that lift air, stable and unstable air, and condensation.

Reading Strategy (page 510)

As you read, write the main idea for each topic in the table below. For more information on this Reading Strategy, see the **Reading and Study Skills** in the **Skills and Reference Handbook** at the end of your textbook.

Topic	Main idea
Adiabatic temperature changes	a.
Stability measurements	b. Stability measurements are made using meteorological instruments that measure the temperature profile of the troposphere.
Degrees of stability	c.

Air Compression and Expansion (page 510–511)

1. When a parcel of air is allowed to expand, it _____. Circle the correct answer.

warms   cools   rises

2. Is the following sentence true or false? The rate of heating or cooling of saturated air is the dry adiabatic rate. _____

3. When a parcel of air reaches its dew point, the process of _____ begins. Circle the correct answer.

evaporation   condensation   precipitation

Processes That Lift Air (pages 512–513)

4. Four mechanisms that can cause air to rise are orographic lifting, frontal wedging, _____, and localized convective lifting.

Chapter 18   Moisture, Clouds, and Precipitation

5. Use the terms below to complete the table below.

> Convergence
> Orographic lifting
> Localized convective lifting
> Frontal wedging

Processes That Lift Air		
Process	Cause of Lifting	Typical Resulting Weather Pattern
	mountains block airflow	clouds and precipitation on windward slopes
	cool, dense air blocks warm, less dense air	clouds and rain
	air in the lower atmosphere flows together	mid-afternoon thunderstorms
	unequal heating of Earth's surface	mid-afternoon rain showers

6. A(n) _____ is produced when two air masses collide.

Stability (pages 514–515)

7. ☁ A parcel of air that is less dense than the surrounding air is _____ and will tend to rise.

8. Circle the letter of the sentence that best describes a temperature inversion.

a. Air temperature increases with height.

b. Air temperature decreases with height.

c. Low-altitude air is unstable.

9. Clouds associated with lifting of _____ air often produce thunderstorms.

Condensation (page 516)

10. ☁ For condensation to occur, air must be _____.

11. Is the following sentence true or false? Above the ground, tiny particles called condensation nuclei serve as surfaces for water-vapor condensation. _____

Chapter 18   Moisture, Clouds, and Precipitation

Section 18.3 Cloud Types and Precipitation
(pages 517–522)

This section describes different types of clouds, including fog. It also explains how precipitation forms and describes different types of precipitation.

Reading Strategy (page 517)

As you read, add definitions for the vocabulary terms. For more information on this Reading Strategy, see the **Reading and Study Skills** in the **Skills and Reference Handbook** at the end of your textbook.

Vocabulary Term	Definition
Cirrus	a.
Cumulus	b. clouds that consist of rounded individual cloud masses
Stratus	c.
Collision-coalescence process	d.

Types of Clouds (pages 517–520)

1. Is the following sentence true or false? Clouds are classified based on

    form and height._____

2. Which photograph shows cumulus clouds? _____

3. Which photograph shows cirrus clouds? _____

A.

B.

Chapter 18   Moisture, Clouds, and Precipitation

4. Circle the letter of each cloud type that is a low cloud.

a. stratus

b. stratocumulus

c. nimbostratus

Fog (page 520)

5. 👁 Define *fog*. _____

_____

_____

6. Is the following sentence true or false? Fogs can be formed by cooling

or by evaporation. _____

How Precipitation Forms (pages 520–521)

7. 👁 What must happen for precipitation to form? _____

_____

8. Formation of precipitation in cold clouds is called the

_____ process.

9. Is the following sentence true or false? In warm clouds, raindrops form

by the Bergeron process. _____

10. Circle the letter of the word that describes water in the liquid state below 0°C.

a. supersaturated

b. saturated

c. supercooled

Forms of Precipitation (page 522)

Match each description with its form of precipitation.

Description	Form of Precipitation
_____ **11.** small particles of ice	a. hail
_____ **12.** drops of water that fall from a cloud and have a diameter of at least 0.5 mm	b. sleet
_____ **13.** ice pellets with multiple layers	c. rain

Chapter 19 Air Pressure and Wind

Summary

19.1 Understanding Air Pressure

☙ Air pressure is exerted in all directions—down, up, and sideways. The air pressure pushing down on an object balances the air pressure pushing up on an object.

- **Air pressure** is simply the pressure exerted by the weight of air above.
- A **barometer** is a device used for measuring air pressure (*bar* = pressure, *metron* = measuring instrument).

☙ In a mercury barometer, a tube is filled with mercury, then turned upside down in a dish of mercury. When air pressure increases, the mercury in the tube rises. When air pressure decreases, so does the height of the mercury column.

☙ Wind is the result of horizontal differences in air pressure. Air flows from areas of higher pressure to areas of lower pressure.

☙ The unequal heating of Earth's surface generates pressure differences. Solar radiation is the ultimate energy source for most wind.

☙ Three factors combine to control wind: pressure differences, the Coriolis effect, and friction.

- **Pressure gradient** is the amount of pressure change occurring over a given distance.
- Isobars are lines on a map that connect places of equal air pressure.

☙ Closely spaced isobars indicate a steep pressure gradient and high winds. Widely spaced isobars indicate a weak gradient and light winds.

☙ The Coriolis effect describes how Earth's rotation affects moving objects. All free-moving objects or fluids, including the wind, are deflected to the right of their path of motion in the Northern Hemisphere. In the Southern Hemisphere, they are deflected to the left.

- **Jet streams** are fast-moving rivers of air near the tropopause that travel between 120 and 240 km per hour in a west-to-east direction.

19.2 Pressure Centers and Winds

☙ In cyclones, the pressure decreases from the outer isobars toward the center. In anticyclones, pressure increases from the outside toward the center.

- Lows, or **cyclones,** are centers of low pressure.
- Highs, or **anticyclones**, are centers of high pressure.

Chapter 19   Air Pressure and Wind

👄 When the pressure gradient and the Coriolis effect are applied to pressure centers in the Northern Hemisphere, winds blow counterclockwise around a low. Around a high, they blow clockwise.

👄 In either hemisphere, friction causes a net flow of air inward around a cyclone and a net flow of air outward around an anticyclone.

👄 The atmosphere balances the unequal heating of Earth's surface by acting as a giant heat-transfer system. This system moves warm air toward high latitudes and cool air toward the equator.

- **Trade winds** are two belts of winds that blow almost constantly from easterly directions.
- The **Westerlies** are winds that blow west to east of the poleward side of the subtropical highs.
- The **polar easterlies** are winds that blow from the polar high toward the subpolar low. These winds are not constant winds like the trade winds.
- The **polar front** is the stormy frontal zone in the middle latitudes separating cold polar air masses from warm tropical air masses.
- A **monsoon** is a seasonal reversal of wind direction. In winter, wind blows from land to sea. In summer, the wind blows from sea to land.

19.3 Regional Wind Systems

👄 The local winds are caused either by topographic effects or by variations in surface composition—land and water—in the immediate area.

👄 In the United States, the westerlies consistently move weather from west to east across the continent.

- When the wind consistently blows more often from one direction than from any other, it is called a **prevailing wind**.
- A cup **anemometer** is often used to measure wind speed.

👄 At irregular intervals of three to seven years, a warm current that normally flows from Ecuador to Peru for only a short time, becomes unusually strong and replaces normally cold offshore waters with warm equatorial waters.

- Scientists use the term **El Niño** for these episodes of ocean warming that affect the eastern tropical Pacific.

👄 Researchers have come to recognize that when surface temperatures in the eastern Pacific are colder than average, a La Niña event is triggered that has a distinctive set of weather patterns.

Chapter 19   Air Pressure and Wind

Section 19.1 Understanding Air Pressure
(pages 532–536)

This section explains what air pressure is and how it is measured. It also describes the factors that cause and control wind.

Reading Strategy (page 532)

As you read, write the main ideas for each topic in the table. For more information on this Reading Strategy, see the **Reading and Study Skills** in the **Skills and Reference Handbook** at the end of your textbook.

Topic	Main Ideas
Air Pressure Defined	Air pressure is the weight of air above. It is exerted in all directions.
Measuring Air Pressure	a.
Factors Affecting Wind	b.

Air Pressure Defined (pages 532–533)

1. Use the terms below to fill in the blank. Air pressure is the pressure

   exerted by the _____ of air above a certain point.

weight	thickness	saturation

2. Is the following sentence true or false? Average air pressure is about the same as that produced by a column of water 10 m high.

   _____

Measuring Air Pressure (page 533)

3. Circle the letter of the instrument used to measure air pressure.

   a. thermometer

   b. barometer

   c. anemometer

Chapter 19   Air Pressure and Wind

4. ⬮ When air pressure increases, the mercury in the tube of a mercury

barometer _____. Circle the correct answer.

                    falls   rises   stays the same

5. Is the following sentence true or false? The mercury barometer was

invented by Galileo. _____

Factors Affecting Wind (pages 534–536)

6. ⬮ Wind is caused by horizontal differences in _____.

7. ⬮ Is the following sentence true or false? Pressure differences that
cause wind are generated by unequal heating of Earth's surface.

_____

8. ⬮ Three factors that combine to control wind are pressure differences,
_____, and friction.

9. ⬮ Due to the Coriolis effect, winds in the Northern Hemisphere are

deflected to the _____.

10. Is the following sentence true or false? The Coriolis effect occurs
because Earth rotates underneath the path of moving objects.

_____

11. _____ are high-altitude winds that travel west to east.

12. Use the terms below to complete the table below.

Coriolis Effect	Friction	Pressure Differences

Factors That Affect Wind		
Factor	**Ultimate Cause**	**Effect on Wind**
	unequal heating of Earth's surface by the sun	the greater the pressure difference, the higher the wind
	Earth's rotation	deflects wind to the right in the Northern Hemisphere and to the left in the Southern Hemisphere
	surface terrain	slows air movement, which changes wind direction

Section 19.2 Pressure Centers and Winds
(pages 537–542)

This section describes cyclones, anticyclones, and global wind patterns.

Reading Strategy (page 537)

As you read about pressure centers and winds, complete the table indicating to which hemisphere the concept applies. Use *N* for Northern Hemisphere, *S* for Southern Hemisphere, or *B* for both. For more information on this Reading Strategy, see the **Reading and Study Skills** in the **Skills and Reference Handbook** at the end of your textbook.

Cyclones rotate counterclockwise.	a. N
Net flow of air is inward around a cyclone.	b.
Anticyclones rotate counterclockwise.	c.
Coriolis effect deflects winds to the right.	d.

Highs and Lows (page 537)

1. Cyclones are centers of _____ pressure associated with clouds and precipitation.

2. 👁 Is the following sentence true or false? In an anticyclone, the value of the isobars increases from the center to the outside. _____

3. 👁 Is the following sentence true or false? In the Southern Hemisphere, winds around a cyclone flow outward. _____

4. These figures show side views of the air movement in a high and low. Select the letter of the figure that identifies each of the following air movements.

   _____ surface low
   _____ divergence aloft
   _____ surface high
   _____ surface divergence
   _____ calm, clear weather

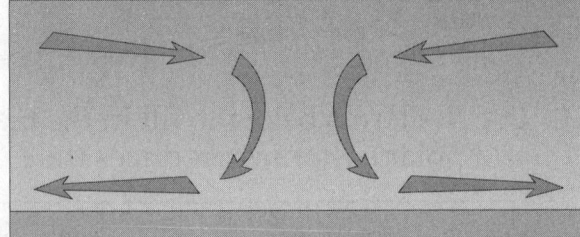

A.

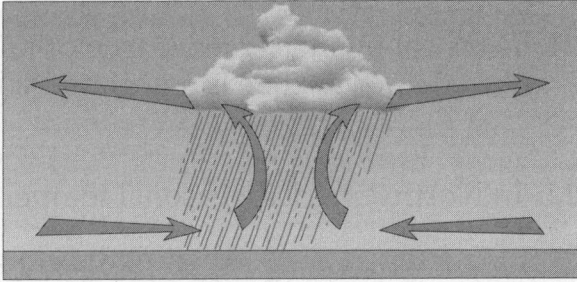

B.

5. Is the following statement true of false? Cyclones often produce bad weather, whereas anticyclones often produce good weather.

_____

Global Winds (page 540)

6. ● The atmosphere moves warm air toward high latitudes and cool air

toward _____. Circle the correct answer.

Antarctica   the equator   high latitudes

7. Is the following sentence true or false? Earth's rotation causes the two-cell

convection system to break down into smaller cells. _____

8. Select the appropriate letter in the figure that identifies each part of the global circulation model.

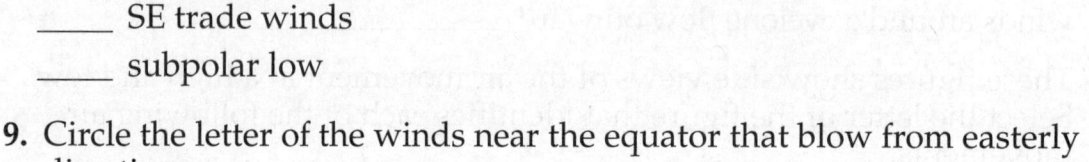

_____ NE trade winds

_____ polar easterlies

_____ equatorial low

_____ westerlies

_____ subtropical high

_____ SE trade winds

_____ subpolar low

9. Circle the letter of the winds near the equator that blow from easterly directions.

a. jet streams   b. westerlies   c. trade winds

10. Use the terms below to fill in the blank. The interaction of westerlies and polar easterlies produces the _____.

trade winds	jet streams	polar front

11. Is the following sentence true or false? Inward and upward airflow at the equatorial zone is associated with clouds and precipitation.

_____

12. In North America, seasonal temperature differences over

_____ disrupt the global pressure pattern.

Chapter 19   Air Pressure and Wind

Section 19.3 Regional Wind Systems
(pages 543–548)

This section discusses local winds and how wind is measured. It also explains El Niño and La Niña.

Reading Strategy (page 543)

Before you read, use Figure 17 on page 547 to locate examples of the driest and wettest regions of Earth. After you read, identify the dominant wind system for each location. For more information on this Reading Strategy, see the **Reading and Study Skills** in the **Skills and Reference Handbook** at the end of your textbook.

Precipitation	Location	Dominant Wind System
Extremely low	a.	b.
Extremely high	c.	d.

Local Winds (pages 543–545)

1. ● Two causes of local winds are _____ and variations in surface composition.

Match each description with its local wind.

Description	Local Wind
_____ 2. During the day, heated air along mountain slopes rises.	a. land breeze
_____ 3. During the day, heated air over land rises, allowing cooler air to move in from over water.	b. sea breeze
	c. valley breeze
_____ 4. At night, air over land cools and moves out over water.	d. mountain breeze
_____ 5. At night, cooled air along mountain slopes moves downward.	

6. Circle the letter of the locations where the coldest air pockets usually can be found.

   a. valley floors   b. mountain peaks   c. mountainsides

Chapter 19   Air Pressure and Wind

7. Does the figure show a land breeze or a sea breeze?

_____

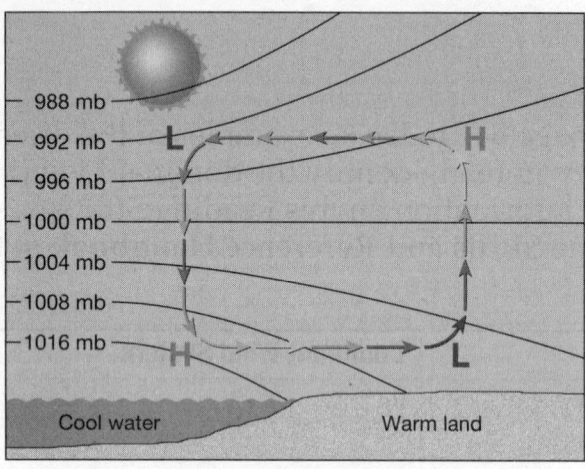

988 mb
992 mb
996 mb
1000 mb
1004 mb
1008 mb
1016 mb

L   H

H   L

Cool water   Warm land

How Wind Is Measured (page 545)

8. What is a prevailing wind? _____

_____

_____

9. In the United States, the _____ move weather from west to east. Circle the correct answer.

trade winds   westerlies   polar easterlies

10. Circle the letter of the instrument used to measure wind speed.

a. thermometer   b. anemometer   c. wind vane

El Niño and La Niña (pages 546–547)

11. An episode of ocean warming that affects the eastern tropical Pacific is

called _____.

12. Is the following sentence true or false? A La Niña episode is triggered by colder than average surface temperatures in the eastern Pacific.

_____

Global Distribution of Precipitation (page 548)

13. Is the following sentence true or false? Areas dominated by subtropical

low-pressure cells are often deserts. _____

Chapter 19 Air Pressure and Wind

WordWise

Use the clues and the words below to help you write the vocabulary terms from the chapter in the blanks. Use the circled letters to find the hidden word.

Clues

1. pressure exerted by the weight of air above a certain point

2. pressure changes occurring over a given distance

3. device used to measure air pressure

4. describes how Earth's rotation affects moving objects

5. center of low air pressure

6. stormy belt where westerlies encounter polar easterlies

7. seasonal change in wind direction due to summer heating of landmasses

8. easterly wind belts on either side of the equator

9. prevailing winds of the middle latitudes

westerlies
barometer
cyclone
polar front
monsoon
air pressure
pressure gradient
trade winds
Coriolis effect

Vocabulary Terms

1. ◯ _ _   _ _ _ _ _ _ _

2. _ _ _ _ _ _ _ _   ◯ _ _ _ _ _ _ _

3. _ _ _ _ _ _ ◯ _ _

4. _ _ _ ◯ _ _ _ _   _ _ _ _ _ _

5. ◯ _ ◯◯ _ _ _ _

6. _ _ ◯ _ _   _ _ _ _ _

7. _ _ _ _ _ ◯ _

8. _ _ _ _ _   _ ◯ _ _ _

9. _ _ _ _ _ _ _ ◯ _ _

Hidden Word: _ _ _ _ _ _ _ _ _ _ _

Definition: _____

Chapter 20 Weather Patterns and Severe Storms

Summary

20.1 Air Masses

● An air mass is an immense body of air in the troposphere that is characterized by similar temperatures and amounts of moisture at any given altitude.

● As it moves, the characteristics of an air mass change and so does the weather in the area over which the air mass moves.

● In addition to their overall temperature, air masses are classified according to the surface over which they form.

- Continental (c) air masses form over land, and are likely to be dry. Maritime (m) air masses form over water, and are humid.
- Polar (P) air masses form at high altitudes and are cold. Tropical (T) air masses form at low latitudes and are warm.

● Much of the weather in North America, especially weather east of the Rocky Mountains, is influenced by continental polar (cP) and maritime tropical (mT) air masses.

● Only occasionally do continental tropical (cT) air masses affect the weather outside their source regions.

20.2 Fronts

● When two air masses meet, they form a front, which is a boundary that separates two air masses of different properties.

- Fronts are classified by the temperature of the advancing front. There are four types of fronts: warm, cold, stationary, and occluded fronts.

● A warm front forms when warm air moves into an area formerly covered by cooler air.

● A cold front forms when cold, dense air moves into a region occupied by warmer air.

● When the flow of air on either side of a front is almost parallel to the front, the surface position of the front does not move, and a stationary front forms.

● When a cold front overtakes a warm front, an occluded front forms.

Chapter 20   Weather Patterns and Severe Storms

☞ **Middle-latitude cyclones are large centers of low pressure that generally travel from west to east and cause stormy weather.**

☞ **More often than not, air high up in the atmosphere fuels a middle-latitude cyclone.**

20.3 Severe Storms

☞ **A thunderstorm is a storm that generates lightning and thunder. Thunderstorms frequently produce gusty winds, heavy rain, and hail.**

☞ **Thunderstorms form when warm, humid air rises in an unstable environment.**

- There are three stages in thunderstorm development: the cumulus stage, the mature stage, and the dissipating stage.

☞ **Tornadoes are violent windstorms that take the form of a rotating column of air called a vortex. The vortex extends downward from a cumulonimbus cloud all the way to the ground.**

☞ **Most tornadoes form in association with severe thunderstorms.**

☞ **Whirling tropical cyclones that produce sustained winds of at least 119 kilometers per hour are known in the United States as hurricanes.**

☞ **Hurricanes develop most often in the late summer when water temperatures are warm enough to provide the necessary heat and moisture to the air.**

- The doughnut-shaped wall that surrounds the center of a hurricane is the **eye wall.** Here the greatest wind speeds and heaviest rainfall occurs.
- At the very center of the storm is the **eye** of the hurricane, where precipitation ceases and winds subside.
- A **storm surge** is a dome of water about 65 to 80 kilometers wide that sweeps across the coast where a hurricane's eye moves onto land.

Chapter 20   Weather Patterns and Severe Storms

Section 20.1 Air Masses
(pages 558–563)

This section describes air masses and explains how they affect weather.

Reading Strategy (page 558)

Building Vocabulary As you read, write a definition for each of the terms in the table. Refer to the table as you read the rest of the chapter. For more information on this Reading Strategy, see the **Reading and Study Skills** in the **Skills and Reference Handbook** at the end of your textbook.

Term	Definition
Air mass	a. an immense body of air characterized by similar temperatures and amounts of moisture at any given altitude
Source region	b. area over which an air mass gets its chaacteristic properties of temperature and moisture
Polar air mass	c.
Tropical air mass	d.
Continental air mass	e.
Maritime air mass	f.

Air Masses and Weather (page 559)

1. Changes in weather patterns are often caused by movement of

   _____. Circle the correct answer.

   winds   air masses   fronts

2. Circle the letter of a common size for an air mass.

   a. 600 km or less across

   b. 1600 km or more across

   c. 16,000 km or more across

Chapter 20   Weather Patterns and Severe Storms

Classifying Air Masses (page 560)

3. Identify each labeled
   air mass on the figure
   as continental tropical,
   continental polar,
   maritime polar, or
   maritime tropical.

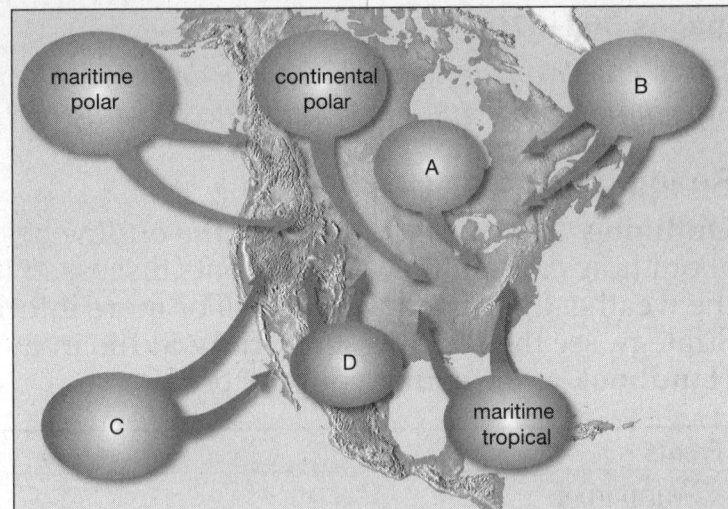

   A. _____

   B. _____

   C. _____

   D. _____

4. Circle the letter of the
   terms that describe
   the temperature characteristics of an air mass.

   a. continental and maritime

   b. polar and maritime

   c. polar and tropical

Weather in North America (pages 561–563)

5. ◉ Is the following sentence true or false? Much of the weather in
   eastern North America is influenced by continental tropical and

   maritime polar air masses. _____

6. Circle the letter of the type of air mass that is the source of much of the
   precipitation that falls on the eastern United States.

   a. continental tropical

   b. maritime tropical

   c. maritime polar

7. Is the following sentence true or false? In the winter, maritime polar air
   masses often bring rain and snow to the west coast of North America.

   _____

8. Is the following sentence true or false? The movement of continental
   tropical air masses into the Great Lakes region in the fall causes Indian

   summer. _____

Chapter 20   Weather Patterns and Severe Storms

Section 20.2 Fronts
(pages 564–570)

This section explains how fronts form, describes different types of fronts, and explains how mid-latitude cyclones affect weather in the United States.

Reading Strategy (page 564)

Outlining As you read, complete the outline below. Include information about how each of the weather fronts discussed in this section forms and the weather associated with each. For more information on this Reading Strategy, see the **Reading and Study Skills** in the **Skills and Reference Handbook** at the end of your textbook.

Fronts
I. Warm front
A. _____
B. _____
II. Cold front
A. _____
B. _____
_____
A. flow of air parallel to front
_____
_____
_____
B. light precipitation

Formation of Fronts (page 564)

1. 🔵 A front is a(n) _____ that separates two air masses.

2. Is the following sentence true or false? Like air masses, most fronts are

   very large. _____

Types of Fronts (pages 565–567)

Match each description with its front.

Description	Front
_____ 3. 🔵 Cold, dense air moves into a region occupied by warmer air.	a. warm front
_____ 4. 🔵 Warm air moves into an area formerly covered by cooler air.	b. cold front
_____ 5. 🔵 A cold front overtakes a warm front.	c. occluded front

6. A warm front often produces a(n) ______________ increase in temperature. Circle the correct answer.

sudden immediate gradual

7. Is the following sentence true or false? Forceful lifting of air along a cold front can lead to heavy rain and strong winds. ______________

Middle-Latitude Cyclones (pages 567–568)

8. The middle-latitude cyclone shown in the figure is a center of low ______________.

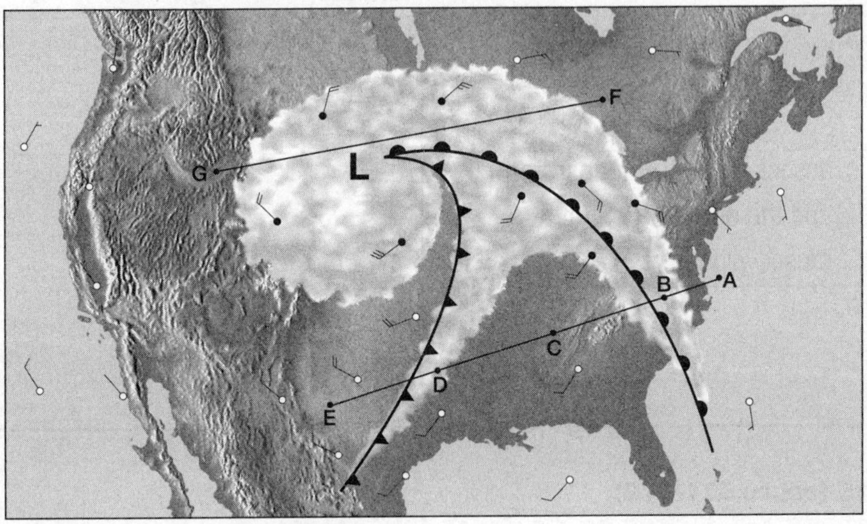

9. Label the type of front shown at each of these locations in the figure as either a warm front or a cold front.

location B: ______________ location D: ______________

The Role of Airflow Aloft (pages 568–570)

10. In the figure of a stage of a middle-latitude cyclone, changes in air flow and ______________ cause a counterclockwise flow of air.

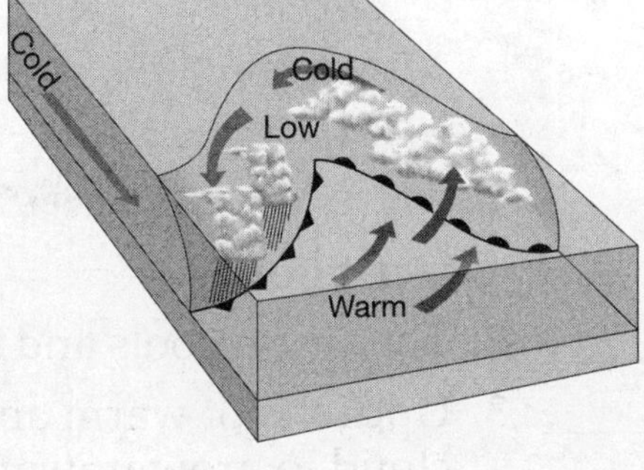

Name _____ Class _____ Date _____

Section 20.3 Severe Storms
(pages 571–577)

This section discusses the causes and nature of thunderstorms, tornadoes, and hurricanes.

Reading Strategy (page 571)

Identifying Cause and Effect Complete the table as you read this section. For more information on this Reading Strategy, see the **Reading and Study Skills in the Skills and Reference Handbook** at the end of your textbook.

Severe Storms		
	Causes	**Effects**
Thunderstorms	a.	b. gusty winds, heavy rain, hail
Tornadoes	c. associated with thunderstorms and the development of a mesocyclone	d.
Hurricanes	e.	f.

Thunderstorms (pages 571–572)

1. ● A thunderstorm generates _____ and thunder.

Using the figure, match each description to its thunderstorm stage.

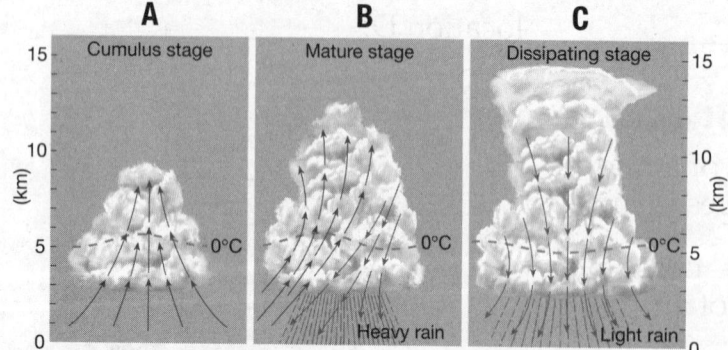

Description

_____ 2. The storm cools and dies down.

_____ 3. Updrafts of warm air cause the cloud to grow upward.

_____ 4. Heavy precipitation falls.

Thunderstorm Stage

a. cumulus stage

b. mature stage

c. dissipating stage

Chapter 20   Weather Patterns and Severe Storms

Tornadoes (pages 573–574)

5. 👁 A tornado is a violent windstorm in the form of a(n)

   _____ column of air.

6. Is the following sentence true or false? Tornadoes occur mainly in the

   winter. _____

7. 👁 Circle the letter of the type of storm usually associated with
   tornadoes.

   a. hurricane

   b. thunderstorm

   c. typhoon

8. A tornado _____ is issued when a tornado has actually
   been sighted in an area.

Hurricanes (page 575)

9. 👁 To be considered a hurricane, a tropical _____ must
   produce sustained winds of at least 119 km per hour.

10. Is the following sentence true or false? Hurricanes are the most

    powerful storms on Earth. _____

11. 👁 Hurricanes usually develop in late summer because they are fueled

    by _____ and moisture from warm water.

12. Is the following sentence true or false? The greatest wind speeds and

    heaviest rainfall in a hurricane occur in the eye. _____

13. Circle the letter of the center of a hurricane.

    a. eye wall   b. eye   c. surge

14. Use the terms below to fill in the blanks. When a hurricane's eye lands,

    a dome of water about 65 to 80 km wide, called a _____,
    sweeps across the coast.

eye wall	storm surge	typhoon

15. A hurricane weakens when it moves over cool ocean waters and when it

    moves over _____.

Chapter 21 Climate

Summary

21.1 Factors That Affect Climate

◉ **As latitude increases, the average intensity of solar energy decreases.**

- The **tropical zones** are located where the sun's rays are most intense, between about 23.5° north and 23.5° south of the equator. These regions are warm year-round.
- The **temperate zones** are located where the sun's energy strikes Earth at a smaller angle than near the equator, between about 23.5° and 66.5° north and south of the equator. These regions have hot summers and cold winters.
- In the **polar zones**, which are between 66.5° north and south latitude and the poles, the energy strikes at an even smaller angle, resulting in cold temperatures year-round.

◉ **The higher the elevation is, the colder the climate.**

◉ **Topographic features such as mountains play an important role in the amount of precipitation that falls over an area.**

◉ **Large bodies of water such as lakes and oceans have an important effect on the temperature of an area because the temperature of the water body influences the temperature of the air above it.**

◉ **Global winds are another factor that influences climate because they distribute heat and moisture around Earth.**

◉ **Vegetation can affect both temperature and precipitation patterns in an area.**

21.2 World Climates

◉ **The Köppen climate classification system uses mean monthly and annual values of temperature and precipitation to classify climates.**

◉ **Humid tropical climates are climates without winters. Every month in such a climate has a mean temperature above 18°C. The amount of precipitation can exceed 200 cm per year.**

- A **wet tropical climate** has high temperatures and much annual precipitation.
- **Tropical wet and dry climates** have temperatures and total precipitation similar to those in the wet tropics, but experience distinct periods of low precipitation.

Chapter 21   Climate

☞ **Climates with mild winters have an average temperature in the coldest month that is below 18°C but above –3°C. Climates with severe winters have an average temperature in the coldest month that is below –3°C.**

- Located between about 25° and 40° latitude on the eastern sides of the continents are the **humid subtropical climates.** They are hot and sultry in the summer, and winters are generally mild, though frosts are common in higher-latitude areas.
- Coastal areas between about 40° and 65° north and south latitude have **marine west coast climates.** These climates have mild winters and cool summers with ample rainfall throughout the year.
- Regions between about 30° and 45° latitude are **dry-summer subtropical climates.** They are humid climates with strong winter rainfall.
- North of the humid continental climate and south of the tundra is an extensive **subarctic climate** region. Winters are long and bitterly cold; summers are warm but very short. This region has the highest annual temperature ranges on Earth.

☞ **A dry climate is one in which the yearly precipitation is not as great as the potential loss of water by evaporation.**

☞ **Polar climates are those in which the mean temperature of the warmest month is below 10°C.**

☞ **In general, highland climates are cooler and wetter than nearby areas at lower elevations.**

21.3 Climate Changes

☞ **Geologic changes in Earth's land and oceans due to plate tectonics cause changes in climate over very long time scales.**

☞ **Changes in the shape of Earth's orbit and the tilt of Earth's axis of rotation affect global climates over intermediate time scales.**

☞ **Changes in ocean circulation also can result in short-term climate fluctuations.**

☞ **Over short time scales, fluctuations in the amount of solar radiation can change global climates.**

☞ **Volcanic ash, dust, and sulfur-based aerosols in the air increase the amount of solar radiation that is reflected back into space. This causes Earth's lower atmosphere to cool.**

☞ **The greenhouse effect is a natural warming of both Earth's lower atmosphere and Earth's surface.**

Chapter 21   Climate

⬭ **As a result of increases in carbon dioxide levels, as well as increases in other greenhouse gases, global temperatures have increased. This increase is called global warming.**

- Scientists predict that by the year 2100, Earth's average temperature could increase by more than 5° C.
- Scientists use complex computer programs called climate models to make predictions about global warming. Climate models cannot describe Earth's atmosphere completely, so their results are only an approximation.
- Some of the possible effects of global warming are higher temperatures that could melt sea ice, leading to increasing sea levels, which could lead to shoreline erosion and coastal flooding. The oceans could warm, further increasing global temperature and causing stronger storms. Weather patterns could change, leading to more extreme weather around the world.

Name _____ Class _____ Date _____

Chapter 21 Climate

Section 21.1 Factors That Affect Climate
(pages 588–591)

This section explains how latitude, elevation, topography, water, winds, and vegetation affect climate.

Reading Strategy (page 588)

Summarizing Information As you read, summarize the effect(s) each factor has on climate. For more information on this Reading Strategy, see the **Reading and Study Skills** in the **Skills and Reference Handbook** at the end of your textbook.

Factor	Effect(s) on Climate
1. Latitude	a. Climates get cooler as latitude increases.
2. Elevation	b. Climates get cooler as elevation increases.
3. Topography	c.
4. Water bodies	d.
5. Global wind	e.
6. Vegetation	f.

Factors That Affect Climate (pages 588–591)

1. ○ Circle the letter of the answer that correctly completes the following sentence. As latitude increases, the average intensity of solar energy

   a. decreases.

   b. increases.

   c. stays the same.

2. Temperate zones have _____ summers and

   _____ winters because of the angle of the sun's rays and the length of daylight in the summer and winter.

3. Is the following sentence true or false? The polar zones are located between 66.5° north and south latitudes and the poles.

   _____

4. Circle the letter of the region between the Tropic of Cancer and the Tropic of Capricorn.

   a. polar zone

   b. tropics

   c. equator

Earth Science Guided Reading and Study Workbook ▪ **209**

© Pearson Education, Inc., publishing as Pearson Prentice Hall. All rights reserved.

5. What effect does elevation have on precipitation? _____

_____

6. 🌐 Is the following sentence true or false? The higher the elevation is, the colder the climate. _____

7. Circle the correct answer. The sun's rays strike the surface of Earth in the tropics at _____.

    a. almost a 45° angle

    b. almost a right angle

    c. more than a right angle

8. The figure below shows the rain shadow effect. Use the terms below to identify the labeled items on the lines provided.

leeward side   warm, dry air   windward side   rain shadow

a. _____

b. _____

c. _____

d. _____

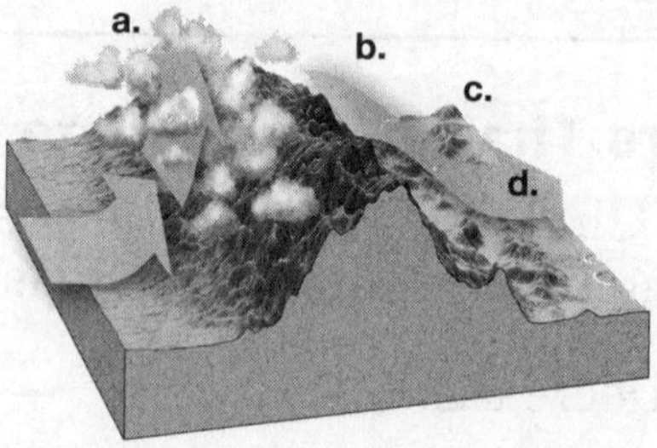

Match each sentence with the term that completes it.

Sentence

_____ **9.** In the temperate zones, the sun's rays strike the Earth at a _____ angle than near the equator.

_____ **10.** 🌐 _____ distribute(s) heat and moisture around Earth.

_____ **11.** 🌐 Plants influence _____ through transpiration, which releases water vapor from their leaves into the air.

Term

a. global winds

b. precipitation

c. smaller

Chapter 21   Climate

Section 21.2 World Climates
(pages 592–599)

This section discusses the Köppen climate classification system and the various types of climates in the world.

Reading Strategy (page 592)

Outlining As you read, complete the outline for each climate type discussed in this section. Include temperature and precipitation information for each climate type, as well as at least one location with that climate type. For more information on this Reading Strategy, see the **Reading and Study Skills** in the **Skills and Reference Handbook** at the end of your textbook.

I. World Climates

    A. Humid Tropical

        1. Wet tropics

        2. _____

    B. Humid mid-latitude

        1. Humid Mid-Latitude/Mild Winters

        2. _____

    C. Dry

        1. _____

        2. _____

The Köppen Climate Classification System (page 592)

1. The Köppen climate classification system uses mean monthly and annual values of _____ and precipitation to classify climates.

2. Circle the letter of the climate that is NOT one of the principal groups in the Köppen system.

    a. humid tropical   b. dry   c. wet

Humid Tropical Climates (page 593)

3. Humid tropical climates are climates without _____. Circle the correct answer.

    summers   rain   winters

4. Is the following sentence true or false? Tropical wet and dry climates have temperatures and total precipitation similar to those in the wet tropics, but experience distinct periods of low precipitation.

_____

Chapter 21   Climate

Humid Mid-Latitude Climates (pages 596–597)

5. Circle the letters of the climates that are classified as humid mid-latitude with mild winters.

   a. humid subtropical

   b. marine west coast

   c. dry-summer subtropical

6. Use the climate diagram for St. Louis, Missouri, on the right to answer the following questions.

   a. When does the highest temperature occur? What is the highest temperature?

   _____

   b. When does the lowest temperature occur? What is the lowest temperature?

   _____

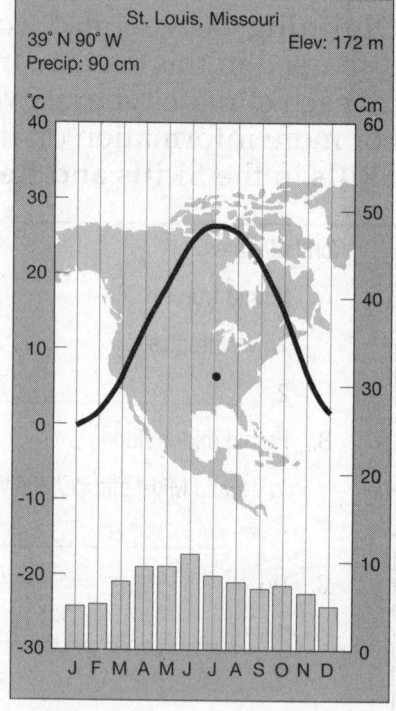

Dry Climates (page 598)

7. 👁 A dry climate is one in which the yearly precipitation is not as great as the potential

   loss of water by _____.

8. The two types of dry climate are arid,

   or _____, and semi-arid, or _____.

Polar Climates (page 599)

9. 👁 Is the following sentence true or false? Polar climates are those in which the mean temperature of the warmest month is above 10°C.

   _____

10. Circle the letters of the two types of polar climates.

   a. tundra   b. Antarctic   c. ice cap

Highland Climates

11. 👁 Is the following sentence true or false? Highland climates are localized areas that are cooler and wetter than nearby areas at lower

   elevations. _____

Chapter 21   Climate

Section 21.3 Climate Changes
(pages 600–603)

This section describes natural processes and human activities that affect climate.

Reading Strategy (page 600)

Identifying Cause and Effect As you read, complete the table below. For more information on this Reading Strategy, see the **Reading and Study Skills** in the **Skills and Reference Handbook** at the end of your textbook.

Climate Changes	
Causes	**Effects**
Plate Tectonics	
	Changes can result in short-term fluctuations.
Earth's Orbital Motions	
	Eruption emissions can reflect more solar radiation, lowering temperatures.

Natural Processes That Change Climate (pages 600–601)

1. ◯ Is the following sentence true or false? El Niño or a change in ocean circulation can result in short-term climate fluctuations.

   _____

2. Use the words below to fill in the blank. The formation of sunspots appears to correspond with _____ periods in Europe and North America.

cool	warm	rainy

3. ◯ Circle the letter of the motions of Earth that result in climatic changes.

   a. rotations

   b. plate tectonics

   c. changes in the shape of Earth's orbit

Human Impact on Climate Changes (pages 602–603)

4. ⬤ Circle the letter of the term for the natural warming of both Earth's lower atmosphere and Earth's surface.

    a. greenhouse effect
    b. tropical warming
    c. polar thawing

5. The major gases involved in the greenhouse effect are water vapor and

    _____ .

6. Is the following sentence true or false? The burning of fossil fuels and the clearing of forests may have added to an increase of oxygen in the

    atmosphere. _____

7. Use the graph below to answer the following questions.

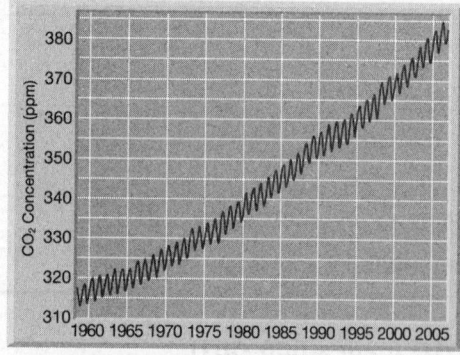

a. What was the approximate concentration of carbon dioxide in the

   atmosphere in 1960? _____

b. What was the approximate concentration of carbon dioxide in the

   atmosphere in 2007? _____

c. What is the approximate difference in carbon dioxide concentration

   between 2007 and 1960? _____

8. ⬤ What is global warming? _____

_____

_____

_____

_____

Chapter 21   Climate

WordWise

Use the clues and the words below to help you write the vocabulary terms from the chapter in the blanks. Then find and circle the terms in the puzzle. The terms may occur vertically, horizontally, or diagonally.

T	I	N	Z	W	L	Z	V	L	W	S	L	I	M		
G	E	N	E	L	R	F	I	E	K	A	V	D	O		
B	X	M	A	P	C	V	S	F	C	B	I	H	P		
I	G	C	P	D	P	T	Q	I	R	M	S	B	S		
M	V	M	K	E	C	O	P	X	U	Q	C	L	U		
C	E	R	Q	O	R	O	K	H	D	K	G	K	B		
A	E	T	A	K	R	A	P	J	Y	M	K	R	A		
W	T	S	L	T	M	I	T	O	S	Y	M	A	R		
L	T	U	B	Z	F	P	A	E	D	V	W	L	C		
A	B	U	S	L	A	C	I	P	O	R	T	O	T		
S	S	C	H	M	N	A	F	W	B	K	B	P	I		
O	P	N	S	R	A	E	P	H	I	U	D	E	C		

Köppen
temperate
tropical
subtropical
polar
humid
subarctic
west coast

Clues

The _____ zone experiences warm weather year-round.

The region located north of the humid continental climate and south of the

tundra has a _____ climate.

The _____ climate classification system uses mean monthly and annual values of temperature and precipitation.

The _____ zone is a region that experiences hot summers and cold winters.

The dry-summer _____ climate is sometimes referred to as a Mediterranean climate.

Coastal areas between about 40° and 65° north and south latitude have

marine _____ climates.

The southeastern United States has a _____ subtropical climate.

The _____ zone is a region that experiences very cold temperatures year-round.

Chapter 22 Origin of Modern Astronomy

Summary

22.1 Early Astronomy

- **Astronomy** is the science that studies the universe. It deals with the properties of objects in space and the laws governing the universe.

In the geocentric model, the moon, sun, and known planets—Mercury, Venus, Mars, and Jupiter—go around Earth.

- The Greeks believed in a **geocentric** universe, in which Earth was a sphere that stayed motionless at the center.
- The path of an object around another object in space is called an **orbit**.

In the heliocentric model, Earth and other planets orbit the sun.

- Aristarchus (312–230 B.C.) was the first Greek to propose a sun-centered, or **heliocentric**, universe.
- **Retrograde motion** is the apparent westward motion of the planets with respect to the stars.

Copernicus concluded that the Earth is a planet. He proposed a model of the solar system with the sun at the center.

Tycho Brahe's observations, especially of Mars, were far more precise than any made previously.

Kepler discovered three laws of planetary motion.

- The oval-shaped path created by the orbit of the planets around the sun is called an **ellipse**.
- The **astronomical unit (AU)** is the average distance between Earth and the sun. It is about 150 million kilometers.

Galileo's most important contributions were his descriptions of the behavior of moving objects.

Although others had theorized the existence of a force that keeps the planets from going in a straight line, Newton was the first to formulate and test the law of universal gravitation.

- The law of universal gravitation states that every body in the universe attracts every other body with gravitational force. The greater the mass of the object, the greater the gravitational force.

22.2 The Earth-Moon-Sun System

The two main motions of Earth are rotation and revolution.

- **Rotation** is the turning, or spinning, of a body on its axis.

Chapter 22   Origin of Modern Astronomy

- **Revolution** is the motion of a body, such as a planet or moon, along its orbit around some point in space.
- At **perihelion**, Earth is closest to the sun—about 147 million kilometers away.
- At **aphelion**, Earth is farthest from the sun—about 152 million kilometers away.
- **Precession** is the slow motion of Earth's axis as it traces a circle in the sky. The period of precession, or the amount of time the axis takes to complete one circle, is 26,000 years.
- At a point known as **perigee**, the moon is closest to Earth.
- At a point known as **apogee**, the moon is farthest from Earth.

◯ **Lunar phases are caused by the changes in how much of the sunlit side of the moon faces Earth.**

- The **phases of the moon** are the monthly changes in the amount of the moon that appears lit.

◯ **During a new-moon or full-moon phase, the moon's orbit must cross the plane of the ecliptic for an eclipse to take place.**

- A **solar eclipse** occurs when the moon moves directly between Earth and the sun, casting a dark shadow on Earth.
- A **lunar eclipse** occurs when the moon moves within Earth's shadow.

22.3 Earth's Moon

◯ **Most craters on the moon were produced by the impact of rapidly moving debris or meteoroids.**

- **Craters** are round depressions in the surface of the moon.
- Splash marks that radiate outward for hundreds of kilometers from a crater are called **rays**.

◯ **Maria, ancient beds of basaltic lava, originated when asteroids punctured the lunar surface, letting magma "bleed" out.**

- A dark, relatively smooth area on the moon's surface is called a **mare** (plural: maria).
- Long channels called **rilles** are associated with maria. Rilles look somewhat similar to valleys or trenches.
- The **lunar regolith** is a soil-like layer on the moon composed of igneous rocks, glass beads, and fine lunar dust.

◯ **A widely accepted model for the origin of the moon is that when the solar system was forming, a body the size of Mars hit Earth.**

Chapter 22 Origin of Modern Astronomy

Section 22.1 Early Astronomy
(pages 614–621)

This section outlines the early history of astronomy, especially changing ideas about Earth's place in the universe.

Reading Strategy (page 614)

Comparing and Contrasting As you read about the geocentric and heliocentric models of the solar system, complete the table. For more information on this Reading Strategy, see the **Reading and Study Skills** in the **Skills and Reference Handbook** at the end of your textbook.

	Location of Earth	Location of Sun	Supporters of Model
Geocentric Model	center of universe	a.	b.
Heliocentric Model	c.	d. center of universe	e.

Ancient Greeks (pages 614–616)

1. The study of the properties of objects in space and the laws under which the universe operates is called _____.

2. Is the following sentence true or false? Eratosthenes is considered to be the first person to calculate the size of Earth. _____

3. ◉ The idea that the moon, sun, and known planets orbit Earth is called the _____ model of the universe. Circle the correct answer.

   Ptolemaic   Heliocentric   Geocentric

4. The figure shows the apparent motion of Mars as seen from Earth. What type of motion is occurring between points 3 and 4? _____

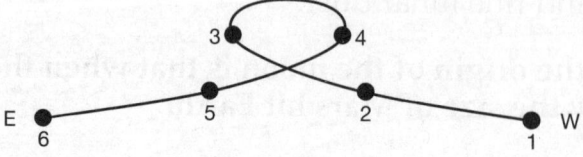

Chapter 22   Origin of Modern Astronomy

The Birth of Modern Astronomy (pages 617–621)

Match each description with its astronomer.

Description	Astronomer
_____ 5. ⬭ developed a model of the solar system with the sun at the center	a. Johannes Kepler
_____ 6. ⬭ formulated and tested the law of universal gravitation	b. Isaac Newton
_____ 7. ⬭ discovered three laws of planetary motion	c. Galileo Galilei
_____ 8. ⬭ described the behavior of moving objects	d. Nicolaus Copernicus

9. Circle the letter of the word that describes the shape of the planet's orbit as shown in the figure.

   a. circle   b. retrograde   c. ellipse   d. focus

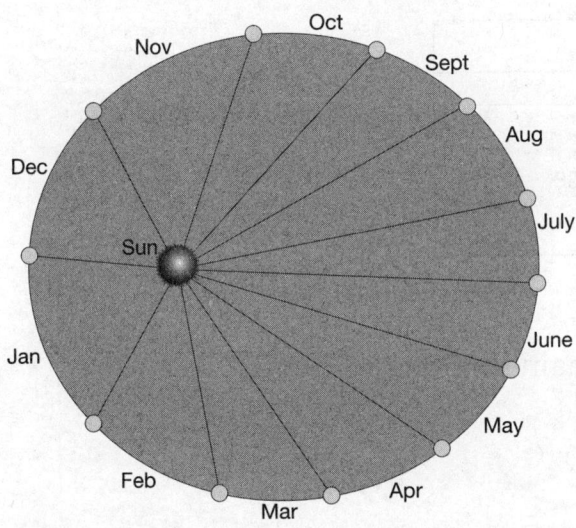

10. Is the following sentence true or false? During December and January on the figure, the planet is moving the fastest. _____

11. The two factors that Newton showed combined to keep the planets in their elliptical orbits are the force of _____ and the tendency of a planet to remain in straight-line motion.

Chapter 22   Origin of Modern Astronomy

Section 22.2 The Earth-Moon-Sun System
(pages 622–629)

This section describes how Earth moves in space and how changes in the relative positions of Earth, the sun, and the moon cause seasons, phases of the moon, and eclipses.

Reading Strategy (page 622)

Monitoring Your Understanding As you read, complete the flowchart to show how eclipses occur. For more information on this Reading Strategy, see the **Reading and Study Skills** in the **Skills and Reference Handbook** at the end of your textbook.

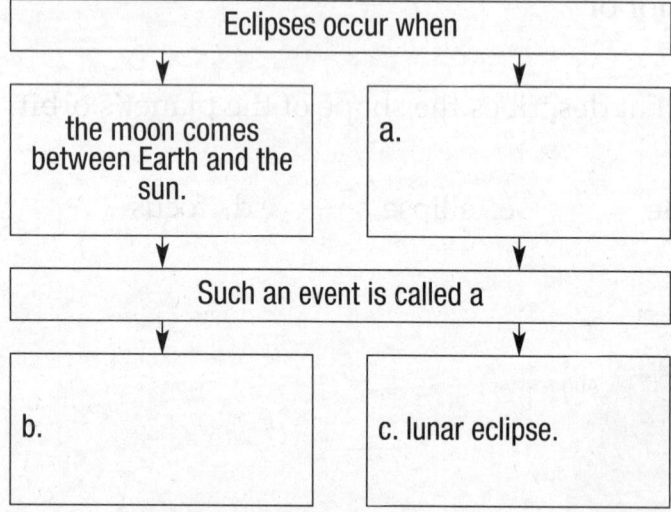

Motions of Earth (pages 622–625)

1. 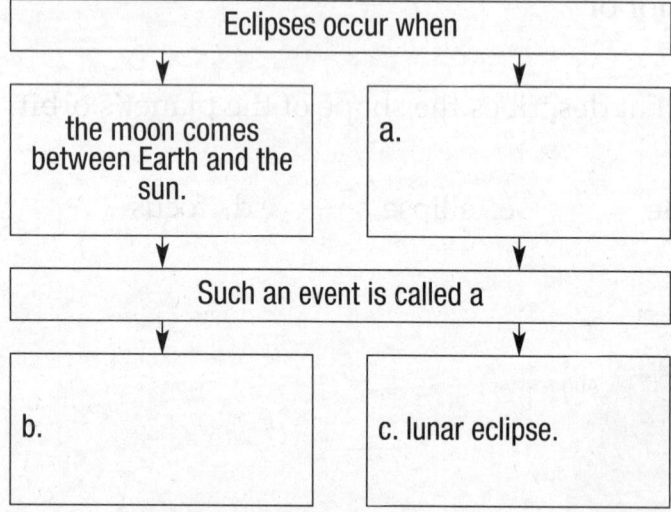 Circle the letter of the two main motions of Earth.

   a. rotation and precession
   b. rotation and revolution
   c. rotation and aphelion

2. Is the following sentence true or false? Day and night are caused by Earth's revolution on its axis. _____

3. Is the following sentence true or false? Seasons are caused in part by the tilt of Earth's axis of rotation. _____

Motions of the Earth-Moon System (pages 626–627)

4. Circle the letter of the term that describes the point at which the moon is farthest from Earth.

   a. apogee   b. aphelion   c. perigee

Chapter 22   Origin of Modern Astronomy

6. Identify each numbered phase on the figure as one of the following: waning crescent, waxing gibbous, new, waxing crescent, full, third quarter.

1. _____   3. _____   5. _____

2. _____   4. _____   6. _____

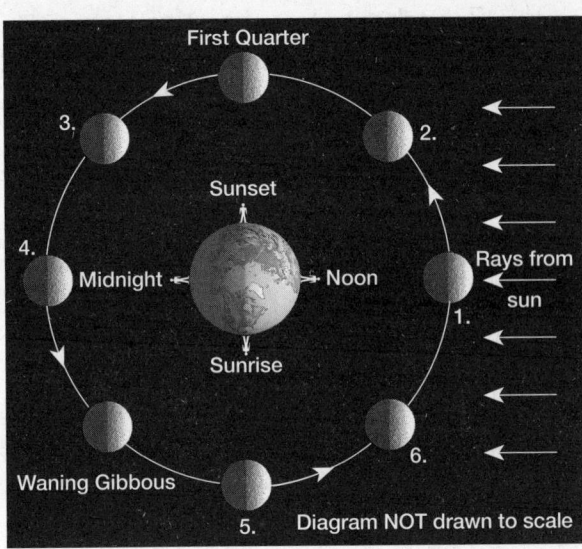

7. ◉ Lunar phases are caused by changes in how much of the sunlit side

of the _____ faces Earth.

8. Is the following sentence true or false? The cycle of the phases takes about two days longer than the moon's revolution around Earth.

_____

9. Two reasons why the moon's surface has extremely high and low temperatures are long periods of daylight and darkness and the absence

of an _____.

Eclipses (page 628)

10. A(n) _____ eclipse occurs when the moon passes between Earth and the sun and casts a shadow on Earth. Circle the correct answer.

lunar   total   solar

11. Is the following sentence true or false? A lunar eclipse occurs when the

moon passes into Earth's shadow. _____

12. ◉ In order for an eclipse to take place, the moon's orbit must cross the

plane of the ecliptic during a new-moon or _____ phase.

Chapter 22   Origin of Modern Astronomy

Section 22.3 Earth's Moon
(pages 630–634)

This section describes the moon's structure, surface, and ideas about its origin.

Reading Strategy (page 630)

Sequencing As you read, complete the flowchart showing the stages leading to the formation of the moon. For more information on this Reading Strategy, see the **Reading and Study Skills** in the **Skills and Reference Handbook** at the end of your textbook.

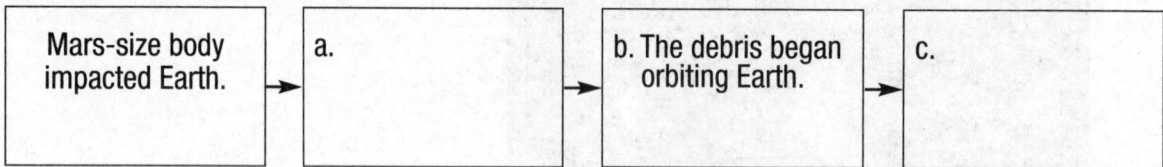

| Mars-size body impacted Earth. | → | a. | → | b. The debris began orbiting Earth. | → | c. |

1. The density of the moon is comparable to that of mantle rocks on

   _____. Circle the correct answer.

   the sun   Mars   Earth

The Lunar Surface (page 631)

Match each description with its moon feature.

Description

_____ 2. densely pitted, light-colored areas containing mountain ranges

_____ 3. 🌑 dark, relatively smooth areas made of ancient beds of basaltic lava

_____ 4. 🌑 splash marks that radiate outward for hundreds of kilometers

_____ 5. long channels similar to valleys or trenches

_____ 6. soil-like layer of igneous rock, glass beads, and fine lunar dust

_____ 7. 🌑 round depressions produced by the impact of rapidly moving debris or meteoroids

Moon Feature

a. regolith
b. maria
c. craters
d. rays
e. highlands
f. rilles

8. 🌑 The maria on the moon's surface formed when asteroids punctured

   the lunar surface, letting _____ "bleed" out.

   | regolith | magma | rays |

Chapter 22   Origin of Modern Astronomy

9. Select the appropriate letter in the figure that identifies each of the following moon features.

_____ crater   _____ highland   _____ mare

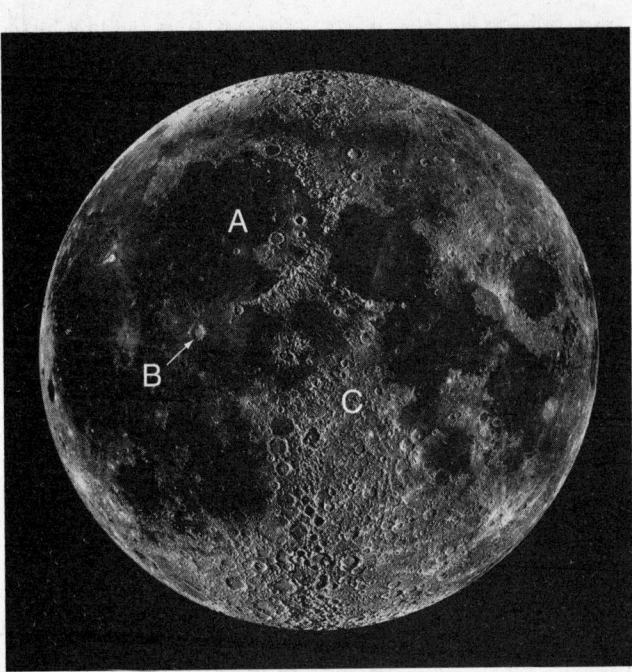

Lunar History (page 633)

10. 👁 Is the following statement true or false? The most widely accepted theory of the moon's origin states that when the solar system was

forming, a body the size of Mars hit Earth._____

11. The greater the density of craters on the moon, the _____ the surface must be.

12. Number the three phases in which the moon evolved in order from oldest to youngest.

_____ a. maria basins

_____ b. rayed craters

_____ c. original crust (highlands)

13. Is the following sentence true or false? Lava flows on the moon sometimes overlap highlands, showing that maria deposits are younger

than highlands. _____

Chapter 22 Origin of Modern Astronomy

WordWise

Use the terms and clues below to identify vocabulary terms from Chapter 22. Write the terms, putting one letter in each blank. Use the circled letters to find the hidden word.

Clues

1. apparent westward drift of a planet as seen from Earth
2. an oval-shaped path
3. average distance between Earth and the sun
4. spinning of a body on its axis
5. motion of a body along a path around some point in space
6. point at which Earth is farthest from the sun
7. point at which the moon is farthest from Earth
8. cycle of changes in the amount of the moon that appears lit
9. splash mark radiating outward from a crater

ellipse
ray
rotation
phases of the moon
retrograde motion
astronomical unit
aphelion
revolution
apogee

Vocabulary Terms

1. _ _ _ _ _ _ ◯ _ _ _ _ _ _ _ _
2. _ _ _ _ _ ◯ _
3. _ ◯ _ _ _ _ _ _ _ _ _ _ _ _ _ _
4. ◯ _ _ _ _ _ _ _
5. _ _ _ ◯ _ _ _ _ _ _
6. _ _ _ _ _ _ _ ◯ _
7. _ _ ◯ _ _ _
8. _ _ _ _ _ _ _ _ _ _ _ ◯ _ _ _
9. _ _ ◯

Hidden Word: _ _ _ _ _ _ _ _ _ _

Definition: _____

Chapter 23 Touring Our Solar System

Summary

23.1 The Solar System

👁 Size is the most obvious difference between the terrestrial and the Jovian planets.

- The **terrestrial planets**—Mercury, Venus, Earth, and Mars—are relatively small and rocky.
- The **Jovian planets**—Jupiter, Saturn, Uranus, and Neptune—are huge gas giants.

👁 Density, chemical makeup, and rate of rotation are other ways in which the two groups of planets differ.

👁 According to the nebular theory, the sun and planets formed from a rotating disk of dust and gases.

- A cloud of dust and gas in space is called a **nebula.**
- As solid bits of matter began to clump together, they formed small, irregularly shaped bodies called **planetesimals.**

23.2 The Terrestrial Planets

👁 Mercury has the greatest temperature extremes of any planet.

- Mercury is only slightly larger than our moon, has cratered highlands and smooth terrains like maria. It's very dense, with a large iron core.

👁 Data have confirmed that basaltic volcanism and tectonic activity shape Venus's surface.

- Venus is similar to Earth in size, mass, and density. It is covered by thick clouds, and has a surface temperature of 475° C.

👁 Although the atmosphere of Mars is very thin, extensive dust storms occur and may cause the color changes observed from Earth.

- The surface features on Mars, including volcanoes and canyons, are 1–4.5 billion years old. Recent evidence points to the possibility that liquid water once existed on the surface.

23.3 The Outer Planets (and Pluto)

👁 Jupiter has a mass that is $2\frac{1}{2}$ times greater than the mass of all the other planets and moons combined.

- Although called a gas giant, Jupiter is believed to be an ocean of liquid hydrogen. Jupiter has a ring system, large storms, and 63 moons.

👁 The most prominent feature of Saturn is its system of rings.

- Saturn's atmosphere is very active with winds of 1500 kilometers per hour. It has 56 moons, the largest of which, Titan, has its own atmosphere.

◉ **Instead of being generally perpendicular to the plane of its orbit like the other planets, Uranus's axis of rotation lies nearly parallel with the plane of its orbit.**

◉ **Winds exceeding 1000 kilometers per hour encircle Neptune, making it one of the windiest places in the solar system.**

◉ **Pluto is considered a dwarf planet because it has not cleared the neighborhood around its orbit.**

- A **dwarf planet** is a round object that orbits the sun but has not cleared the neighborhood around its orbit.

23.4 Minor Members of the Solar System

◉ **Most asteroids lie in the asteroid belt between the orbits of Mars and Jupiter. They have orbital periods of three to six years.**

- **Asteroids** are small rocky bodies that orbit the sun.
- **Comets** are pieces of rocky and metallic materials held together by frozen water, ammonia, methane, carbon dioxide, and carbon monoxide.
- The glowing head of a comet, called a **coma,** is caused by vaporized frozen gases.

◉ **A small glowing nucleus with a diameter of only a few kilometers can sometimes be detected within a coma. As comets approach the sun, some, but not all, develop a tail that extends for millions of kilometers.**

- Comets originate in two regions of the outer solar system. Those with short orbital periods come from the Kuiper belt, and those with long orbital periods come from the Oort cloud.

◉ **Most meteoroids originate from any one of the following three sources: (1) interplanetary debris that was not gravitationally swept up by the planets during the formation of the solar system, (2) material from the asteroid belt, or (3) the solid remains of comets that once traveled near Earth's orbit.**

- A **meteoroid** is a small solid particle that travels through space.
- Meteoroids that enter Earth's atmosphere and burn up are called **meteors.**
- A meteoroid that actually reaches Earth's surface is called a **meteorite.**
- Scientists used evidence from meteorites, moon rocks, and Earth rocks to determine the age of the solar system.

Chapter 23   Touring Our Solar System

Section 23.1 The Solar System
(pages 644–648)

This section gives an overview of the planets of the solar system and describes the nebular theory of the formation of the solar system.

Reading Strategy (page 644)

Relating Text and Diagrams Complete the flowchart on the formation of the solar system. For more information on this Reading Strategy, see the **Reading and Study Skills** in the **Skills and Reference Handbook** at the end of your textbook.

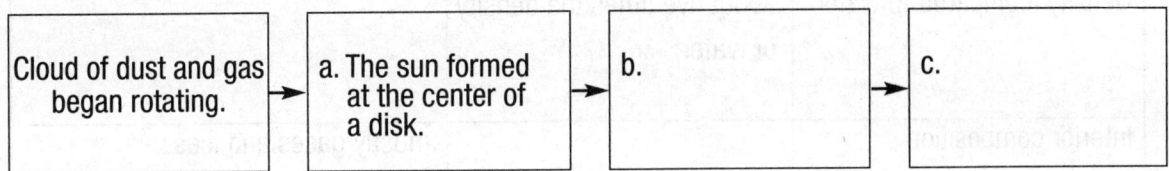

1. Use the terms below to fill in the blank. Almost all of the mass of the

   solar system is within the ——————————.

sun	moon	Jovian planets

2. Is the following sentence true or false? The farther a planet is from the

   sun, the shorter its period of revolution. _____

The Planets: An Overview (pages 645–647)

3. ● Which is NOT one of the differences between terrestrial and Jovian planets? Circle the correct answer.

   rate of rotation   size   density   shape   composition

4. Indicate whether each of the following planets is a terrestrial planet or a Jovian planet.

   a. Saturn _____   e. Mars _____

   b. Venus _____   f. Neptune _____

   c. Mercury _____   g. Jupiter _____

   d. Uranus _____

5. The _____ planets are relatively small and rocky.

6. Is the following sentence true or false? The Jovian planets are huge,

   rocky giants. _____

Chapter 23   Touring Our Solar System

7. The Jovian planets have much thicker atmospheres than the terrestrial planets because they have much higher surface gravities and

_____.

8. Complete the table below.

Characteristic	Terrestrial Planets	Jovian Planets
Comparative size		
Density (compared to water)	about five times the density of water	
Interior composition		mostly gases and ices
Atmosphere thickness		

Formation of the Solar System (pages 647–648)

9. Use the terms below to fill in the blank. A(n) _____ is a cloud of dust and gas in space.

Jovian planet	nebula	planetesimal

10. ⬤ Is the following sentence true or false? The nebular theory says that the sun and planets formed from a rotating disk of dust and gases.

_____.

11. Circle the letter of the term for small, irregularly shaped bodies.

a. planet

b. ice

c. planetesimal

12. Is the following sentence true or false? The inner planets formed mainly from metals and silicate minerals because of the high temperatures near

the sun. _____

Chapter 23   Touring Our Solar System

Section 23.2 The Terrestrial Planets
(pages 649–653)

This section describes the features of Mercury, Venus, and Mars.

Reading Strategy (page 649)

Using Prior Knowledge Before you read, add to the web diagram properties that you already know about Mars. Then add details about each property as you read. Make a similar web diagram for each of the other terrestrial planets. For more information on this Reading Strategy, see the **Reading and Study Skills** in the **Skills and Reference Handbook** at the end of your textbook.

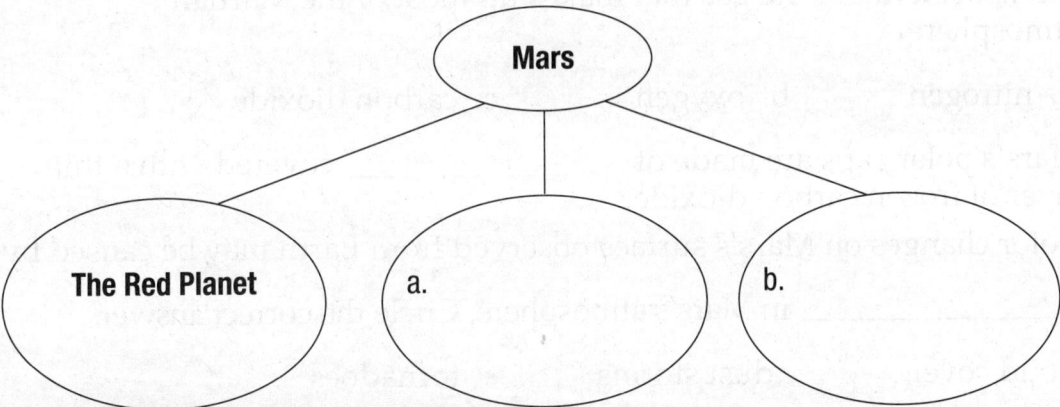

Mercury: The Innermost Planet (pages 649–650)

1. Circle the letter of Mercury's position in the solar system.

   a. innermost terrestrial planet

   b. innermost Jovian planet

   c. outermost terrestrial planet

2. Is the following sentence true or false? Like our moon, Mercury absorbs most of the sunlight that strikes it, has cratered highlands, and has vast smooth areas similar to maria. _____

3. Mercury is a very _____ planet, because it contains a large iron core for its size.

4. ⬲ Mercury has the greatest _____ extremes of any planet.

Venus: The Veiled Planet (pages 650–651)

5. Venus's size, _____, mass, and location in the solar system are similar to Earth's.

6. Venus's topography has been mapped from space and Earth, using

   _____ pulses. Circle the correct answer.

   radar   light   wave

Earth Science Guided Reading and Study Workbook ▪ **229**

Chapter 23   Touring Our Solar System

7. Is the following sentence true or false? Most of Venus's surface consists

of plains covered by lava flows. _____

8. 🜨 The surface of Venus was shaped by basaltic volcanism and

_____ activity.

Mars: The Red Planet (pages 651–653)

9. Is the following sentence true or false? Mars's atmosphere is 90 times

the density of Earth's. _____

10. Circle the letter of the gas that makes up most of the Martian
atmosphere.

    a. nitrogen   b. oxygen   c. carbon dioxide

11. Mars's polar caps are made of _____ covered with a thin
layer of frozen carbon dioxide.

12. Color changes on Mars's surface observed from Earth may be caused by

_____ in Mars's atmosphere. Circle the correct answer.

    cloud cover   dust storms   tornadoes

13. Is the following sentence true or false? The largest volcano on Mars is

over $2\frac{1}{2}$ times higher than Mount Everest. _____

14. Select the appropriate letter in the figure that identifies each of the
following Mars features.

    _____ Valles Marineris or canyon

    _____ Volcanoes

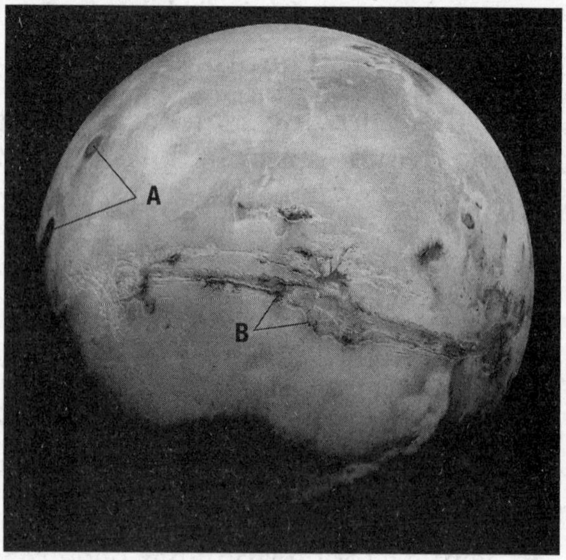

15. 🜨 One piece of evidence that
there was once water on Mars is
that some areas have drainage
patterns similar to those made by

_____ on Earth.

16. Is the following sentence true or
false? The finding of evidence of
liquid water on Mars is important
because water is essential for life.

_____

Chapter 23   Touring Our Solar System

Section 23.3 The Outer Planets (and Pluto)
(pages 654–659)

This section describes the features of Jupiter, Saturn, Uranus, Neptune, and Pluto, the dwarf planet.

Reading Strategy (page 654)

Summarizing In the table, write a brief summary of the characteristics of each planet. For more information on this Reading Strategy, see the **Reading and Study Skills** in the **Skills and Reference Handbook** at the end of your textbook.

Outer Planet	Characteristics
Jupiter	largest, most mass, Great Red Spot
	axis titled more than 90º

Jupiter: Giant Among Planets (pages 654–656)

1. ● Circle the letter of the answer that correctly describes Jupiter's mass.

   a. the same mass as the sun

   b. $2\frac{1}{2}$ times greater than the mass of all of the other planets and moons combined

   c. the same mass as all of the other planets and moons combined

2. Is the following sentence true or false? Jupiter's surface is thought to be a giant ocean of liquid water. _____

3. One of Jupiter's moons, _____, is one of only four volcanically active bodies in the solar system. Circle the correct answer.

   Io   Europa   Callisto

Saturn: The Elegant Planet (pages 656–657)

4. ● Circle the letter of Saturn's most prominent feature.

   a. moon system

   b. ring system

   c. liquid oceans

Chapter 23   Touring Our Solar System

5. Describe the features of Saturn's main rings, labeled A and B in the figure.

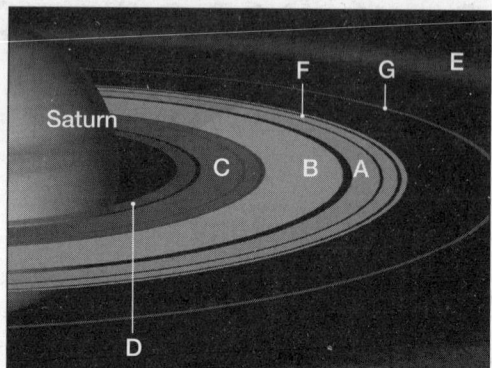

_____

_____

6. Describe the features of Saturn's outer rings, labeled E in the figure.

_____

_____

7. Is the following sentence true or false? Saturn has large cyclonic "storms" similar to Jupiter's Great Red Spot. _____

Uranus: The Sideways Planet (page 658)

8. ◉ Uranus's axis of rotation is _____ to the plane of its orbit. Circle the correct answer.

perpendicular   nearly parallel   at a right angle

9. Is the following sentence true or false? Uranus's rings were discovered when Uranus passed in front of a distant star and blocked its view.

_____

10. Uranus's moon Miranda has a greater variety of _____ than any solar system body yet examined. Circle the correct answer.

a. clouds   b. landforms   c. rings

Neptune: The Windy Planet (page 658)

11. ◉ Is the following sentence true or false? Neptune has winds exceeding 1000 km per hour. _____

12. Circle the letter of the substance that most likely makes up Neptune's upper cloud layer.

a. water droplets   b. ice crystals   c. frozen methane

Pluto: Dwarf Planet (page 659)

13. Pluto is small, dense, and has a solid surface that is a mixture of

_____ and rock.

OM

Chapter 23   Touring Our Solar System

Section 23.4 Minor Members of the Solar System
(pages 660–664)

This section describes the characteristics of asteroids, comets, and meteoroids.

Reading Strategy (page 660)

Building Vocabulary As you read this section, write a definition for each vocabulary term in your own words and enter it in the table. For more information on this Reading Strategy, see the **Reading and Study Skills** in the **Skills and Reference Handbook** at the end of your textbook.

Vocabulary	Definition
asteroid	
	glowing head of a comet
meteor	
	meteoroid that reaches Earth's surface

Asteroids (page 661)

1. Is the following sentence true or false? Asteroids are small, rocky bodies in space. _____

2. ● Most asteroids are found between the orbits of _____ and Jupiter.

Comets (pages 661–663)

3. _____ are pieces of rocky and metallic materials held together by frozen gases. Circle the correct answer.

   Comas   Comets   Meteoroids

4. Circle the letter of the term for the glowing head of a comet formed when frozen gases vaporize.

   a. coma   b. gas tail   c. dust tail

Chapter 23   Touring Our Solar System

5. Select the appropriate letter in the figure that identifies each of the following parts of a comet.

_____ nucleus

_____ tail of ionized gases

_____ coma

_____ tail of dust

6. The two regions from which comets originate are the _____ and the Oort cloud.

7. Is the following sentence true or false? The nucleus of Halley's comet is spherical. _____

Meteoroids (page 663)

Match each description with its object.

Description	Object
_____ 8. small, solid particle from space that reaches Earth's surface	a. meteor
_____ 9. small, solid particle from space that burns up in Earth's atmosphere	b. meteoroid
_____ 10. small, solid particle that travels through space	c. meteorite

11. ● The three sources of most meteoroids are interplanetary debris that

was not swept up by planets, _____, and solid remains of comets that once traveled near Earth's orbit.

12. A(n) _____, or display of frequent meteor sightings, can result when Earth encounters a swarm of meteoroids.

13. Large craters on Earth such as Meteor Crater in Arizona were formed

when very large _____ hit Earth's surface.

14. Is the following sentence true or false? Meteorites are now the only extraterrestrial materials scientists have to examine directly.

_____

Chapter 24 Studying the Sun

Summary

24.1 The Study of Light

◉ **Electromagnetic radiation includes gamma rays, X-rays, ultraviolet light, visible light, infrared radiation, microwaves, and radio waves.**

- The arrangement of electromagnetic radiation according to their wavelengths and frequencies is called the **electromagnetic spectrum.**
- In some instances, light behaves like waves.
- In some cases, light acts like a stream of particles called **photons.** Photons can push on matter, and they exert radiation pressure.
- **Spectroscopy** is the study of the properties of light that depend on wavelength.
- A **continuous spectrum** is an uninterrupted band of light produced by an incandescent solid, liquid, or gas under high pressure.
- An **absorption spectrum** is produced when visible light is passed through a cool gas under pressure. Because the gas absorbs some wavelengths, the spectrum appears continuous with dark lines running through it.
- An **emission spectrum** is a series of bright lines of particular wavelengths produced by a hot gas under low pressure.

◉ **When the spectrum of a star is studied, the spectral lines act as "fingerprints." These lines identify the elements present and thus the star's chemical composition.**

◉ **In astronomy, the Doppler effect is used to determine whether a star or other body in space is moving away from or toward Earth.**

- The **Doppler effect** refers to the apparent change in frequency of electromagnetic or sound waves that are emitted from a source that is moving away or toward an object.

24.2 Tools for Studying Space

◉ **The most important lens in a refracting telescope, the objective lens, produces an image by bending light from a distant object so that the light converges at an area called the focus.**

- A **refracting telescope** uses a lens to bend or refract light.
- The **chromatic aberration** is an effect caused by the fact that when a refracting telescope is in focus for red light, blue and violet light are out of focus and vice versa.

◉ **Most large optical telescopes are reflectors. Light does not pass through a mirror so the glass for a reflecting telescope does not have to be of optical quality.**

Chapter 24   Studying the Sun

- **Reflecting telescopes** use a concave mirror that focuses the light in front of a mirror, rather than behind it, like a lens.
- Both refracting and reflecting telescopes have three properties: light-gathering power, which makes brighter images; resolving power, which makes sharper images; and magnifying power, which makes larger images.

👄 **A radio telescope focuses incoming radio waves on an antenna, which absorbs and transmits those waves to an amplifier, just like a radio antenna.**

👄 **Space telescopes orbit above Earth's atmosphere and thus produce clearer images than Earth-based telescopes.**

24.3 The Sun

👄 **We can divide the sun into four parts: the solar interior; the visible surface, or photosphere; and two atmospheric layers, the chromosphere and corona.**

- The **photosphere** (*photos* = light, *sphere* = ball) radiates most of the sunlight we see and can be thought of as the visible "surface" of the sun.
- Just above the photosphere lies the **chromosphere**, a relatively thin layer of hot gases a few thousand kilometers thick.
- The outermost portion of the solar atmosphere, the **corona** (*corona* = crown) is visible only when the brilliant photosphere is covered.
- The streams of protons and electrons that flow from the corona constitute the **solar wind.**

👄 **Sunspots appear dark because of their temperature, which is about 1500 K less than that of the surrounding solar surface.**

- **Sunspots** are the dark regions on the surface of the sun.

Chapter 24   Studying the Sun

◉ **Prominences are ionized gases trapped by magnetic fields that extend from regions of intense solar activity.**

- **Prominences** are huge cloudlike structures consisting of chromospheric gases and appear as great arches that extend into the corona.

◉ **During their existence, solar flares release enormous amounts of energy, much of it in the form of ultraviolet, radio, and X-ray radiation.**

- **Solar flares** are brief outbursts that normally last about an hour and appear as a sudden brightening of the region above a sunspot cluster.
- An **aurora** is a bright display of ever-changing light in the poles caused by solar radiation interacting with the upper atmosphere.

◉ **During nuclear fusion, energy is released because some matter is actually converted to energy.**

- **Nuclear fusion** occurs when four hydrogen nuclei combine to make the nucleus of one helium atom. This releases a tremendous amount of energy and is how the sun produces its energy.

Chapter 24   Studying the Sun

Section 24.1 The Study of Light
(pages 674–677)

This section describes the electromagnetic spectrum and how scientists use spectroscopy to study it. It also explains the Doppler effect and how it is used in astronomy.

Reading Strategy (page 674)

Predicting Before you read, predict the meaning of the term *electromagnetic spectrum* and write your definition in the table. After you read, revise your definition if it was incorrect. For more information on this Reading Strategy, see the **Reading and Study Skills** in the **Skills and Reference Handbook** at the end of your textbook.

Vocabulary Term	Before You Read	After You Read
electromagnetic spectrum	a.	b.

1. Why is an understanding of light important to astronomers?

   _____

   _____

Electromagnetic Radiation (pages 674–675)

2. The arrangement of electromagnetic waves according to their

   wavelengths and frequencies is called the _____. Circle the correct answer.

   emission spectrum   continuous spectrum   electromagnetic spectrum

3. ◕ The types of energy that make up the electromagnetic spectrum are

   gamma rays, _____, ultraviolet light, _____,
   infrared radiation, microwaves, and radio waves.

4. Is the following sentence true or false? Different electromagnetic waves

   travel through a vacuum at different speeds. _____

Chapter 24   Studying the Sun

5. Particles of light are called _____.

6. Circle the letter of the waves in the figure that have the highest frequency.

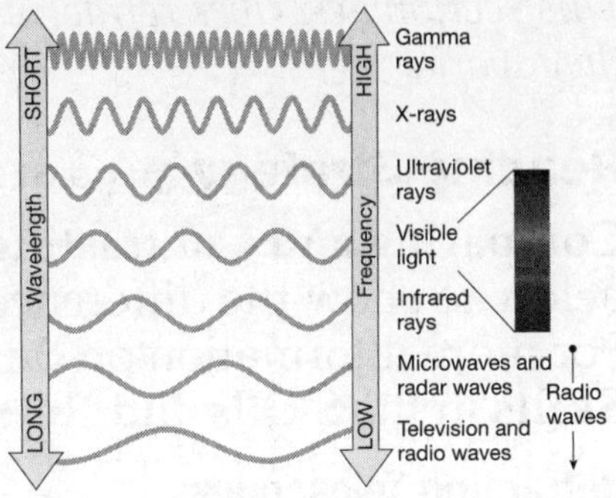

   a. gamma rays

   b. ultraviolet rays

   c. infrared rays

Spectroscopy (page 676)

Match each description with its spectrum.

Description	Spectrum
_____ 7. band of color with a series of dark lines running through it	a. absorption spectrum
_____ 8. uninterrupted band of color	b. emission spectrum
_____ 9. series of bright lines of particular wavelengths	c. continuous spectrum

10. Spectroscopy is the study of the properties of light that depend on

    _____.

11. ⬤ A star's spectrum can tell astronomers the star's elements and

    _____.

The Doppler Effect (page 677)

12. When a wave source is moving toward or away from an object, the

    wavelength changes, a phenomenon known as the _____.

Match each situation with its type of change in a wave.

Situation	Change in Wave
_____ 13. sound source approaches an observer	a. pitch becomes lower
_____ 14. light source moves away from an observer	b. pitch becomes higher
_____ 15. sound source moves away from an observer	c. light becomes redder

Chapter 24   Studying the Sun

Section 24.2 Tools for Studying Space
(pages 678–683)

This section describes refracting, reflecting, radio, and space telescopes and how they work.

Reading Strategy (page 678)

Comparing and Contrasting As you read, complete the Venn diagram below to show the differences between refracting and reflecting telescopes. For more information on this Reading Strategy, see the **Reading and Study Skills** in the **Skills and Reference Handbook** at the end of your textbook.

Refracting Telescopes   **Reflecting Telescopes**

a.

light-gathering, resolving, and magnifying power

b.

Refracting Telescopes (pages 678–679)

1. 🔘 Is the following sentence true or false? The objective lens of a refracting telescope produces an image by bending light from a distant

   object so that the light converges at the focus. _____

2. Select the appropriate letter in the figure that identifies each of the following features.

   _____ objective lens

   _____ focus

   _____ focal length of the eyepiece

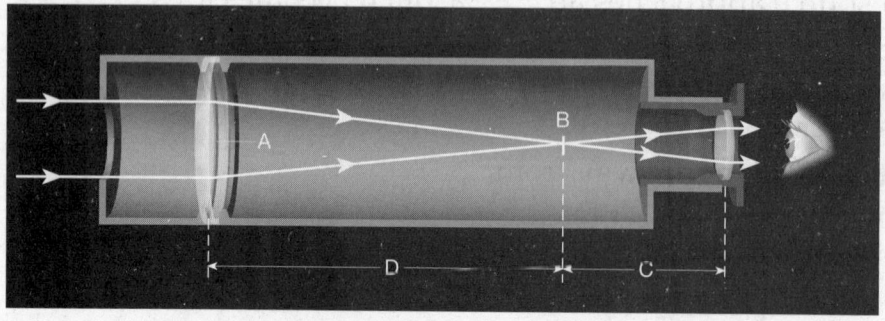

3. Refracting telescopes got their name because they refract, or

   _____, light.

Chapter 24   Studying the Sun

4. Is the following sentence true or false? Astronomers usually study

an object by looking directly through a telescope. _____

5. Is the following sentence true or false? Refracting telescopes suffer

from an optical defect called chromatic aberration. _____

Reflecting Telescopes (page 680)

6. Use the terms below to fill in the blank. The main difference between a reflecting telescope and a refracting telescope is that a reflecting

telescope uses a(n) _____ to focus the incoming light.

| mirror | antenna | lens |

7. ☞ Is the following sentence true or false? Most large optical telescopes

are reflectors. _____

8. Three properties of optical telescopes that aid astronomers in their work

are light-gathering power, resolving power, and _____.

Detecting Invisible Radiation (pages 681–682)

9. Circle the letter of the type of invisible radiation from space that can be detected from Earth's surface.

   a. gamma rays   b. X-rays   c. radio waves

10. ☞ Is the following sentence true or false? A radio telescope works in a

similar way to a radio antenna. _____

11. Is the following statement true or false? The surfaces of radio telescopes

need to be as smooth as a mirror. _____

Space Telescopes (pages 682–683)

12. ☞ Space telescopes produce clearer images than telescopes on Earth

because space telescopes are above the _____, which distorts
images made by most Earth telescopes.

13. Circle the letter of the first space telescope.

   a. Hubble Space Telescope
   b. Chandra X-ray Observatory
   c. Compton Gamma-Ray Observatory

Chapter 24   Studying the Sun

Section 24.3 The Sun
(pages 684–690)

This section describes the structure of the sun, features on the sun's surface, and nuclear fusion in the interior of the sun.

Reading Strategy (page 684)

Preview the Key Concepts, topic headings, vocabulary, and figures in this section. In the table, list two things you expect to learn. After reading, complete the table, stating what you have learned about each item you listed. For more information on this Reading Strategy, see the **Reading and Study Skills** in the **Skills and Reference Handbook** at the end of your textbook.

What I Expect to Learn	What I Learned
a.	b.
c.	d.

Structure of the Sun (pages 685–686)

1. ⬤ The four main parts of the sun are the solar interior, the visible surface (photosphere), the chromosphere, and the _____.

2. The solar wind is a stream of _____ and electrons that boil from the corona.

Match each description with its sun layer.

	Description	Sun Layer
_____	3. outermost part of the sun's atmosphere	a. chromosphere
_____	4. relatively thin layer of the sun's atmosphere	b. photosphere
_____	5. layer that radiates most of the sunlight we can see	c. corona

Chapter 24   Studying the Sun

6. Select the appropriate letter in the figure that identifies each of the following features.

_____ prominence
_____ chromosphere
_____ sunspots
_____ corona
_____ core

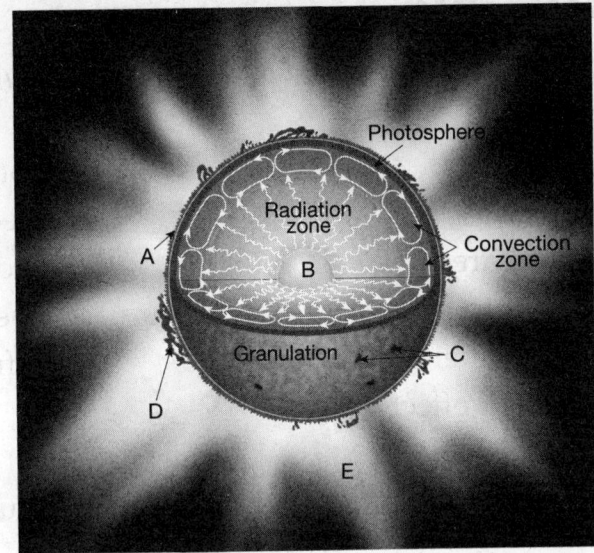

The Active Sun (pages 687–688)

Match each description with its sun feature.

Description	Sun Feature
_____ 7. dark region on the surface of the photosphere	a. solar flare
_____ 8. brief outburst associated with sunspot clusters	b. sunspot
_____ 9. huge cloudlike structure of chromospheric gases	c. prominence

10. Is the following sentence true or false? Different parts of the sun rotate

at different speeds. _____

11.  Prominences are ionized gases trapped by _____ extending from regions of intense solar activity. Circle the correct answer.

sun spots   magnetic fields   solar flares

12. ● The three main forms of energy released by solar flares are

_____, radio, and X-ray radiation.

13. Solar flares can cause spectacular _____, or northern and southern lights, in Earth's atmosphere.

The Solar Interior (pages 689–690)

14. Is the following sentence true or false? The sun produces energy by

nuclear fission. _____

15. ● During nuclear fusion, _____ is converted into energy.

Chapter 24   Studying the Sun

WordWise

Complete the sentences by using the vocabulary terms below.

corona   continuous spectrum
photons   electromagnetic spectrum
solar flares   radio telescope
sunspots   spectroscopy
photosphere   refracting telescope
Doppler effect

Sunspots are associated with brief outbursts called _____.

_____ are dark regions on the surface of the photosphere.

The study of the properties of light that depend on wavelength is

_____.

A(n) _____ uses wire mesh as a reflector to collect radiation from space.

The siren from an ambulance that is approaching you seems louder because

of the _____.

Galileo used a(n) _____ that had a lens to bend light.

The _____ is the outermost part of the sun's atmosphere.

Most of the sunlight we can see comes from the _____ of the sun.

The _____ is the arrangement of electromagnetic waves according to their wavelengths and frequencies.

_____ are particles of light.

An uninterrupted band of color produced by a prism is a(n)

_____.

Chapter 25 Beyond Our Solar System

Summary

25.1 Properties of Stars

◉ Color is a clue to a star's temperature.

◉ Binary stars are used to determine the star property most difficult to calculate—its mass.

- The word **constellation** is used to designate an area of the sky that contains a specific pattern of stars.
- Two stars that orbit each other, pulled toward each other by gravity, are called **binary stars.**

◉ The nearest stars have the largest parallax angles, while those of distant stars are too small to measure.

- **Parallax** is the slight shifting in the apparent position of a nearby star due to the orbital motion of Earth. Parallax is the most basic way to measure star distance.
- The **light-year** is the distance light travels in one year—about 9.5 trillion kilometers.

◉ Three factors control the apparent brightness of a star as seen from Earth: how big it is, how hot it is, and how far away it is.

- A star's brightness as it appears form Earth is called its **apparent magnitude.**
- Astronomers are also interested in how bright a star actually is, or its **absolute magnitude.**

◉ A Hertzsprung-Russell diagram shows the relationship between the absolute magnitude and temperature of stars.

- A **main sequence star** is a star that falls into the main sequence category on the Hertzsprung-Russel diagram. This category contains 90 percent of stars.
- **Red giants** are very bright stars that lie above and to the right of the main sequence in the H-R diagram.
- **Supergiants** are very large, very bright red giants.
- **Cepheid variables** are stars that get brighter and fainter in a regular pattern.
- A **nova** is a sudden brightening of a star.
- **Nebulae** are clouds of dust and gases found in "the vacuum of space."

25.2 Stellar Evolution

- A medium-mass star like the sun goes through several stages of development. It starts as a nebula, which contracts into a **protostar**—a developing star not yet hot enough for nuclear fusion to occur.

Chapter 25   Beyond Our Solar System

🔵 **When the core of a protostar has reached about 10 million K, pressure within is so great that nuclear fusion of hydrogen begins, and a star is born.**

- At some point after fusion begins, a star becomes a balanced, main-sequence star. For an average star, this stage lasts 90 percent of the star's life.
- Once all of the hydrogen in a star's core is consumed, the star expands and cools, becoming a red giant.

🔵 **All stars, regardless of their size, eventually run out of fuel and collapse due to gravity.**

- The final stage of a star's life cycle depends on the star's mass. Low-mass stars go from being a main-sequence star to becoming a white dwarf. Medium-mass stars become planetary nebulae. Massive stars end in a supernova.
- A **supernova** is a brilliant explosion that causes a star to become millions of times brighter than its prenova stage.
- The process that produces chemical elements inside stars is called nucleosynthesis.

🔵 **The sun began as a nebula, will spend much of its life as a main-sequence star, and then will become a red giant, planetary nebula, white dwarf, and finally, a black dwarf.**

- **White dwarfs** are the remains of low-mass and medium-mass stars.
- **Neutron stars**, which are smaller and more massive than white dwarfs, are thought to be the remnants of supernova events.
- A spinning neutron star that appears to give off pulses of radio waves is called a **pulsar.**
- Dense objects with gravity so strong that not even light can escape their surface are called **black holes.**

Chapter 25 Beyond Our Solar System

25.3 The Universe

◉ **The Milky Way is a large spiral galaxy whose disk is about 100,000 light-years wide and about 10,000 light-years thick at the nucleus.**

- **Galaxies** are large groups of stars, dust, and gases held together by gravity.
- There are three types of galaxies. Spiral galaxies are disk shaped with arms extending from the center. Most galaxies are elliptical galaxies, which range in shape from round to oval. A small percent of galaxies have irregular shapes, and are called irregular galaxies.

◉ **In addition to shape and size, one of the major differences among different types of galaxies is the age of their stars.**

- A **galaxy cluster** is a group of galaxies.

◉ **The red shifts of distant galaxies indicate that the universe is expanding.**

- **Hubble's law** states that galaxies are retreating from us at a speed that is proportional to their distance.

◉ **The big bang theory states that at one time, the entire universe was confined to a dense, hot, supermassive ball. Then, about 13.7 billion years ago, a violent explosion occurred, hurling this material in all directions.**

- According to the **big bang theory,** the universe began as a violent explosion from which the universe continues to expand, evolve, and cool.

Chapter 25   Beyond Our Solar System

Section 25.1 Properties of Stars
(pages 700–706)

This section describes the characteristics of stars, explains how astronomers measure distances to stars, and describes the Hertzprung-Russell diagram.

Reading Strategy (page 700)

Previewing Before you read, write two questions about the Hertzprung-Russell diagram on page 704. As you read, write answers to your questions. For more information on this Reading Strategy, see the **Reading and Study Skills** in the **Skills and Reference Handbook** at the end of your textbook.

| Questions About the Hertzprung-Russell Diagram ||
Question	Answer
a.	b.
c.	d.

Characteristics of Stars (page 701)

1. Three properties of stars are their _____, temperature, and mass.

2. ☁ Is the following sentence true or false? A star's color can tell you what its approximate temperature is. _____

3. ☁ Binary stars can be used to determine the _____ of a star. Circle the correct answer.

mass   color   temperature

Measuring Distances to Stars (page 702)

4. The apparent change in position of a star when seen from opposite sides of Earth's orbit is called _____. Circle the correct answer.

light-year   parallax   absolute magnitude

5. ☁ Circle the letter of each statement that is true.

a. Nearby stars have large parallax angles.

b. Nearby stars have larger parallax angles than distant stars have.

c. The parallax angles of distant stars are too small to measure.

6. Is the following sentence true or false? Astronomers have calculated the parallax angles of millions of stars. _____

Chapter 25   Beyond Our Solar System

Stellar Brightness (page 703)

7. ● Three factors that control the apparent brightness of a star

   as seen from Earth are how big the star is, how _____ the star
   is, and how far away the star is.

8. Is the following sentence true or false? A third-magnitude star is ten

   times as bright as a fourth-magnitude star. _____

9. A star's actual brightness is its _____.

   density   absolute magnitude   apparent magnitude

Match each definition to its term.

Definition	Term
_____ **10.** a star's brightness as it appears from Earth	a. absolute magnitude
	b. apparent magnitude
_____ **11.** how bright a star actually is	

Hertzsprung-Russell Diagram (pages 704–706)

12. ● Circle the letter of what a Hertzsprung-Russell diagram shows.

   a. the location of stars in the sky
   b. the absolute magnitude and temperature of stars
   c. the apparent magnitude and temperature of stars

13. Select the appropriate letter in the figure that identifies each of the
    following features.

   _____ the sun

   _____ cool, small,
         red stars

   _____ white dwarfs
         (small faint
         stars)

   _____ red giants
         (bright cool
         stars)

   _____ hot, large, blue
         stars

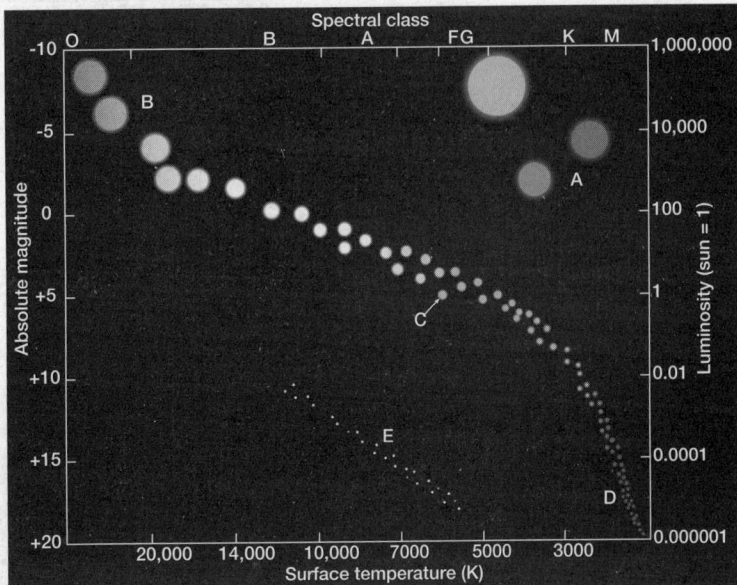

Idealized Hertzsprung-Russell Diagram

Section 25.2 Stellar Evolution
(pages 707–714)

This section describes the evolution of stars from birth to burnout and death. It also discusses types of stellar remnants.

Reading Strategy (page 707)

Sequencing As you read, complete the flowchart to show how the sun evolves. Expand the chart to show the evolution of low-mass and high-mass stars. For more information on this Reading Strategy, see the **Reading and Study Skills** in the **Skills and Reference Handbook** at the end of your textbook.

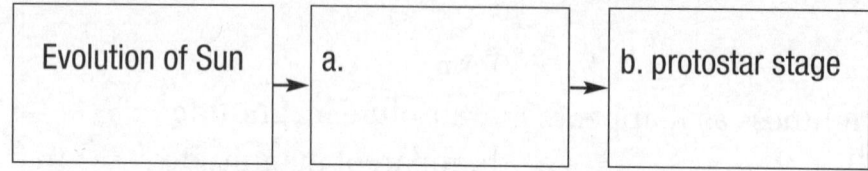

Star Birth (pages 707–709)

1. List in order the labeled stages shown on the figure that a medium-mass star goes through during its "life." (*Hint:* It may be helpful to draw arrows on the figure from stage to stage.)

a. dust and gases

b. protostar

c. _____

d. _____

e. _____

f. _____

g. _____

h. _____

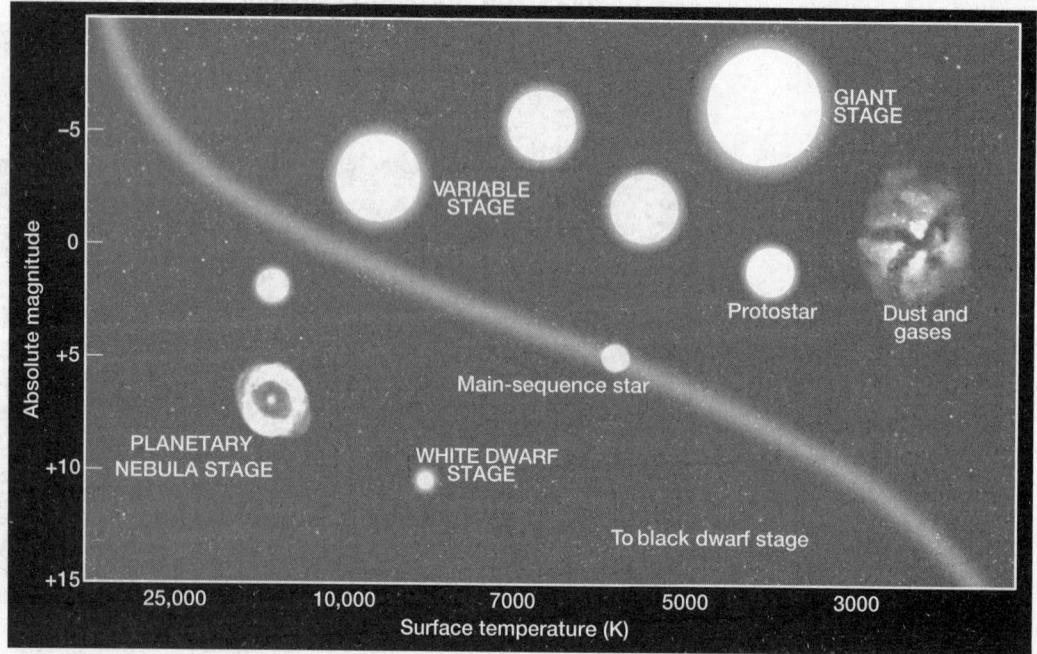

Chapter 25   Beyond Our Solar System

2. A(n) _____ is a developing star not yet hot enough to engage in nuclear fusion. Circle the correct answer.

white dwarf   protostar   pulsar

3. Is the following sentence true or false? An average star spends 90 percent of its life as a helium-burning main-sequence star.

_____

Burnout and Death (pages 710–712)

4. ● Is the following sentence true or false? All stars eventually run out of

fuel and collapse due to gravity. _____

Match each death description with its star.

Death Description	Star
_____ 5. forms a red giant, which then collapses into a red dwarf and forms a planetary nebula	a. low-mass star
	b. medium-mass star
_____ 6. blows up in a supernova explosion	c. massive star
_____ 7. does not form a red giant; collapses directly into a white dwarf	

Stellar Remnants (pages 712–714)

8. ● The stages the sun has gone through and will go through during its

evolution are nebula, main-sequence star, _____, planetary

nebula, _____, and black dwarf.

Match each description with its stellar remnant.

Description	Stellar Remnant
_____ 9. remnant of a supernova event; similar to a large atomic nucleus	a. black hole
	b. white dwarf
_____ 10. small dense object formed from the remnants of a star at least three times as massive as the sun	c. neutron star
_____ 11. remnant of a low-mass or medium-mass star	

Chapter 25   Beyond Our Solar System

Section 25.3 The Universe
(pages 715–721)

This section describes the Milky Way galaxy and types of galaxies. It also explains how we know the universe is expanding, how the universe probably began, and how it might end.

Reading Strategy (page 715)

Outlining As you read, complete the outline of the most important ideas in this section. For more information on this Reading Strategy, see the **Reading and Study Skills** in the **Skills and Reference Handbook** at the end of your textbook.

I. The Universe
  A. Milky Way Galaxy
    1. _____ 100,000 light-years wide and 10,000 light-years thick
    2. Structure—_____
  B. _____
    1. Spiral Galaxy
    2. Elliptical Galaxy _____
    3. _____
    4. _____ groups of galaxies
    _____
    1. Red Shifts—_____
    2. _____

The Milky Way Galaxy (pages 715–716)

1. ◯ Circle the letter of the type of galaxy that the Milky Way is.

   a. spiral galaxy   b. elliptical galaxy   c. cluster galaxy

Types of Galaxies (pages 716–718)

Match each description with its galaxy.

Description	Galaxy
_____ 2. ranges in shape from round to oval; most are small	a. spiral
_____ 3. ◯ composed mostly of young stars	b. elliptical
_____ 4. usually disk-shaped with many variations	c. irregular

Chapter 25   Beyond Our Solar System

5. ○ Is the following sentence true or false? The disk of the Milky Way galaxy is about 100,000 light-years wide and about 10,000 light-years thick at the nucleus. _____

6. A(n) _____ of thin gas and clusters of stars surrounds the disk of the Milky Way galaxy.

7. The larger galaxy in the photograph is a(n)

_____ galaxy. Circle the correct answer.

elliptical   irregular
        spiral

8. ○ Is the following sentence true or false? The larger galaxy in the photograph probably contains mostly young stars.

_____

The Expanding Universe (pages 718–719)

9. Is the following sentence true or false? The Doppler effect can tell us whether a galaxy is moving toward or away from us.

_____

10. ○ Is the following sentence true or false? The red shifts of distant galaxies show that the universe is collapsing. _____

The Big Bang (pages 720–721)

11. Is the following sentence true or false? All distant galaxies are moving away from ours because our galaxy is at the center of the universe.

_____

12. ○ The _____ theory states that the universe began when a dense, hot, supermassive ball violently exploded.

13. Circle the letter of each item that is evidence for the big bang theory.

a. red shift of galaxies

b. supernova explosions

c. cosmic background radiation